Mary and the Seawolf

The true WWII Story of the
Submarine U.S.S. Seawolf
Fearless Freddy Warder
And his wife Mary

SAM STAVROS

Seawolf

and the Seawolf

Stavros

Mary and the Seawolf
Copyright © Sam Stavros 2007
By: Sam Stavros

All rights reserved. Printed in the United States of America. No part of this book may be used or reproduce in any manner whatsoever without written permission except in the case of brief quotations embodied in critical articles or reviews.
Any pictures or material in this book are the authors's or given to the author for all purposes in regard to this book including but not limited to writing, publication, and publicity. The comic strips are likewise used by permission.

StavrosMusic@gmail.com

ISBN 978-0-578-36455-1 (paperback)
ISBN 979-8-218-01240-3 (hard cover)

Cover design: Sam Stavros

First Edition: February 2022

10 9 8 7 6 5 4 3 2 1

Seawolf

For all the Sailors and Marines,
throughout our country's history,
that have left loved ones behind
while traveling across the seas,
that our Freedom might be preserved.

Table of Contents

1. Mary and Fred...1

2. Separation...18

3. Storms..33

4. Wilderness..45

5. Endings...56

6. Dark Days...73

7. Frustration..93

8. Renewal..108

9. Breakthrough..125

10. Hunting...147

11. Bad Omens...162

12. On All Fronts..194

13. Success...210

14. Last Patrol..234

Epilogue...257

Notes..260

Preface

"I wish we could all pull together like we did in World War II," That is the sentence I read in a newspaper around the time that the "war on terrorism" began, that got me really thinking about writing this book. Because of personal connections, I well knew of the heroics of "Fearless Freddy" Warder and the famous Submarine "U.S.S. Seawolf" he commanded during the first year of fighting in the Pacific, during WWII. And knowing the reality of what he and his family went through, made it prescient that this book should be written. From the serious torpedo failures and unrealistic training, to housing shortages, work stoppages, and discrimination of families whose husbands were in combat zones, that refrain of "I wish we could all pull together like we did in World War II," rang especially hollow and needed some correction.

Additionally, this story is interesting on the human level. The real and serious strains that warfare causes civilian life, even in areas not under immediate bomb or general attack, as was the case on the United States mainland, are real and deserve some attention. After all those left behind in civilian life are the people that make the ordinance, farm the land, and create the ongoing wealth to support the fighter at the front lines. Without that effort and the willingness to say farewell to loved ones perhaps forever, there is no ability to successfully fight war - even necessary war to defend our freedoms here in America. That is Mary Warder's part of the story

Being personally connected to relatives of Mary and Fred brought me a treasure trove of personal correspondence the two exchanged during the war. Further they corresponded with relatives who were both colorful and hardworking, which helps to bring the story to life.

Acknowledgments

First, one of Fred Warder's daughters Grace Harde made available to me important correspondence between Fred and Mary, as well as photographs and insights that are unavailable to anyone else; in that sense this book is also her book. Henry Thompson, who served aboard the Seawolf under Fred Warder's command had invaluable stories and insights concerning the war patrols of the Seawolf as well as when docked in the Philippines, Malaysia, and Perth. My personal interviews with him at his home in Southern California gave this book a first-person perspective that is so important in bringing history and biography to life. Lucienne Aarsen gave extremely important assistance and criticism reading through several drafts, making important changes and corrections, and generally helped put this book into readable shape. Finally, my wife Hieu Stavros, who was always encouraging through every stage of writing, travel, research, and the long search for publishers. Without her this book would not be read by you today.

Seawolf

Seawolf

Chapter 1
Mary and Fred

"So, this is the Navy," thought Ensign Fred Warder as he hiked through the hot humid jungles of Nicaragua. Following narrow paths made slippery by torrential rains he grabbed hold of vines and tree branches to keep himself from falling yet again on the uncertain terrain. Suddenly behind him, Fred heard a thrashing of leaves and some swearing, not uncommon in the Navy, so he halted his small column of sailors-turned-soldiers and looked back. Sure enough one of his men had fallen a short distance into a shallow ravine. By the time Fred carefully made his way back to lend a hand, the sailor had already clawed his way back up to the path. Wordlessly the two men stared at each other for a brief moment as the thick rain quickly dissolved the gooey mud that had plastered itself onto the face and uniform of the sailor. Fred returned to the head of the column and the march continued.

After a few more hours of hiking, the rain ceased as suddenly as it had commenced, like a light switch being flipped from "on" to "off." The men looked up through cracks in the jungle canopy to blue sky and the blistering sun. Soon steam rose out of the tangled vegetation followed by huge flying insects, which used to unnerve the men, but familiarity had bred boredom to the point that nobody cared anymore.

After tramping a few more miles Fred halted the column with a sharp command that belied the crushing atmosphere. He checked his map.

"Okay, we are not to go any further," Fred told his men.

A few sighs of relief could be heard as the men took a short break from their march. At least they would not have to fight through the rain on their return trip to Bluefields, a town located on the east coast of Nicaragua, where their ship was anchored.

After about five minutes of rest Ensign Warder's not loud but commanding voice ordered the sailors to get up and start moving. With only a little bit of grumbling, a prerequisite for any duty performed by enlisted men, they got up and began to march. As Fred led the way, taking occasional swipes at the thick vegetation with his machete, the word "march" stuck in his mind.

"Why am I marching?" he asked himself. "I am in the Navy, one of the reasons people join the Navy is so that they do not have to march everywhere." Fred Warder thought back through his so-far short life and through his even shorter Navy career, trying to figure out how exactly he had been placed at the head of an "infantry" column in Nicaragua.

Fred was born in Grafton, West Virginia where he lived an unremarkable childhood with three brothers and a sister. His father, Hugh Warder, was a well to do attorney. The family was raised commensurate with the fairly high level of education and public responsibility possessed by their father. Amongst Hugh Warder's most important clients was the B&O Railroad, the most important early railroad in America.

Fred attended schools in Grafton and was a good student all the way through high school, making a college education a forgone conclusion. As with most Americans, when thinking about attending college, finances played a significant role in deciding where to attend. The military academies, at West Point for the Army and Annapolis for the Navy, have no tuition, which makes them attractive to parents and students alike. However, both Academies are extremely difficult to get into. Fred possessed very high grades and an excellent character; but more importantly he had an appointment to the Navy Academy from the local congressman, all of which are required to get into the Navy Academy.

Fred Warder first entered the massive Bancroft Hall of Annapolis in 1921 as an engineering student. He excelled in his studies and made close lifelong friends as so often happens at our military academies. Fred was very interested in sports during his years at the academy and became a proficient boxer, fighting in the bantamweight classification. He also enjoyed tennis and usually got in a set or two per day. During football season Fred watched some practices and attended the games played by the Midshipmen. Fred enjoyed the challenges that the academy presented to him, but sometimes did think about the warmth of home writing to his mother,

> Kind of miss you & Dad this week, you can bet your life, but one nice thing about the N.A. we never have a chance to get homesick. They take up too much of our time for that.[1]

Fred did not mind the discipline of the Academy,

> Don't be surprised if you see me "braced up" when you see me next. Whenever we're outside our rooms we have to keep shoulders back "gut up," chest out, chin in. We are given considerable assistance in doing so – a punch in the stomach; pull in the shoulders, etc. It's great stuff & will be the making of me.[2]

Mary and Fred

Fred Warder certainly enjoyed all of his experiences at Annapolis and when his four years came to an end, he threw his hat in the air with the rest of the graduating class of 1925 and was officially commissioned an Ensign in the United States Navy. His first assignment put him on board the cruiser U.S.S. Milwaukee.

The future Mary Warder was the daughter of Grace and Louis Brydon. Louis' father William had created a mini empire in the coal and lumber business in West Virginia. All could view William's success after he built a fantastic mansion in 1865 called "Borderside" in Bloomington, Maryland appropriately located on the border between Maryland and West Virginia. The coal and lumber business created by William necessarily stretched the family across those two states as they continued to prosper. That explains why Louis Brydon and his family lived in Grafton, West Virginia much of the time. In addition to attending to the family businesses in West Virginia, Louis was on the board of directors of the B&O Railroad – the very same railroad that retained Hugh Warder Esq. As one of their attorney's.

Mary's early life was much like Fred's: typical of any American youth born into a family that is prosperous in business or successful in profession. As a girl she rode tricycles and had "tea parties" with her friends. As Mary grew up her beauty matured. Her thick curly hair darkened to a rich auburn color, which she wore either long or combed straight and put up. Her high check bones and doe-like eyes made her very attractive to all the boys at Grafton High School where she met Fred. Having a few common friends and having inadvertently taken a few classes together, it would not be unusual for Mary and Fred to be in the same cheering group at the high school football or basketball game.

When high school came to an end Mary might have considered Fred her "Beaux," but college soon separated them with no firm future in sight for them. Fred went to the United States Naval Academy, while Mary attended Goucher College in Baltimore. Admittedly that was not much of a separation since the two schools were within twenty-five miles of each other. Mary thoroughly enjoyed her college days at Goucher, which included many short jaunts to Annapolis for dances, socializing, and Fred Warder. In fact, social events held at Annapolis attracted many young women who enjoyed good bands, food, and a chance to escape the steady flow of college classes and study. Of course all of those white uniforms and the young men tucked into them might have also lured the ladies of Goucher College to evenings of relaxation at Annapolis.

Unfortunately for the young couple, Mary's parents thought the proximity between Goucher and Annapolis, and Fred and Mary, to be a little too close. After two years Mary's parents relocated her to an all-female school called Sweet Briar College, located in Virginia near Lynchburg. At that school over three hundred miles of poor roads separated Mary from Fred and all those splendid events at the Navy Academy. Mary lasted just two weeks at Sweet Briar College for Women. Her parents then decided to send her to Mount Holyoke College, which is located in the Connecticut River Valley in Massachusetts, just north of Springfield. Like Sweet Briar, Mount Holyoke is a women's college. One needn't be a genius to discern a pattern in the strategy devised by Mary's parents. In the end Mary bowed to the inevitability of it all, raised her white flag in surrender, and went north. She enjoyed very much her time up at Holyoke but could not be away from her beloved for too long. During "June Week," a time of general festivities surrounding the graduation of a class from the Navy Academy, Mary cut her classes, and her final exams, and left for Annapolis to be with Fred during that big moment in his life.* The two thoroughly enjoyed the dances and ceremonies during Fred's final days there as well as solidifying their own plans for the future. During the festivities and happy times only one casualty could be counted, Mary's college career.

Not all was lost though as Mary possessed talent to excess, a love of life, and no fear of adventure. As Fred went on board his first ship the U.S.S. Milwaukee, Mary went to New York City. As the song goes, "If you can make it here [New York] you can make it anywhere," and Mary "made it" in New York. When she arrived there Mary was a well-educated and confident young woman. She stood about five feet and five inches tall and possessed a slim attractive figure with long graceful arms. Mary's warm smile and good conversation skills made her popular with everyone she met.

Mary always loved literature and writing. Sometimes it seemed her best friend was a typewriter. Naturally she gravitated to a job where she could use her talent as a writer. Mary soon found work at the *New York Times*, the most important newspaper in America at the time. She wrote some of the standard copy items such as the obituaries with the occasional column when an editor needed something fast. Meeting people, writing about them, and rubbing shoulders with some of the most important journalists in the United States made the vivacious Mary Brydon even more exhilarated in one of the

---

* Since 1865 the graduation festivities were called June week. In 1979 the graduation of a class was moved to May. The period of graduation is now called Commission Week.

most exhilarating cities in the world. When not working Mary and her many friends often attended plays and other shows; day trips to Coney Island would not be out of the question nor would a stroll through the Metropolitan Museum of Art.

For Mary life was good, even better than good. But an even better and happier life was soon to come. After being at Sea for about a year, the U.S.S. Milwaukee was coming into port in New York City. When the cruiser docked and the gangway came down, Fred Warder walked off the ship right into the waiting arms of his intended Mary Brydon. They had agreed to be married before Fred left on his cruise, but circumstance caused them to be secretive of their intentions. Mary's family was Protestant and Fred's was Catholic. The two had already easily resolved that issue, love being a great lubricant in sticky situations, however both were pretty sure that their union might cause a hurricane amongst their families – or at least a small gale. The two married in a small chapel in New York City with just a few friends on hand. A small dinner celebration ensued followed by a short honeymoon. Having been irrevocably married, Mary and Fred Warder sent word of their nuptials to the folks back home in West Virginia via the U.S. Mail. The two families, separated by religion, fared okay with the fathers taking things in stride while the mothers cried for a few days. In the end they reconciled themselves to each other and as they say, "Lived happily every after." As for Mary and Fred, he got back onto the U.S.S. Milwaukee returning to his sea duty while Mary stayed behind in New York, pounding away at her typewriter. Life would never be the same again.

After Fred had been several days at sea, the Captain of the Milwaukee got an urgent message from the Chief of Naval Operations directing that ship to Nicaragua. In 1926 a civil war had flared up in that part of the world with the leftists and rightists going at each other catching Americans in the middle. Sailors and Marines from the ship U.S.S. Galveston landed in August. They created a small protective enclave for Americans at Bluefields on the east coast of Nicaragua. After about six months things calmed down and the two sides agreed to terms. Everybody seemed satisfied except for a small group of fighters that still held out using guerrilla tactics while skirmishing amongst the banana trees. That group brought the Corinto and Managua railway under pressure and came close to cutting it. Additional Marines and Sailors were needed to protect the railway. The U.S.S. Milwaukee soon anchored near Bluefields and discharged a landing party. Fred was in the landing party leading his men through the steamy jungles to look for the renegade fighters and to protect the railroad.

That is how is how Fred Warder ended up in Nicaragua marching in un-Navy-like fashion, through the jungle while slapping mosquitoes from his face. While struggling with insects and jungle, he probably wondered more than once, "How can I get an assignment that seems less like the Army and more like the Navy?" It occurred to him that serving on a submarine might be the answer. Those vessels travel in the water. It logically occurred to Fred that a crewman on such a ship reduced his chances of fighting on land. He applied and was accepted to submarine school in 1927.

The United States Submarine School is in Groton, Connecticut, and has a military history that dates to the War of Independence. During that war Groton and the nearby town of New London came under serious military pressure from the British. They were trying to stop patriot sea raiders based in Groton from attacking British shipping. The turncoat Benedict Arnold led a British raid against New London and Groton in 1781. After a fierce fight at Fort Griswold on top of Groton Heights, the British forced the patriots to surrender. Later Arnold ordered the town burned to the ground.

In 1868, Connecticut gave this land to the United States to build a navy base there. Four years later the Navy built two buildings and a dock to be used primarily as a coaling station for the Atlantic Fleet. In 1915 the first submarines showed up and after World War I submarine schools and training facilities were installed. The near success of the German U-boat campaign in the Atlantic during World War I convinced the United States Navy to develop a reliable submarine of its own, but a reluctant congress needed some convincing. After all the Germans did not exactly endear the Americans with a love of submarine warfare. The Americans viewed the ambush tactics of the U-boats in a very poor light. Indeed the sinking of the Lusitania by a German submarine during World War I caused a great outcry from the American public. So instead of ambushing enemy merchant shipping, the United States Navy envisioned submarines that would travel with the main battle fleet and attack enemy warships in conjunction with surface actions. This took care of any scruples possessed by congress. Construction of a new generation of submarines, designated "S-Boats," began in late 1918. Unfortunately, the submarines did not perform well enough to work closely with the surface fleet. Construction of S-Boats came to an end in 1924 after 51 had been built.

In addition to their poor performance an S-boat could be quite dangerous to the crew. For instance, the S-5 sank in 190 feet of water during a routine dive near the Delaware Capes in 1920, when a valve malfunctioned, stuck open, and allowed water to rush into the ship. Franticly the quick-thinking crew confined the flooding to the torpedo room in the bow of the boat. The crew then attempted to drain the flooded torpedo room, but a gasket on the pump broke. Without the ability to pump the water out of the ship, the submarine remained on the bottom with little hope for rescue. Survival now depended solely on the trapped crew.

Lt. Commander Charles Cook, the Commanding Officer of the S-5, devised a scheme to raise the stern of the ship out of the water by blowing all of the ballast water and fuel out of the boat. He figured that the bow of the ship, weighed down by the water contained in the flooded torpedo room, would remain on the bottom of the ocean while the stern floated to the top. Being that the S-5 was about 230 feet long, but trapped in only 190 feet of water, Cook calculated that the stern would rise above the water line giving the crew some chance to get out of the boat. With no other alternative he decided to risk it.

The crew began to blow air into the ballast and fuel tanks. Slowly the stern of the ship began to rise, just as planned. Then unexpectedly the stern of the ship shot straight up. Deck plating, desks, chairs, pans, cups, and anything else not bolted down, fell down through the now upright boat. In the dim light provided by handheld flashlights, the men clawed there way upwards to the stern of the ship. Crewmembers banged a pipe on the side of the hull and determined from the sound that the stern did indeed rise about 17 feet out of the water. The crew then used crude tools to try and cut there way out of the boat to safety. After 36 hours they managed to cut a small hole of only about 3 inches in diameter.

Through the small hole the trapped crew could see various ships passing nearby. Imagine the frustration of being so close to rescue and yet go unnoticed! Undeterred, the crew continued to yell out of the small hole hoping to attract some attention. Finally, the captain of the S.S. Alanthus spotted what he thought was a buoy. Noting they were too far from shore for buoys to be present he ordered the Alanthus to turn so he could investigate. Entering lifeboats, crew members of the Alanthus rowed up to the S-5. The Alanthus crew shouted through the small hole and enquired where the S-5 was headed. "To hell by compass," came the exasperated answer. Alanthus sent out a distress call as their crew tried to enlarge the hole in S-5. The S.S. Goethals answered the call, and by nightfall her crew had removed a plate from S-5 and the submarine crew was able to escape.

Such were the trials and tribulations of the early submarine service, the same branch of the Navy that Fred Warder joined when he went to Submarine School in 1928. He was a natural engineer, which made him especially suited to the quirky unreliable submarines of the era. He would later find that in an emergency, the most outrages solution, such as that devised by Lt.

Commander Cook on the S-5, was sometimes the most correct solution to a problem.

After submarine school, Fred was assigned to the S-16. That boat suffered the problems that other S-boats suffered, including bad ventilation, extremely cramped and hot quarters, diesel engines that worked part time, and malfunctioning valves that put the crews in constant peril. In other words, it was the perfect assignment for a young engineering officer who wanted to prove his worth. Countless things went wrong every day on the ship giving Fred nearly endless opportunities to showcase his great skill in keeping the ship seaworthy and running. Fred had a love of engineering and an inherent curiosity that caused him to be interested in every part of the ships he served on. More importantly he had a lot of energy. Working extra hours to study machinery never bothered him. Fred never let down the Navy or the taxpayers. During the period 1930-31, the S-16 won the engineering trophy for its class. The next year the S-16 came in second. Both years Warder's Commanding Officer named him as the officer most responsible for the high efficiency ratings. These experiences of keeping the submarine going despite the many problems intrinsic in their manufacture later meant the difference between life and death when Fred became commander of his own submarine.

The S-16 was stationed on the east coast of the contiguous United States. The ship made regular cruises to the Gulf of Mexico visiting several ports, but most often Corpus Christi. In 1931 they were assigned to duty protecting the Panama Canal. Mary moved down to Panama, as did the families of most of the married crew, to stay close to her husband. This is the typical life of a navy spouse, lots of moving. Mary Connsetman wrote a short poem about the "Navy Wife."

> *You who have never packed and moved away,*
> *From where your grandsire saw the light of day,*
> *I envy you! I have not lived so long,*
> *In any house to listen for the song*
> *Of certain birds each spring: to note the height*
> *A tree has grown: to memorize the sight*
> *Of flowers along a fence, and watch them fade*
> *In autumn's hand. My feet have never made*
> *A pathway, trod again and yet again,*
> *Going and coming home in snow or rain.*
> *Briefly I stay. Then swiftly I must come*
> *To find another house, and call it "home."*

Mary and Fred

Being able to move a family and household rapidly is a special skill acquired fairly early in the careers of military officers and their families. However, the uninitiated did sometimes fall prey to the more experienced, as witnessed by Mamie Eisenhower, who upon her not yet famous husband's first reassignment, sold all her furniture, that cost about $900, to a more experienced army wife for $90. Mamie had been told that whenever somebody is reassigned, the furniture was generally sold, and new furniture was purchased at the new base to avoid the hassle of moving furniture.[3] After that Mamie remained somewhat leery of other military wives offering advice.

As for Mary, she had the adventurous spirit and traveled light, and Panama was quite the adventure. There were lots of animals down there, but not the cute and cuddly kind that Mary liked. Cockroaches, bedbugs, lizards, and snakes made up most of the animal population in Panama. And then there were the bats, lots and lots of bats. The French imported bats to Panama during their attempt to dig the canal in the 1880's to eat away at the clouds of mosquitoes that proved to be such a nuisance to the workmen. The French did not know that the mosquitoes were the killers that caused Malaria and Yellow Fever. That lack of knowledge, and the fact that the bats simply could not eat enough mosquitoes, resulted in more than 20,000 deaths to canal workers during the French period of construction, most of those deaths being attributed to Yellow Fever. Where the French failed, the American doctors William Gorgas and Jesse Lazear succeeded and finally conquered Yellow Fever and Malaria. However, the bats did remain in Panama. Those bats tended to be very clever in finding their way from outdoors into indoors, much to the horror of many service families. Indoor bat catching became a sort of sport practiced in the Canal Zone.

In addition to the trouble caused by the local wildlife, the hot rainy weather could be withering. Luckily it only rained during the rainy season, which lasted a mere ten months. Mary did not mind the rain so much, but the mold and mildew that it so readily spawned annoyed her to no end. She developed a sixth sense in detecting mold and mildew after her stay in Panama. This became an important talent as she followed her husband around the world, moving from house to house and having to make rapid decisions to "take it or leave it."

For the Warders life in Panama took its natural turn for a young married couple. Mary became pregnant and Fred reported the happy news to his mother back in West Virginia. She was overjoyed at the news; however, she was not too sure Panama was a good place for Mary to have a child and told the young couple that Mary and the baby were most welcome at her house in West Virginia if they thought that best. Fred assured his mother that there would be no problem with Mary down in Panama. This being Mary's first child though, it was an uncomfortable situation. She gave birth to a daughter and named the child Mary in honor of the mother. Later they would refer to her as "Mary B." or sometimes "Mary Jr."

While the birth of their new baby girl brought much happiness, Fred received a scare when he found out his father was deathly ill. After Hugh Warder was out of danger Fred wrote him from Panama,

> I'm certainly elated tonight to get word from mother that you are better and I know as healthy as you are that you'll pull right out of it. It's the first time I've ever known you to be ill and it certainly frightened me.[4]

Maybe it was the sudden shock of realizing up close his father's mortality coupled with some professional frustration that caused him to soon after write,

> I like the actual operating much better than fooling around the office here on paper work...Strange to say, I still get homesick and particularly at a time like this when both you and Mary are under the weather. I wish to heaven I were out of the Navy and really accomplishing something. But as yet I don't know enough to do anything. Ten more years and I will.[5]

Little did Fred know that in ten years he would be a nationally acclaimed war hero, and a few years after that he would be training all of the submarine crews in the United States Navy. In the beginning though, the uncertainties of being a new father together with the health problems of his own father caused doubts in the man that would one day be known as "Fearless Freddie."

In 1932 Fred was taken off his ship and reassigned back to the Navy Academy where he attended the Post Graduate School working towards his Masters Degree in marine engineering. While there he received his second letter of commendation from the Secretary of the Navy "as the officer who contributed most to the efficient performance of that vessel [S-16]."[6] Mary as usual was in charge of moving the family, which took a huge burden off of Fred and allowed him to concentrate on his job.

Fred worked hard and showed outstanding engineering ability. He was always at the top or near the top of his class and his efficiency ratings were always the highest possible. His efficiency in returning library books did not however come up to his engineering standards. The library peppered him

Mary and Fred

with letters demanding that he return some late books or face overdue fines. During this time Mary was also late, but there were no overdue fines, just a new baby boy aptly named, Fred. Like his older sister he had a nickname. When not called Fred Jr., his parents referred to him as "Bub." The very next year Fred, Mary, Mary Jr., and Fred Jr. went to the West Coast where Fred completed his Masters Degree at the University of California, at Berkley. Wherever he went Fred Warder always made lifelong friends and Berkley proved to be no exception.

With his formal education over, Fred wanted an assignment overseas to help advance his career. The Navy obliged and sent him to the Philippine Islands in 1935. Fred joined the crew of S-40 as the Executive Officer, or as the navy refers to that position, the X/O. Generally speaking, the X/O is second in command of the submarine whose primary responsibility is navigation. It is also somewhat traditional in the U.S. Navy that a Commanding Officer of a ship be a calm sort of person, or at least act calm and serene, while the X/O does all the yelling. Fred Warder definitely had the lungs to give a good chewing out, however he rarely resorted to such traditional methods. Warder's way to get his men to do what he wanted them to do was based more on inspiring and teaching. He led by example and his men respected and even loved him for it.

Being stationed in the Philippines meant summers in the China stations and winters in Manila. Fred Warder's first cruise landed him in Shanghai where U.S. sailors enjoyed a fairly routine schedule, despite an ongoing war instigated by Japan against China, as well as a civil war between the Chinese Communists led by Mao Tse-Tung and the Nationalists led by Chiang Kai-shek. Tensions between the Japanese and Chinese were focused north of Peking and the Communists had just completed their "long-march" to the west. Therefore, coastal cities remained secure and families of the crew felt safe to accompany their men to the eastern cities such as Shanghai. During those years Mary and the children accompanied Fred to his various Oriental stations enjoying the variety and adventure a career in the Navy sometimes offered.

The contrasts of the International Settlement in Shanghai made living there exciting and topsy-turvy. The climate included bitterly cold winters, then oppressive heat and humidity in summer. The rich ate caviar and drank vodka at Kafka's, the best Russian restaurant in Shanghai, for $1.50 American. After dinner people strolled along the Bund,* Shanghai's most famous street, which followed the curve of the Huangpu River as it flowed

---

* Now called Zhongshan Lu

toward the Yangtze River, one of China's most important rivers. Back in the day, a person could walk from the Shanghai Club to the manicured lawns of the British Consulate about a mile away, passing all the great trading houses including Sassoon, Butterfield & Swire, Jardine Matheson, and The Glen Line. Interspersed with those building were a few hotels including the magnificent Cathey where Noel Coward wrote *Private Lives* in four days. The International Settlement had a decidedly European flavor; even the police and court system were European.

After the workday ended most people congregated, in the English fashion, to their various clubs. The British Country Club and the Dome attracted the up-and-coming young crowd. The most important club, and the one that everybody aspired to, was the Shanghai Club located at 1 Bund. This is where the movers and shakers drank their gin, made their deals, and socialized. A person's position at the Shanghai Club's "Long Bar" denoted their position in society. The farther up the bar toward the windows that looked out upon the Bund, the more important the person.

When they were on their summer Chinese stations the Warder's lived 17 miles away from Shanghai where Huangpu and the Yangtze Rivers met. That is one of the places where the United States Navy anchored its ships while in China.

When not in Shanghai the submariners went north to Tsingtao, which is located on the Shandong peninsula. Ceded to Germany in 1897, the same year Hong Kong went to the British and Macau went to the Portuguese, Tsingtao had a decided Teutonic flavor to it including a brewery. The beer the Germans produced there is still world famous. Unlike the British, the Germans did not remain in China for long being forced out in 1914 due to events surrounding World War I.

The Warder's loved the summer months they spent in Tsingtao. A very genial German named Mr. Boethe rented a small house to the Warders during their stays in that city. Mary Warder spoke a little German, learned in her college days, which made communication a lot easier and caused the Boothe's and the Warders to become very close. The children played at the nearby beach. The families of fellow officers socialized regularly sharing meals and drinks at each other's houses. Later in life Fred and Mary reminisced fondly of Tsingtao.

In the winters the Warders moved back to the Philippines where they generally rented apartments or hotel rooms in Manila. That kept them close to the submarine base located at Cavite. The family also spent time in Camp John Hay, located near Baguio, about an hour-long train ride from Manila. The military provided nice bungalows for the service families and a common

Mary and Fred

dining area for meals. Mary played golf there with her friends, sometimes joined by her husband during his off-duty days. Aside from those activities Mary and Fred enjoyed hiking and of course socializing with fellow officers and their families. This was a happy time for everybody. So happy was the Warder family that it expanded by one, Grace being born in Manila.

After about one year aboard the S-40, Fred joined the crew of the S-37 where he assumed the duties of squadron engineer. His excellent performance in that capacity caused him to be quickly promoted to Commanding Officer of S-38. On that ship he distinguished himself by coming in second place in torpedo practices.

Fred Warder had been in the Orient just three years and achieved a promotion each of those years as well as garnering distinctions for his work. Things were going very well for Fred. Then at the end of 1939 it got even better. The Navy transferred him back to Portsmouth, Maine. In Portsmouth Warder oversaw the construction of the U.S.S. Seawolf and was her perspective commanding officer. From this beginning at Portsmouth the ship and the man would be wholly intertwined. In a little over two years both would be famous, and the two names tied together forever.

While Warder worked at the Navy Yard his family moved into a nice two-story house in York, Maine. Aside from their stays in Tsingtao, York would be the place that Mary most treasured. She enjoyed the stable family life without the constant packing up and moving. Mary and Fred both enjoyed the garden parties and other socializing with their good friends who Fred had shared assignments with all around the world. Most importantly Mary's husband was not out to sea and able to come home every evening. After three children and more travel than most people experience in three lifetimes, Mary and Fred were still deeply in love, and would remain so.

The keel of the U.S.S. Seawolf was laid down in September of 1938, a short time before Fred arrived at Portsmouth. When he did get to Portsmouth, Fred could be seen everyday at the navy yard overseeing the construction of the new submarine. It was exciting for him as he watched the ship rising upward everyday, surrounded by the massive timbers of the building-ways that held the Seawolf steady in her dry dock. One day while working on the Seawolf, Fred unfortunately fell from a ladder badly injuring his knee, the same knee he had injured several months early when he slipped on some ice. Fred stayed in the hospital several weeks recuperating. Though healed, Fred's bad knee continued to be a health problem for him over the next several years. At one point that little slip on the ice nearly cost him his command as being "physically unfit for duty."

Then, as if to remind everybody of the extreme hazards of serving onboard a submarine, tragedy struck. On May 23th, 1939 U.S.S. Squalus, like Seawolf a Sargo-Class submarine, sank in 240 feet of water. The main induction valve of Squalus malfunctioned causing water to rush into the engine room. As the submarine rapidly sank the watertight doors had to be shut, trapping twenty-six men in the engine room where they drowned. Thirty-three crewmen remained alive but confined to the front part of the ship now laying on the bottom of the ocean. Those men, including the Commanding Officer Lieutenant Oliver F. Naquin, made their way to the forward compartments of the submarine and formulated their survival plan.

The crewmembers did have some "Momsen lungs," but those devices were generally best for emergency escapes in less than 100 feet of water. Furthermore, Naquin theorized that the cold-water temperature would not allow for a prolonged survival time on the surface of the ocean; therefore, he decided that the remaining crew should sit tight and confidently wait for rescue.

The Navy did mount a maximum effort to rescue the crew. However, locating the submarine proved difficult without reliable sonar. After several hours another submarine searching on the surface found Squalus' rescue buoy. After establishing communication with the trapped crew through the phone lines on the rescue buoy's cables, they waited for the submarine rescue ship U.S.S. Falcon to arrive. That ship carried a diving bell, specifically designed for this type of emergency, called a McCann Rescue Chamber.

But before the U.S.S. Falcon could arrive the cables on the emergency buoy broke. The men on the rescue ships resorted to grappling hooks to relocate the lost submarine. After several hours, in what amounts to a miracle, one of the hooks caught something that everybody hoped to be the Squalus. Upon the arrival of the U.S.S. Falcon the next morning, an initial dive in the diving bell confirmed that Squalus had been found. Three round trips in the diving bell brought 25 men to the surface; only one trip remained to get the rest of the survivors. On the fourth dive the remaining eight crewmen climbed into the diving bell, with Commander Naquin of course the last to leave Squalus. Unluckily, as the diving bell ascended to the surface of the ocean, the cable jammed. Workers on the rescue ship could not un-jam it, so the diving bell returned to Squalus. For the next four hours the rescue crew worked to get the diving bell working properly. The men below could only wait and wonder; would they return to those living on the surface, or join their shipmates now drowned in the engine room. Finally at midnight the diving bell did make it to the surface and the last of the survivors climbed out into the fresh air.

Mary and Fred

The rescued crew was brought to Portsmouth. Some weeks later salvage crews raised the Squalus and brought her back to Portsmouth and set her in a drydock about 300 yards from Flatiron Pier where workers continued to build the Seawolf. The Seawolf crew witnessed the removal of the dead sailors from the ill-fated submarine.

In the military, few days are spent mourning fallen comrades as work continued in the navy yards, and on the Seawolf. On August 15, 1939, construction workers knocked the building-ways away launching the Seawolf under the sponsorship of Mrs. Edward C. Kalbfus. After that Seawolf moored at a construction dock for "fitting out." At this time the soon-to-be-crew of the Seawolf began to report for duty to familiarize themselves with the new ship. As the shipyard workers continued to build, the crew of the Seawolf pored over the Seawolf's blueprints to make sure they new everything about the internal machinery of the ship. Warder joined the crew going over every nook and cranny of the ship. Warder's credentials as a submarine engineer, his natural curiosity of machinery, and his complete commitment to a quality job helped everyone working on the submarine.

Finally On December 1, 1939, exactly three months after the Germans invaded Poland starting World War II, Seawolf was commissioned. The crew spent the next couple of months taking the ship out for short daylong cruises. They did this both for training and to make sure that Seawolf was seaworthy. On February 15th the Seawolf went into the Atlantic Ocean for its first dive. All submarine dives have risk to them. Even in our modern times most submarine crewmen have been aboard a submarine that experienced problems while submerged. Back in the World War II era a first dive always carried with it some trepidation. Nobody needed to be reminded of the Squalus.

Happily, the initial dive went perfectly. Seawolf came into port. Warder checked over the ship and decided to schedule a "test depth" dive for the next day. Fleet boats such as Seawolf had a test depth of about 250 feet but generally operated no deeper than 120 feet below the surface of the ocean. If the boat went deeper than 250 feet, the immense pressure on the hull could implode the boat killing everybody on board. For that reason, test depth dives were always of concern to the crew.

Seawolf left port the next morning as scheduled. After arriving at an appropriate place in the ocean the crew closed the hatches. The diving officer checked the indicator lights on the "Christmas tree," confirming that the Seawolf was watertight. Warder ordered the Seawolf down to her test depth. As the ship slipped past the 200-foot level eerie noises began to echo throughout the boat. As the pressure built and the steel shell warped every so slightly, the creaking noises grew louder as they reached the test depth. They stayed at 250 feet for a few minutes, declared success, and headed back to the surface as the crew breathed a sigh of relief.

The next month the crew did more training, more dives, gunnery practice, and torpedo attacks. Every emergency was anticipated, and solutions rehearsed as the sailors became experts at maneuvering and controlling the Seawolf. Then disaster struck. During a routine dive Warder called for a power outage drill on the bow and stern seaplanes. The seaplanes are the little wings on the outside of the ship that direct it up or down depending on the angle of the planes. If power is cut off from the seaplanes they can still be controlled manually by manipulating large wheels located at the bow and stern of the ship.

For some reason when the power was cut off, the Seawolf started to descend rapidly. This in turn caused extreme pressure to build up on the top side of the bow planes, which sent the Seawolf into a hard dive. Chief Machinists Mate Otis Dishman, the man controlling the bow planes, could not overcome the water pressure and straighten out the planes. Two other men came to his aid, but all three men together could not budge the bow planes. As the ship's angle of dive increased the men started to look at the depth gauge as it rose to 70 feet…90…120…150…170 feet. Papers, pencils, seats, and coffee cups started to slide towards the bow of the boat as disaster loomed. If Seawolf fell another 80 feet she would pass her test depth of 250 feet and implode. Fortunately, the ship was in only about 240 feet of water making it impossible to go past its test depth and disintegrate; yet, at the high rate of decent the Seawolf could splinter into a million pieces once it hit the bottom of the ocean. The crewmen did not need to be reminded of those dead Squalus crewmembers they witnessed being carried away on stretchers about six months before.

As the emergency heightened Warder came sliding down the ladder from the conning tower to the control room. He immediately ordered that the number one ballast tank be blown. A deafening scream ensued as the crew activated the high-pressure pumps, which forced air into the number one ballast tank and blew the water right out of it. The men waited for the ship to stop sinking but instead the dive continued. Warder then commanded that all the tanks be blown including the emergency tank. Still nothing changed as the depth gauge dutifully reported that Seawolf fell past 200 feet beneath the surface of the ocean.

Fred Warder's next order, "All back emergency," was repeated in the maneuvering room as the propellers reversed. This was the crew's last chance for survival. The giant propellers churned and finally grabbed hold of the sea. Ever so slowly the men could hear the cavitation sounds as the great screws pulled the ship level, stern first. The men gave a sigh of relief. However, the danger did not end there. With no water ballast left, the buoyancy of Seawolf was far too great. The ship began to head straight up, rapidly gaining speed toward the surface of the ocean as the men were tossed around in the unstable submarine. Crewmen grabbed hold of what they could, bracing themselves while being flung back and forth as debris flew in their faces. Then Seawolf broke the surface of the ocean, popping out like a formerly recalcitrant Champaign cork in a gigantic geyser of whitewater spray. The atmosphere in the ship became foggy and thick as the sudden change in pressure condensed the moisture in the air. The crew struggled through the fog and opened a hatch. Cool air rushed down through the opening and the crew breathed the fresh air.

Submariners live in extreme circumstances at times. One second it looks like there is no way out of a crisis then literally the next second brings the opposite emergency that also threatens to kill them. Most of the time deliverance comes, sometimes only by chance, and the crew returns to the surface of the ocean only to begin the struggle again

Chapter 2
Separation

On April 12, 1940, Seawolf embarked on its first extended cruise, the traditional "shakedown cruise," where the crew worked the final bugs out of the ship. They planned to be at sea at sea for two months visiting the ports of Galveston, Tampa, Corpus Christi, Cristobal, Annapolis, and the Brooklyn Navy Yard. After those stops they planned to return to their homeport of Portsmouth, New Hampshire. Mary and the children came down to the pier with the rest of the wives and families of the Seawolf crew and waved goodbye.

The voyage proved uneventful with the Seawolf performing well. When Fred arrived at Corpus Christi the city's fathers came out and greeted him. For a few days the officers were treated to dances and dinners while the enlisted men enjoyed several days of liberty. On Seawolf's return trip, Fred and the other officers made a homecoming of sorts when they entered the Chesapeake Bay, went to the Severn River, and docked at Annapolis. Many of the midshipmen at the Naval Academy came out to look at the new submarine. James Calvert, then a student at the Navy Academy, met Fred briefly then received an hour-long tour of the Seawolf. The tour changed Calvert's life as he immediately, upon graduation from the Naval Academy, volunteered for submarine duty and served on board the U.S.S. Jack during World War II. Calvert went on to become a Vice-Admiral.[7]

After a few days at Annapolis the Seawolf entered the Atlantic Ocean and headed north on route to Portsmouth, New Hampshire. Unfortunately, on the way up Fred became seriously ill and Seawolf had to dock in Boston and drop him off at the Naval Hospital at Chelsea. Fred was literally floored for a few weeks with some kind of infection. Mary made plans to come and see him right away, but Fred cautioned her,

> Your note of Wednesday just received. I'm gradually feeling better and might be able to sit up tomorrow but I can't today – so I'm glad your not coming before Saturday. Visiting hours are 1 to 9 pm. I do wish you were here to read to me and to rest my eyes by letting them look at you.[8]

Separation

After a few weeks and a few visits from Mary, Fred recovered and returned to his ship at Portsmouth where Seawolf received a post-shakedown overhaul. Any errors in construction were corrected, gears replaced, and leakages fixed. While this was going on Mary and Fred returned to their house in York as well as their nine to five routine, which agreed with the whole family very much. Mary loved York, she loved her children, and of course she adored her husband. When on cruise a sailor spends countless days away from his family; therefore, when he returns from the sea he and his family must make the most of their time in anticipation of the next long separation. Fred and Mary always made the most of their time together knowing that Fred's sea duty would constantly conspire to keep them apart.

With the work on the Seawolf finished, the ship left for six weeks of intensive torpedo marksmanship training at Newport, Rhode Island. It was the fall of 1940, and the problems of the world were catching up to the United States. War raged in Europe while there was trouble in the Pacific. President Roosevelt decided to create a larger navy presence on the west coast of the United States in order to send a message to the Empire of Japan that he was watching them and aware of their war-like ways. As part of the President's plan the Seawolf was reassigned to Long Beach, California immediately after the crew finished their training in Newport.

As usual the families had to make decisions about where to live. Questions arose: How long is the assignment? Will Seawolf be coming back to the East? Will she end up in the far-east? Nobody knew for sure. Mary wanted to be with her husband and Fred wanted to be with his family, so they decided to pack up and move west. The Seawolf cruised through the Panama Canal while Mary and the children took the three-day train trip across the country. When the whole family met up in Long Beach, they discussed their plans and looked forward to a nice stay in sunny California. The Warders had spent some time in California during a previous assignment and looked forward to spending a lot of good times there now.

Two days later everything changed. The officers of the Seawolf rounded up the crew and told them that they were leaving the next morning. Although they were not told exactly where they were going, most of the crew guessed the destination to be Pearl Harbor. For the single members of the crew it was no big deal. For the married crewmembers it was a hardship, but for the crewmembers with both wives and kids, the news was shocking and amounted to a major disaster. Everybody scrambled as best they could making arrangements just twenty hours before the Seawolf left.

The next morning Mary and the children waved as the Seawolf pulled out of Long Beach Harbor. Of course Mary was apprehensive. It is not too often in peacetime that military orders changed on twenty-four hours notice stranding families at various quaysides. Ironically the perils of war did not immediately touch Fred and the crew. Instead, a long dark shadow fell over Mary and the family in that last year of peace in America.

Except for those members of the crew who continued to recover from their Panama Canal contracted diseases, the five-day cruise to Pearl Harbor was pleasant and uneventful. Once in Pearl Harbor new crewmembers came aboard, including Quartermaster Henry Thomson and radio operator Paul Maley.

A third man, an Auxiliary Machinist named Zircle, or "Jew" as he wished to be called, also came aboard. An old-time submariner, probably the oldest man on the Seawolf, with duty in almost every port of call including the Asiatic Stations, Jew seemed to know that Seawolf's stay in Pearl Harbor would be short. No one knew for sure but rumor had it that he had a Chinese wife and child trapped in China. Jew hoped that Seawolf would be assigned to the Philippines, putting him closer to his family. The war in China – instigated by the Japanese – made that country a dangerous place. Jew wanted to get his family out of China to a safer country.

The Empire of Japan started its modern wars of territorial conquest against China in 1894. After the dust from that first incursion settled in 1895, the Japanese helped themselves to Formosa Island. In 1904-05 they beat the Russians in a short war acquiring the Russian interests in China at Port Arthur. In 1910 the Japanese annexed Korea and started that country's long enslavement. When WW I began Japan quickly acquired the German interests in Shantung province including the important port town of Tsingtao. In 1931 the Japanese overran all of the Manchurian section of China and installed a puppet government there. When the League of Nations criticized Japan for their imperialist grab, instead of withdrawing from China, the Japanese withdrew from the League of Nations.

The 1930's could be referred to as "the age of appeasement." We most associate appeasement with Britain's Prime Minister Neville Chamberlain and his concessions to Hitler in his hope to avoid a European war. Hitler remilitarized the Rhineland, took Austria, and stole the Sudetenland all with the blessing of Chamberlain. The bullying politics of the Third Reich are well known and Prime Minister Chamberlain's attempts to appease Hitler are generally acknowledged as at least partially responsible for starting World War II.

Long before anybody knew the name Adolph Hitler, the Japanese had perfected those tactics. They also developed unhealthy "master race" theories even before the Germans thought of them. Indeed, the Japanese thought

Separation

themselves to be the master race of the Orient looking down upon the Occidentals as a sort of mongrel people with no racial integrity. Historian Barbara Tuchman described General George Stilwell's experiences in China and Japan.

> Stillwell found an aggressive chauvinism in Japan that was lacking in China. As the only people of the East to be completely sovereign in their own land and effective in modern terms as well, the Japanese were feeling the pricking in their blood of the master-race sensation. Besides requiring a subject people to validate it, this expressed itself in seizing every available bureaucratic contact to annoy and domineer foreigners...[9]

In July of 1937 the Japanese started another series of full-scale military operations against China. Those actions included the bombing of Shanghai and the cold-blooded killing of about 250,00 Chinese in that city. Those events culminated in the installation of another puppet government, this time in Nanking. Shortly after that atrocity the Emperor Hirohito and his fellow band of killers, most notably Hideki Tojo, directed the Japanese army into Indochina. That is when the Roosevelt administration became extremely alarmed about the Japanese and their deeds in the far-east.

As stated before, President Roosevelt responded to the Japanese challenge by directing many of our naval assets away from California to Hawaii. That is the reason for Seawolf's rapid redeployment to Hawaii, but that westward movement proved not enough for the impatient Roosevelt. Seawolf stayed in Hawaii only about four days before receiving new orders sending her to the Philippine Islands. In late December 1940, Seawolf passed the dominating bluffs of Bataan and the tadpole shaped island of Corregidor, then proceeded to the Navy base at Cavite, just south of the city of Manila, in the Philippine Islands.

Back before the time of swift and inexpensive jet airplane travel and vacations hawked by travel agents, Manila presented the unusual to western eyes. The Filipino people looked different and ate different foods than the occidentals of America. The purple bougainvillea, frangipani, white gardenias, and the orchids – orchids everywhere – gave newcomers to Manila a swirling exhibition of the exotic. Luzon, the largest island in the Philippine Archipelago, possessed five Army bases and two Navy bases, giving American service men and women ample opportunities to live for a while in a tropical paradise. Tales of weekly polo matches at Ft. Stotsenberg and the relaxed atmosphere of Ft. John Hay, located at the base of the cool Cordillera Central Mountains, enticed free spirits to request duty in the Philippines. Weekend jaunts into the mountains and jungles, presented hikers with monkeys chattering in the trees in the company of Toucans and parrots, which displayed more colors than the daily rainbows. The soldiers at Ft. McKinley had streetcar service to take them to the pool, bowling alley, movie theater, and the golf course.[10]

For those who preferred their oriental evenings mixed with a bit of the occident, movie theaters such as the Ideal, Lyric, and Metropolitan, ran not-too-old Hollywood movies. Those theaters that lined the Escolta, Manila's main street, gave off a glow and encouraged cheery nighttime moods. After the movies the Americans congregated at the many parties and dances given in private homes, or at the Army-Navy club. White tunics mixed with evening gowns as gin mixed with tonic, the islands preferred drink. The warm relaxed atmosphere continued out of doors where perfect sunsets rewarded evening strolls along the beaches. If one lingered past the gloaming and into the dark of night, star-studded skies covered those below with its crystalline show. For those in the U.S. Navy, a short ferry ride across the bay brought people to the Cavite Navy Yard, Sangley Point Airfield, and the U.S. Navy Hospital at Canacao. The nursing staff there had an enviable schedule. Their day started with the morning newspaper and some fresh squeezed papaya juice brought by servants. Those nurses stationed at Ft. Mills on Corregidor, spent evenings sitting on the veranda of the officer's club with their dates, and the ever-present gin and tonic.[11]

While docked at Cavite, the Seawolf crew spent evenings in town and enjoyed what Manila offered. "The Luzon Bar" was a favorite for some members of the Seawolf crew. A couple of Americans, old hands from the Chinese stations, owned and operated that bar. Plenty of friendly faces could be found there. Other members of the crew enjoyed eating at a restaurant owned by a Russian Jew. Nobody quite knew how that man ended up in Manila, but his excellent Beef Stroganoff brought many patrons to his hospitable door.[12]

As for Fred Warder, his workdays were long, seldom under ten hours. After work he and a few friends might visit a club or see a movie. One movie he particularly liked was "Chad Hanna," which starred Henry Fonda, Dorthy Lamour, and Linda Darnell. Fred Warder's friend, David Buttolph, wrote the musical score for the movie. Back in the early days when Mary and Fred lived in Washington Heights, Buttolph and his then girlfriend Vic, frequently socialized with Mary and Fred. It made for a nice set of four that Warder sometimes reminisced about. In addition to the attractions of Manila, Fred got away on some weekends. Usually he went to Ft. Stotsenberg for a hike in the mountains with his friend Dick Voge. Fred especially liked that Ft. Stotsenberg as it reminded him of when He and Mary lived in the Philippines. Together they had spent many nice weekends in the mountains. Now that Fred was alone, he tended to be even more adventurous. One trek took him to Pagsanjan where he tried his skill at running the rapids.*

The Philippines agreed with Warder for the moment. He confessed to Mary that he had not saved a cent. Spending money on club entrance fees, enlisted men's club, income tax (unavoidable), crew's party, keeping up with the other skippers, "and in addition I have been having one helluva good time (as good as I could without you)."[13] In spite of Warder's "sailor's bravado," he in fact missed Mary and the four children very much. He taped their pictures to a bulkhead in his quarters so he could constantly see them. Warder attempted to call Mary a couple of times a week during those first few months in the Philippines without success. In mid February he finally spoke with her and described the occasion; "Last night was a red-letter day in my life – which I will never forget."

At times famous people showed up in Manila and Warder sometimes received orders to play tour guide for them. On one occasion Warder showed Clair Boothe around. She was the wife of Henry Luce, the founder of *Time* and *Life* magazine. However, Clair was a star in her own right, being an excellent writer and experienced journalist as well as the managing editor of *Vanity Fair* in 1933. In 1936 she wrote the famous Broadway play, *The Women*, that later became a very successful movie starring Joan Crawford and Norma Shearer. Warder liked Boothe and enjoyed her visit. Not only did he take her around to see the submarine base at Cavite, but he also gave her a tour of the Seawolf showing and explaining the various machinery on the ship. According to Warder, Booth was very interested and interesting.[14] Aside from those duties Warder took some time to play golf. He reported improvement in his game to Mary, shooting a 117 at the course in Olongapo.[15] Warder must have been a very optimistic man pointing to such a poor score with pride. Later when the war started, that great optimism alone, would be responsible for his and the crew's survival and success.

Although the crew enjoyed the diversions of Manila they did concentrate on their main purpose, training for war. The crew generally showed up at about 7:00am and made necessary preparations and inspections for taking the ship out to sea. Usually, they left the harbor around midday.

---

* The waterfall there is fairly famous, and the river was used in the filming of the movie Apocalypse Now.

Then the crew usually did some target practice and ran safety drills, the most important being the response to a chlorine gas leak, one of the worst possible scenarios on a submarine. If anybody detected chlorine gas an alarm sounded and all compartments were closed and dogged, all air circulation was closed, and the louvers on the ducts closed. A man in respiratory gear would enter the battery compartment while the submarine surfaced as rapidly as possible. The battery compartment was a dangerous place. On February 3rd, 1941, battery acid splashed the face of Electricians Mate L. Crane sending him to the base hospital.

Overboard drills also were practiced. If a person fell off the left side of the ship a crewmember shouted, "Man-over-board-starboard." The Officer of the Deck (OOD) then ordered, "all stop right full rudder," in order to swing the stern of the ship away from the fallen crewmember. The quartermaster then threw out a life ring. After clearing past the overboard person, the ship turned around and brought the man back onto the ship using a line.

A submarine had little chance of getting into a collision, but none the less drills had to be run for that possibility. A collision exercise consisted of reversing engines, closing all compartments, closing all louvers, holding on tight, crossing fingers, and hoping nothing bad would happen. Seawolf could go from 18 knots to "dead in the water" in about 80 seconds. If that seems quick imagine if it took an automobile 80 seconds to stop after the driver put his foot on the brake. It was always best to simply stay away from other ships.

Warder ran a tight ship and was admired by his crew. In turn Warder liked his superior offices with one exception, his squadron commander John Wilkes. The two men got into a few scrapes, as Warder did not agree with much of Wilkes training regimen. One of the things that most irked Warder, and his fellow officers for that matter, was Wilkes' insistence that the submarine squadron do surface maneuvers together. For some reason he thought that submarines should be able to maneuver together on the surface in squadron tactics. Seawolf spent many prewar training hours performing "column left," and "column right" with other submarines. Those types of maneuvers, while suited for surface vessels, had no purpose for submarines. The crews of the various boats thought these exercises to be exceptionally stupid. After one of these exercises Lt. Kinsella, the officer in charge of engineering and electrical on the Seawolf, started to make some disparaging remarks about Wilkes and the maneuvers. The tenor of his tirade increased in volume until his bellows could be heard throughout the Seawolf. Unknown to Kinsella somebody left the "Talk Between Ships" (TBS) radio on. His upbraiding remarks did not confine themselves to the Seawolf and could be heard on several submarines including the Pickerel, where Wilkes just happened to be at the time. Just as Kinsella reached the height of his crescendo a soft voice came over the TBS saying, "Seawolf turn off your radio." Kinsella turned off the radio with a look of "oops" in his eyes. Kinsella then looked around at the now wide-eyed people in the conning tower of Seawolf, each of them wondering how long Kinsella would be in the brig. Luckily it had been a fellow junior officer that tipped him about the radio. Wilkes never became the wiser. Good thing too as Kinsella was a great officer enjoying the complete confidence of Seawolf's officers and crew. Warder could not afford to lose a man of his abilities.

During the year prior to the war the crew went through other types of training. Faithfully recorded in the deck logs of January 3rd, "8:00am, moored as before. Mustered crew at quarters. Instructed crew in first aid and Venereal Prophylaxis."[16] One can only imagine the hooting and drollery Warder endured from the toughened and not so toughened sailors. Many crewmembers did note how Warder sometimes took a fatherly interest in their lives, this being but one example. Unfortunately, some of his crew did disappoint him when it came to venereal disease. He wrote to Mary about the problem,

> The venereal list has been taking a heavy toll among our unmarried people. It speaks pretty well for the faithfulness of the married ones (and the respect they have for their families) that more of them have come down with nothing.[17]

While extending a kindly hand Warder could also be a terror and he knew it. He liked and defended crewmembers to the last inch when they performed their jobs on the Seawolf correctly; but if anybody messed up his job he was withering, maybe too much so. After one especially rough incident he related to his wife, "You know my disposition is not of the sweetest, I think they take my sour moments very well indeed."[18]

In other personal matters Warder also set the example by taking regular exercise on the deck of the Seawolf. He had his own routine of deep knee bends and general limbering up type exercises. Those exercises inspired a little laughter from the crew, yet Warder was good-natured about the ribbing. He lived to be 95 years of age, so maybe he had the last laugh on that.

Notwithstanding Warder's best efforts, sometimes crewmembers did get into some problems. This tended to be very rare, not because sailors in general are angels, but rather because submariners received bonus pay. The CO of a submarine during WW II could disqualify any member of the crew at anytime, even for no reason. Certainly a crewmember did not want to give a CO a reason to send him to surface ships, thus losing the bonus, which amounted to about 1/3 more than a surface fleet sailor earned. It took four months in the East before the first minor infraction had to be adjudicated aboard the Seawolf. Seaman 1st class, J. Scott, was found guilty of being absent from quarters. A warning sufficed his punishment.

In addition to maneuvers in and around Manila Bay, Seawolf spent time in Subic Bay just north of Manila Bay. That body of water stays relatively calm in even the stormiest weather, making it a great training area. After maneuvers during the day in Subic, Seawolf often moored at Alava Dock in Olongapo where the battery overhaul facility was located. While at Olongapo liberty was restricted to 12:00 am. That was fine since that port offered only limited nighttime entertainment in the form of one dance hall/bar. Drinks were not too expensive and the food half decent. There were plenty of females at the bar too. Unfortunately, the female patrons were not really patrons at all; they worked there. Typically, it cost the men 10 centavos, (about 5 cents U.S. at the time), to dance with one of the "ballerinas," a title probably not exactly fitting the occidental interpretation of that word. If you didn't dance with the "ballerina" it cost you 5 centavos to talk. This of course begs the question, how much English did those "ballerinas" know, and just how good dancers were they?

If trouble ever arose at any of the "night-clubs," the shore patrol might be able to help. In the movies shore patrol are sometimes portrayed as heavy-handed "cops." But in reality, most men on a ship as small as a submarine served as shore patrol from time to time. Far from being heavy handed, the shore patrol were just members of the crew who, more than likely, tried to look out for their friends. If a sailor got a little rowdy, possibly the shore patrol would intervene before anything got serious. If things got serious, they might hustle the sailor away from crafty natives trying to get into Uncle Sam's pockets.

The men on shore patrol also had to be very aware. Some of the less savory natives knew that any consumption of alcohol resulted in a general court-martial for a shore patrol. A few of those club owners and bar tenders tried to slip some alcohol into the coffee of an on-duty shore patrol to have something "on him." Ordinary sailors would not be above this tactic either. Sometimes high-ranking officers had a "brush with propriety" causing the shore patrol, an enlisted man by the way, to make some tough decisions. On one occasion Fred Warder, John Wilkes, and two other COs in division 202 came into the dance club at Olongapo. A young beautiful Mastiso, half German and half Filipino, walked in. They had some drinks, no problem.

Separation

Then a couple of the "ballerinas" came over. The officers were not in the mood to dance but the girls sat down anyway. Time passed and the owner of the club was getting very agitated. Maybe a fight would break out. One nod from the club owner to the huge bouncers and trouble would soon follow. Hank Thomson, Seawolf's quartermaster and the shore patrol that night,* noticed the club owner's face getting redder and redder. He went over and enquired as to the problem. According to the club owner the officers had not yet paid for the "conversation" of the "ballerinas." What to do? The last thing an enlisted man/shore patrol wanted to do is have to arrest or even "advise" officers. But what had to be done, had to be done. Thomson straightened his shoulders, marched over to the officers and informed them that the club owner expected them to pay for the pleasant conversation of the "ballerinas." He then turned on his heel and left. Although he thought he might catch hell for his action, Thompson never heard about it again.

By mid January Warder's training routine had the Seawolf and her crew in tip-top shape. The approach team, the five men in the conning tower that tracked and then set up shots against the enemy, worked together most everyday. During exercises Warder rarely missed a shot. The Seawolf would stalk its tender, the Canopus, and fire practice torpedoes at her. Sometimes a cruiser such as the Houston would be around, and the submarines could take a few shots at her. Practicing against a cruiser gave the submarine crews a better awareness of what to expect in battle because a cruiser moved so much faster than a tender.

But this training proved to be a problem in itself. Everyone wanted to sink big ships. The high command designated capital ships as the priority targets. Unfortunately, most of the capitol ships in the Japanese Navy, or any navy for that matter, traveled between 27 and 32 knots while a U.S. fleet submarine traveled at about 19 knots – *on the surface*! Submerged, a submarine's speed decreased to no more than 12 knots, and that for only a short period of time. It's better to figure the submerged speed of a U.S. fleet submarine at about 7 knots. On speed alone the U.S. submarines could not match the Japanese capitol ships.

Devising a strategy that called for something that could not be physically accomplished on paper, let alone in actuality, is poor planning. Strategic planners and ordinance designers created many problems for the submarine fleet in the Pacific, but this early blunder unquestionably hurt the war effort. If the United States and Britain had committed their entire

---

* Out on station generally the shore patrol was one man whereas Stateside the shore patrol traveled in pairs.

submarine forces to commerce raiding in Empire waters from the beginning, the war might have been shortened. Only later in the war when concentrations of U.S. submarines practically clogged the sea-lanes in empire waters, did Japan seriously suffer the burden of blockade. The failure to go after Japan's merchant marine early in the war is especially egregious considering that Germany had already demonstrated the potential success of such a strategy.

In late April a war scare caused large movements of U.S. warships stationed in the Manila area. Admiral Thomas Hart's complete lack of faith in the Army Air Force's ability to protect the U.S. Navy from aerial attack caused him to send his ships, including the Seawolf, south. Most of the navy's ships took on enough fuel and supplies for an extended period away from Manila. As for Warder he was glad to get away from Manila for a while. For all of the nice attractions that city offered, Warder began to consider it "unhealthy." "Too much whiskey and too little sleep," his succinct judgment read.[19]

For the trip south Seawolf took on a few passengers including the Squadron Commander John Wilkes. Lieutenant Kinsella, Seawolf's electrical and engineering officer, did not like Wilkes' command and training philosophy. For that matter neither did Warder; Occasionally, he got very frustrated with Wilkes. As CO of the ship, Warder needed to use all the charm and decorum he could call on, in order to make a calm passage. Kinsella however took a different tack – he spent most of the voyage trying avoiding Wilkes, a difficult task on a submarine.

Seawolf first stopped at Zamboanga Harbor on the most western part of Mindanao. The Seawolf anchored in 25 fathoms of water next to her tender, the Canopus. Without a pier most crewmembers stayed on board their ship while only a few men took the ship's boat ashore. As those men wondered around the sparsely populated town, a couple of them made a quick acquaintance with two old ladies. Those women knew the territory and politics of Mindanao from long experience. After exchanging pleasantries and rumors, the ladies bestowed a gift on the men consisting of a record player and a couple of records. The ladies, agreeing with Adm. Tommy Hart, thought war would come soon. They didn't want the record player to fall into enemy hands and they thought the sailors might enjoy passing a little time in the Seawolf listening to some music. As the men walked away one of the women shouted, "When the Japs come, give'em hell."[20]

On April 26th the fleet pulled up anchors and moved further south. After a day of cruising, Canopus, Houston, and Seawolf entered Tutu Bay on Jolo Island and for the next fifteen days Seawolf called Jolo home. Other ships

Separation

came and went. At times the bay rivaled Olongapo in activity. Most everyday the Seawolf went for maneuvers and target practice in the open ocean, returning at night. The men did enjoy a day off here and there and on those days the crew ferried themselves to shore with Seawolf's boat. They generally stayed away from town. Jolo wasn't exactly dangerous, but the police did walk their beats armed with shotguns. Those policemen were under the direct control of the Sultan. He was being paid by the United States to keep order in Jolo and he meant to earn his pay. The few taxi drivers in Jolo were also prepared for trouble. They carried pistols in gun-belts, well stocked with ammunition. The taxi drivers considered those items insurance against any Moro's, the native inhabitants of Jolo, which might cause trouble. Jolo was not friendliest of places.

Despite the security and political problems at Jolo, Fred and his friend Dick Voge went for a short shopping tour. Fred bought some grass mats for his mother. Thinking of his wife and daughters he bought, "Some pretty shells for the small girls, [and] some pearls for the big ones." When he sent the items home he did not mention the shotguns.

On board the Seawolf the men played cards or read. Being cramped in a submarine however, impelled the crew to outdoor recreation. Since the they could only stay on shore four or five hours at a time, pick-up baseball games seemed a logical choice to stretch stiff muscles. Henry Hershey, a machinist's mate onboard the Seawolf, usually organized these. When he joined the crew of the Seawolf he brought with him a good supply of bats, balls, and mits. At Jolo the crew put those items to good use. The games, played in fresh air and sunshine, promoted a friendly sporting atmosphere. At times however the competitive nature of the men boiled over. Two crewmembers, Perry and Kibbons, collided after running for a fly ball. The results included one concussion, a set of lacerations that required stitches, and one dropped ball. In spite of those injuries the two crewmen reported back to the ship and four hours later Seawolf weighed her anchors and left for nighttime exercises.

U.S.S. SeaDragen led Seawolf out of Tutu Bay and after a night and morning of exorcizes, returned at about noon the next day only to be ordered back to sea a few hours later for more night training and then daytime drills. Those drills included firing the anti-aircraft machine guns and practicing crash dives. During one of those crash dive rehearsals machinist mate R. Bateman got this leg shut into a watertight door. The chief pharmacist's mate, Frank Loaiza, looked over the injury and decided there were no broken bones. About ten minutes later the crew hustled onto the deck for a "repel boarders drill." One wonders why a submarine crew needs to think about fighting off boarders. Presumably if a ship did get close, Seawolf could simply submerge. Warder, at the very least was going to humor Wilkes on this one. Someone distributed a few Thompson sub-Machine guns stored in the conning tower. Some of the men waved them around a bit. The only thing missing was an eye patch and a cutlass.

Despite the increased tension from strained geopolitics, the men of the Seawolf went through their work in a relaxed and professional manner. Other than Bateman's badly bruised leg the only real problem encountered during the stay at Jolo occurred when ensign Casler cut his finger while closing a coffee tin. This accident momentarily called into question the punctiliousness of the morning coffee. Mutiny however was averted when a seaman, without orders, quickly stepped into the command void and turned the switch on the coffee urn to the "on" position.

On May 10th Cdr. Wilkes inspected the Seawolf's landing forces. A few hours later the fleet pulled out of Jolo, destined for Tawi Tawi. That small island is located in the Sulu archipelago, about 40 miles east of Borneo, and is a very dangerous place. Tawi Tawi, a name derived from the Malay word "jaui" meaning "far," gained some importance as a trading hub between Malaysia, Indonesia, and the Philippines. The first westerners came in the 1300's, and Sheik Karimul Nakdum introduced Islam to the island in 1380. The Spanish conquest of the Philippines in 1564 did not result in the subjection of Tawi Tawi or the Muslims. Quite the opposite, the fierce native Moro's, who were ferocious fighters, resisted all attempts to be conquered. Probably best known for the leather wrapping around their arms to thwart possible bleeding from battle wounds, they became legendary for their viciousness. Making close contact with their enemies they used their krises, which were long curved knives, with stunning effectiveness. Their stature as fighters did not dissipate over the centuries, hence the extra precautions of U.S. personnel in Tawi Tawi as well as Jolo. Today the islands are incorporated into the Autonomous Region in Muslim Mindanao and remain somewhat separate from the Philippines proper.

Seawolf arrived in Tawi Tawi on May 11th. That port had no docking facilities, therefore Seawolf's boat had to be taken out of its storage area in front of the conning tower. With the help of a small derrick the crew soon had the boat in the water for some occasional trips to dry land. But going ashore had a few pitfalls, most notably the ever-present Moros. Additionally, being a strict Muslim area, there was not much nightlife anyway. Despite that Warder wanted to give his men a little break from the grind of constant duty so he treated them to a beer party on the beach. However, in a Muslim area finding an alcoholic beverage proved to be quite a challenge. Certainly Seawolf could not have brought the beer because the U.S. Navy was strictly "dry." However, that policy seemed to be more honored in the breach than the observance, and beer there was.

Bathing at Tawi Tawi proved to be another problem for the men. The Seawolf carried only a small amount of water mainly for cooking and drinking. The ship was able to distill small amounts of fresh water using heat generated from the diesel engines, but only while cruising on the surface. With too little fresh water on the ship and no liberty, the men concocted a bathing plan. Whenever the watch saw a rain squall coming in, (about once a day and thick with water), he would alert the crew. They would then strip down get some soap and take a shower in the rain. One day when the rain stopped a little early a few of the crew had to jump overboard to rinse the last of the soap off. After being in the water for less than a minute one crewmember felt something slimy. A huge water snake slithered by him. It is amazing how superhuman a person can be when confronted by something he doesn't like. The sailor nearly sprang out of the water onto the deck of the Seawolf and swore off swimming in the tropical ocean forever.

The Seawolf spent 11 days at Tawi Tawi. On May 23rd she left on a return trip to Manila, arriving 3 days later. As usual Seawolf docked at Cavite, the main submarine base in the Philippines. Unfortunately during this stay at Cavite, a series of problems occurred that almost ruined Fred Warder's career. Warder was the type of officer that demanded excellence on the job, but the "spit and polish" part of the navy did not interest him too much beyond the necessary. If Warder had confidence in that person's ability to perform under pressure and ultimately in combat, he could put up with a lot of on shore hi-jinx; over the next several months one of his most excellent crewmen, H. H. "Swede" Hanson, tested Warder on that point, to the limit.

On May 31st Hanson reported nine hours absent over leave. Warder made him a prisoner at large pending a mast. On June 3rd Warder awarded Hanson a trial by deck court. The executive officer, James "Catty" Adkins, presided. After hearing testimony Hanson was sentenced to five days of solitary confinement on bread and water. Additionally, he lost thirty dollars pay for one month. Several days of maneuvers went by before Hanson finally stepped off Seawolf and onto the tender U.S.S. Canopus to serve his time. It can't be too pleasant having a diet of only bread and water. However, serving on a submarine is so confining anyway, a sentence of confinement seems a bit redundant. In a way serving solitary confinement was almost a reward; just think, a little privacy, no body else's body odor to smell (a real problem on a WW II submarine), and a little quiet while sleeping.

Unfortunately for Warder this initial incident was only the beginning of a long train of problems that ultimately brought him into a direct confrontation with Admiral Thomas Hart.

Chapter 3
Storms

While Fred Warder wrestled with crewmembers and enjoyed the challenges of commanding a fleet submarine, Mary was left to navigate the sometimes rocky shoals of life as a navy wife. She found herself marooned on the west coast with four children in tow, and little help. After the Seawolf sailed, Mary spent a few nights in Long Beach with some other stranded navy wives also left alone by the sudden departure of ships. As luck or coincidence might have it Mary's brother Bill Brydon lived about forty miles east of Long Beach in Pomona, California. He lived there with his wife Margaret and their two kids. Bill ran a couple of local newspapers, "The Pomona Citizen" and the "Citrus Valley News." He was a man about town who knew all of the important people and was heavily involved in local politics. After a few phone calls Mary decided that moving from Long Beach to Pomona might be best for her and the kids. If nothing else she could count on some help from Bill and Margaret.

The Brydon's lived in a small one-story craftsman style home in Pomona on Huntington Blvd., a street with a wide grassy meridian lined with large graceful Pepper Trees. The architecture is typical of what is known as a "California Bungalow." By modern American standards the house was barely big enough for a family of four. It must have been quite cramped when five more people moved in. Mary, who had a lot of energy, maybe too much, decided to get a place of her own as soon as possible. At first she had difficulty. Landlords did not like renting furnished homes to people with young children. After looking around for a few days she found a small furnished duplex on Eleanor Street in Pomona that allowed children. It was about 5 miles from Bill's house.

What the neighbors on the other side of the duplex must have thought when four kids moved in, separated by only a thin wall, is anybody's guess. Mary did see a look of concern on the faces of their new, very close, neighbors. Unfortunately, after moving in she thought the place was much too small. Fred Jr. referred to the duplex as a "com-partment." Mary thought the whole place could fit into the living room of their old house in York Village, Maine; the "Old Captain Dennet House." That house located on Long Sands Road, became a focus of Mary, the last place she would know happiness for a while. Their new house had only two bedrooms. Mary and

Suzy slept together, while Mary Jr., Grace, and Fred Jr., were issued cots. Putting a very fine point on the situation Mary dubbed the living quarters in Pomona, "The doll house."

Despite the week of setbacks Mary did try to like the area. Pomona is located at the base of a beautiful snow-capped mountain range. On clear days it can look like a post card; unfortunately, there were very few clear days. Long before Mary and the four children showed up in Pomona, the Inland Valley (Claremont, Ontario, Cucamonga, Montclair, Pomona, and San Bernardino) was an agricultural area. Citrus and grapes were the most important crops grown with a smattering of walnut, peach, and apricot groves thrown in. But what looks pristine and ideal in a picture, in this case the almost ceaseless rows of orange and lemon trees, presented many problems for the people that lived amongst the groves. Interspersed with all the trees were oil burning smudge-pots, each about 4 feet high. When the weather got cold the growers lit them to keep frost off the trees. But the smudge-pots created thick black smoke that settled into the valley due to a prevailing inversion layer. Mary referred to the air in Pomona as, "smudgy" when the pots had to be lit. On the bright side, she liked the warmer winter days and appreciated all the, "Greening that is everywhere." Good dinners were available at the local diners for about 50¢. Other good news included the enrollment of Mary jr. and Fred jr. into Lincoln Elementary School with no demotion, always a point of concern for military families that move around so much.

The winter nights in Pomona might have been cold, but Mary heard that the summer months could be hideously hot. This was a big concern of hers and she immediately started to look around for a "summer" home up at one of the mountain resorts called Big Bear. Even to this day the village at Big Bear Lake is a quiet mountain retreat in the summer and a place for alpine sports during the winter. The beaches of California also offered cool recreation during the summer. A train service, the Red Cars of the Pacific Electric Co., made getting around the Los Angeles and Inland Valley easy.

Mary's desire to like Pomona sparked her husband's interest in the place. Shortly after Mary moved there Fred received a new chief Yeoman named Pritchett on board the Seawolf. He had been in Pomona and reported to Fred that it was a very nice town. Fred wrote a cheery note to Mary saying, "I hear many fine things about Pomona. I am glad you are liking the place more all the time."[21]

In spite of Fred and Mary's optimistic attempt to adapt to her accidental domicile, Pomona became a place of some sorrow for Mary.

The international crisis caused Mary's stay in Pomona. Later, the war would have a huge impact on the local economy around the Pomona Valley. Henry Kaiser built a huge steel plant in nearby Fontana, specifically to supply his marine works with material to build his famous prefabricated Liberty Ships. Further into the future Italian and German POWs were interred in Cucamonga, a perfect match since most of that area was covered with vineyards and resembled the Mediterranean climate of Italy. The POW's worked for the Southern California Farmers Association picking oranges and tending vines. Later German POWs would be housed at the Los Angeles County Fairgrounds, located in Pomona.

Mary wanted her stay in the cramped little duplex amongst the orange groves to be a short one, not because Pomona was unappealing, but rather she missed her husband. Just before Thanksgiving, Mary became very sad and lonely. She had enjoyed the "honeymoon," as she called Fred's brief stopover in Long Beach, but by now felt that "My world had fallen on me and left me squashed all over." The four children, sensing their mother's accelerating melancholy, took turns soothing her. On one occasion little Suzy, while patting Mary on the shoulder said to her, "Life will be perfect someday."[22] Unbeknownst to all of them, that someday faded further and further away as the world crisis deepened.

Mary's suffering and loneliness continued and now the tell-tell signs of mental and physical exhaustion began to occur. Mood swings began to appear in her letters to Fred. "I am here because I am here because I am here for the duration," is one mournful passage, but then accompanied with, "California is a paradise for the children." In fact, the children seemed to take to their new surroundings. Fred jr. was at the age where boys enjoy sports the most. According to Mary he had gone, "Football crazy," and at times forgot that football is an outdoor sport. The clothing styles out west also differed from what Mary saw in the East. Most notable was the fabric "blue denim" or blue jeans, which Fred jr. took to wearing, thinking it made him look very grown up. As Christmas approached the kids wrote out lists for Santa Claus with one child wanting to move back east and another wanting some pet mice. Amidst the chaos and excitement Mary received a bit of good news. The Navy shipped some of Mary and Fred's furniture to her from the east, including Mary's favorite writing desk, at no charge. The desk, a symbol of happier times in York, pleased Mary very much.

The day after the desk arrived Mary wrote Fred some comments about President Roosevelt's Lend-Lease plan. President Roosevelt had been trying hard since about 1937 to get the United States on a war footing. At that time Roosevelt had been alone amongst world leaders in power to take the

German's and their Nazi menace seriously. But isolationist sentiment ran very strong in the United States. Who can blame the people for that? The United States fought in World War I to make the world "safe for democracy." By the early 1930's the plethora of dictators on their little European thrones was proof positive to the Americans that the effort had been a waste. Now the Europeans were at it again and the Americans were truly tired of fixing Europe's problems.

Roosevelt was nothing if not determined though. Being a former Secretary of the Navy, he often liked to do his most critical thinking on the water. In early December 1940 President Roosevelt boarded a cruiser, the U.S.S. Tuscaloosa, and went on a ten-day cruise through the Caribbean Sea. He had been working on the problem of how to help the British, while the Americans, whom he was supposed to represent, did not generally want to help the British. That is when he came up with the catch phrase "lend-lease."[23] In our modern times few people think of this phrase as anything but popular and right. In Roosevelt's times however, people were not so enthusiastic. Senator Robert Taft, a giant among isolationists said, "Lending arms is like lending chewing gum, you don't want it back."[24] As for Mary, sitting at the now returned writing desk, she wrote Fred, "I wonder now if we are going to lend the British some submarines." Mary thought the minute we lent anything to the British, Hitler would declare war on the United States, a proper conclusion seeing as lend-lease openly declared that the United States supported Britain in the European war. As it turned out she was wrong on that account. Lend-Lease passed the House of Representatives 260-165 and the Senate 60-31 in February 1941, but no declaration of war from Germany ensued.*

When it came to the United States, Herr Hitler seemed to be on his best behavior, for a while anyway. Things didn't get sticky between Hitler's Reich and the United States for seven more months. Then serious trouble began when a German submarine fired two torpedoes at the USS Greer, a destroyer on a mail run to Iceland. (The Greer's initial mission sounds innocent enough, but while delivering the mail a crewmember on Greer spotted a German submarine. The captain then ordered Greer to follow the German sub and acted as a spotter for a British patrol plane for the next two hours.) On October 17th the U.S.S. Kearny was torpedoed with eleven men killed, and on October 31st the U.S.S. Ruben James was torpedoed and sunk. All three ships had been operating in the Iceland area. Again, no declaration of war ensued, much like in our time where the World Trade Center (first

---

* Senator Taft did in the end vote for Lend-lease.

attempt 1994), two U.S. Embassy's in Africa, and the U.S.S. Cole were bombed, all with no declaration of war against the responsible organization; Al Quieda. Just as then, it does take a lot for the United States to get involved in a full-fledged worldwide war.

While all that European trouble lay many months away, Mary remained unenthusiastic about Roosevelt. His fireside chats did not impress her. Every time she picked up a newspaper, she wondered more and more just how long the "duration" might be. Even though she remained cool to Roosevelt she could not ignore the trouble the Japanese were causing in China. And while concerned about the international situation and how that affected her husband, she also had to contend with domestic conditions such as a family case of the mumps that started with Fred Jr. and didn't stop until everyone had become immune, the hard way.

It had been a tough November for Mary. She had always enjoyed the holiday season, but Thanksgiving in 1940 did not have the happiness and togetherness that Mary found so poignant in the past. Christmas followed and Mary's loneliness deepened as that cheery time of year sank into an unhappy affair with forced smiles. On New Years Eve, only Mary and Fred Jr. managed to stay awake long enough to greet the New Year. The two stood outside of their humble lodgings, with their arms intertwined, standing close against the chill of the cold night air. They wished upon a star, both hoping for a permanent family reunion in the new year of 1941. Mary made a few New Years resolutions; "No more tears, no more quarrels, no more dirty sinks and dishes."

As the holiday season came to an end Mary started to think that the only possible way the family could get together was to go to Manila. But when Admiral Thomas Hart took over command of the Asiatic Fleet in October, he ordered all dependants home. Desperately Mary thought she could take a private ocean liner to the Philippines, but the huge expense associated with such a move proved prohibitive. She dreamt about the Dennet House in York Valley, Maine. That is where she and the children had been happiest, living with Fred as he supervised the building of his future submarine, U.S.S. Seawolf. The summers there were not too hot and encouraged many garden parties attended by Fred's fellow officers and their wives. With the women in their light cotton dresses, children swinging on an old car tire suspended from a tree, and the officers looking on with amusement and satisfaction. A happier scene could not be imagined. Fred often set up a badminton net on the lawn for some not very serious sport and of course there was plenty of good food and drink. The obligatory New England church steeple rose in the distance above the trees in the large yard. Fred kept the very large lawn trim with a push lawn mower, which in turn kept him trim. Harbor Beach was within walking distance making fishing and lobster parties especially easy. At times the adults took off to the lake country around Winnipesauke to enjoy a little solitude. In the winter, snowball fights and sleds occupied the children's time. No wonder memories of York Village often entered Mary's mind during her stay in Pomona.

Mary thought she wanted to go back to that place, but she really wanted to go back to that time. Then those feelings would quickly pass as she thought the only thing to do was to return to West Virginia where her family still lived, an idea she did not much like. Mary's confusion even extended to rationalizations on why she ended up in the "doll house" on Eleanor Street in the first place. Mary wrote Fred,

> Everything else as it was when arrived – ready to reship. I want to be ready to "pull stakes" without expense or trouble. I decided against taking a larger house and getting settled,"

She started to mention going to Manila over and over as the only possible way to save her situation. But her deterioration lay less in her surroundings than within herself as her depression continued to grow.

Mary's inability to understand her own innermost troubles did not interfere with her understanding of other people's problems and the general situation in the world. Mary read newspapers and avidly followed and commented on world events. She took much interest in the surface fleet battles near Montevideo, on the River Platte, between the German ship Graf Spee commanded by Hans Langsdorff, and three English cruisers, Achilles, Ajax, and Exeter. She commented to Fred, "The stories of the German raiders in the South Pacific make me wonder if there will be good hunting for you."

Mary was also very concerned about Fred's demeanor toward his superior officers, most notably with John Wilkes, the squadron commander in Manila. Fred had a habit, for whatever reason, of quarreling with the "brass hats." It just so happened that Wilkes became his prime target. On more than one occasion the two men had argued heatedly. One time Seawolf displayed lettering congratulating another submarine after maneuvers. Wilkes sent Warder a memo stating, "The letters are considered nonessential. This is not a mutual admiration society." Fred blew up but Mary warned him in a letter to hold his temper, "There is much war talk here…this nation needs you in a submarine!" she wrote.

Mary's comments on the European War gives a small window of insight into the American mind at the time. Most Americans followed the war in the news. Most rooted for the British. Few expected a war in the Pacific, and all wanted peace because the Americans really wanted to simply be left alone and take care of their families. Far from our modern nostalgic view of the World War II era, there was little support for a European war to help the British. In February the magazine *Ladies Home Journal*, which Mary read, printed the results of one of their poll questions, "do you think the United States should go to war to help England and France?" The women answering the poll left no ambiguity as to their feelings; 94% said "no" while only 6% responded yes.[25]

During that period President Roosevelt suffered mightily from his political opponents, the owners of mass media (newspapers and radio), and depending on the issue, from most Americans from time to time. Once in October of 1937 Roosevelt gave a speech on the European situation in which he said, "The epidemic of world lawlessness is spreading." The general outcry against just that part of the speech was, in Secretary of State Cordell Hull's words, "Quick and violent."[26] The American Federation of Labor, an organization closely allied with Roosevelt, immediately issued the statement, "American labor does not wish to be involved in European or Asiatic wars." The intense chorus of disapproval caused Roosevelt to not mention things European for the next seven months. And if his friends caused him trouble just imagine what his enemies were up to.

Roosevelt's enemies included Robert McCormick, an old school chum of Roosevelt's at Groton and the owner of the Chicago *Tribune*. Initially McCormick supported Roosevelt, both in the campaign of 1932 and for the year that followed.[27] However Roosevelt's attempt to bring the press under the umbrella of the National Industrial Recovery Act deeply disturbed McCormick. When a *Tribune* reporter asked Roosevelt about freedom of the press, the President, who recognized the source of the question said, "Tell Bert he is seeing things under the bed."[28] After that McCormick's intense and personal criticism of the Commander-in-Chief easily made him the enemy-in-chief. McCormick led the charge on behalf of the isolationists and anybody else who did not like Roosevelt or his policies. Amongst other things, Colonel McCormick served overseas during World War I and never tired of pointing out that Roosevelt, then assistant Secretary of the Navy, served far from the western front.

Cissy Patterson's paper, The Washington *Times-Herald*, tended to follow her brother Joseph Patterson's lead. He owned the New York *Dailey News*. Both papers generally supported Roosevelt's new deal initiatives.[29]

However both violently turned-on Roosevelt when he announced lend-lease. In addition to denouncing lend-lease and President Roosevelt in her paper, Cissy wrote that the Vice-President Henry Wallace was, "A Crystal-gazing crackpot...a harmless kind of nut." She ran photos of draft age men employed by the State Department and called on the Secretary of State Cordell Hull to send them into the army even referring to them as, "the pantywaste brigade."[30] Much of her rage must have been pent-up since she and Roosevelt tangled over the building of the Jefferson Memorial, construction beginning in 1939. Cissy objected to the sight chosen for the memorial by the administration. Forty cherry trees would have to be cut down to accommodate the huge memorial. She thought the trees should be spared. A few female followers agreed and chained themselves to some of the trees just as the bulldozers arrived. But the administration had a strategy. They noticed that the women protesters didn't bring food to sustain themselves through their ordeal of protesting. After awhile the protesters got hungry. The administration, being peopled exclusively by the right kind of gentlemen, sent out food to the demonstrators, even though the administration was the target of the demonstration. The women were grateful for the food because demonstrating is a tough business that can sap ones strength. They were even more grateful for the hot coffee they received, lots of hot coffee. But after so much coffee they had to unchain themselves and visit the rest room. In their absence the bulldozers rolled and the trees were gone. Such are the diversions of the press even during troubled times.[31]

William Hearst also initially supported the President until Roosevelt gave a speech in 1935 where he called on Americans to, "forswear that conception of the acquisition of wealth which, through excessive profits, creates undue private power over public affairs."[32] That is all Hearst, the king of acquisitors, needed to hear. After that the full measure of his newspaper empire came crashing down on Roosevelt. Amongst other things Hearst directed that his editors refer to Roosevelt's programs as the "Raw Deal" instead of the "New Deal." FDR often called newspaper reporters liars, and he did it by name, and he did it in person. At one news conference in 1937 President Roosevelt read a story written by a reporter named Ernest Lindley, who also was at the news conference in his capacity as a reporter. As the President read the offending article he stopped from time to time saying such things as, "Lie number one...This is a statement and it is a lie...If that is based on anything that happened yesterday it is a lie." Far from our gentlemanly give and take in the press today, Roosevelt did not pull any punches. The President went so far as to accuse newspaper reporters of being "sixth columnists" that were aiding fifth columnists with their "propaganda."

He saw nothing wrong with questioning the ethics and patriotism of newspapers and the reporters that wrote for them. The absolute low point came when FDR gave/awarded an Iron Cross to a newspaper reporter named John O'Donnell at a Washington news conference in 1943.[33] To say FDR demonstrated a stunning lack of decorum coupled with an unmitigated gall that could only be described as beneath the behavior of even the most churlish bully, would be the understatement of the century.[34] However, in the President's defense, the United States had to win the war and FDR was going to do whatever it took to win. Thank goodness he did.

This is the real-life world that Mary lived in, not the over-nostalgic perception of perfection that some people today look back and admire so much as a time when, "everybody worked together happily." There was trouble everywhere. The extreme pressure brought on to individual families for instance, is proved by the increased divorce rate in the 1940's; 16 per 100 marriages ended in divorce in 1940 increasing to 27 per 100 marriages by 1944.[35] Mary's problems did not end up in divorce, but they definitely were pushing her into troubled areas.

Mary continued to try to get to Manila and reminded Fred of their visits to camp John Hay years before. Fred responded by telling of all the movies and other entertainment he was enjoying, including a hike with friends around that same camp. "What no women?" headlined one of Mary's letters at that time, obviously asking for reassurance in that area. "These separations have become harder to take – unlike earlier ones," she wrote.[36] As Mary became sadder and sadder, she began to "forget" to take her medicine prescribed to treat her overwrought nerves. One day she would be very sad then another day completely happy. When Mary received four letters from Fred in one day she was, "sitting on top of the world." But within a day she returned to her gloom thinking of ways to get to Manila and commenting on Roosevelt's latest speech, "I gather that we really expect to get into the war. (I pray so hard for peace too.)" But Mary being a realist conceded that a war would be long, "at least a couple of years to lick the Germans." Like most Americans she did not expect any trouble from the Japanese. However, Fred and the Seawolf were quickly ordered to Tawi Tawi at which time he dashed a note off to Mary intimating some problems on the horizon,

> If things should "pop" please be sure that I am proud of you and happy to be in the Seawolf...and that I will always love you.

After about a month in Pomona Mary did not receive much help from her brother Bill and his wife anymore. The Brydon's had their own problems.

Before Bill moved to California, he had been in the family timber and coal business in West Virginia. His grandfather had built a mini-empire complete with a stately mansion called "Borderside," to remind people of his success. But Bill showed no interest in the business and went to Florida. He then did a short stint in the military, where unfortunately an explosion during training blew off part of his right hand. Then Bill made his way to California where he started his two small newspapers. He was a success, but Bill, like most Americans, experienced a lot of pressure during these last months before the Japanese attack on the United States. Right when Mary needed a helping hand from her brother he unfortunately was distracted.

Then the next issue began, what to do with the car. Mary had the family car but did not want it. She did not drive so she did not need a car. This became a sort of focus in her life. She wrote Fred that she wanted the whole thing taken off her hands as soon as possible. Fred, always trying his best to help even at such a great distance, had the car shipped to Manila. For some reason, he thought he had a better chance of selling the car in Manila. Selling the car turned into a sort of career, judging by the length of time and the amount of ink spent getting the papers together and selling the thing. Fred had a lot to do for his family. The distance and slow communication must have really frustrated him at times.

These pressures coming so unexpectedly from so many sources caused Mary to become sadder, even more depressed. On February 14th Mary experienced some serious anxiety. Luckily on that day Margaret Brydon and Mary had plans to meet. When Margaret got to Mary's house, she immediately felt something was not right with Mary. Seeing the condition she was in Margaret tried desperately to call Bill but could not reach him for several hours. Finally, when Bill showed up, he described Mary's house as a place of complete confusion with a "bunch of women milling around trying to help but not knowing what to do."

A doctor was called in who recommended putting Mary in a county facility, which thankfully Bill refused to do. He looked around for a few alternatives but the hospitals he called refused to take anxiety cases. Luckily the clear-thinking Mrs. Watts, wife of Electricians Mate Evan Watts on board the Seawolf, showed up and suggested that they take Mary to the Navy hospital in Long Beach. Mary was admitted under the care of Dr. Mull. But once he examined her, Dr. Mull decided that she should not be in a Navy hospital. He recommended that Mary be placed in Las Campanas, a facility in Compton specializing in anxiety and nervous cases. Tragically, they could not get Mary there for several days, during which time she deteriorated.

Storms

Admitted at last to Las Campanas hospital, Dr. Robert Newhouse oversaw Mary's care. He was a gentle and understanding physician. According to Dr. Newhouse, Mary's recovery would not be swift. For that reason, Bill and Margaret took in Mary's four kids making a total of six children. The house Bill and Margaret had on Huntington Blvd. was too small for all of them, so they rented a much bigger house with three bedrooms. The move however was not smooth as it rained constantly making Bill generally grumpy. On the other hand the new house was located only a block from Lincoln Elementary School making it easy for Fred Jr. and Mary Jr. to walk to school. The school was very nice with a very large play yard ringed with an attractive red brick wall. Fred Jr. and Mary did well there, and things started to calm down for both the Warder's and the Brydon's

Bill was trying his best to help out and keep Fred informed. But communications got jumbled up at times, not that communications in the early 1940's amounted to much. Bill sent a cable to Fred, but he used too much of his newspaper headline creating instinct cabling, "Mary in Las Campanas...nervous breakdown complete. Recovery at hospital not expected for month or more." That must have been comforting to Fred as he was trying to concentrate on his job six thousand miles away. Over a week later Bill wrote a detailed letter to Fred, but it did not arrive until about the second week of March. Fred, obviously very worried, immediately cabled Bill wondering what was going on. Bill then wrote him another letter somewhat surprised that his original letter had not yet arrived. Mail delivery was slow to say the least, a circumstance Mary and Fred already knew from experience. Sending mail by "Clipper," which was the airmail service across the Pacific Ocean, was sometimes as slow as surface or "boat mail" due to weather and other problems.

Despite the initial turmoil with the family Mary responded well to the treatments given to her at the hospital. Those treatments consisted of hot and cold packs, a massage, and a lot of rest. Who wouldn't respond to that favorably? Bill though was unimpressed. Newspaper people tend to be very cynical, it is a sort of job pre-requisite, and Bill was nothing if not cynical. While he expressed confidence in the doctors at Las Campanas, he thought the whole operation was little more than a scam. "All these hospitals like to keep the paying guests as long as possible. To know when these doctors are thinking about their books and when they are thinking about the patient is a problem," was his assessment of the current situation. If the doctors watched their books, Bill Brydon seemed determined to watch his even closer. He wanted to get Mary out of the hospital as soon as possible, even against the Dr. Newhouse's advice.

While Bill explained this to Fred, he could not resist straying into the realm of foreign affairs especially those concerning the Pacific. Bill hoped for a bit of information. Using his newspaper reporter skills by asking questions in a way that might seem that he was not asking a question, "Naturally you can't tell me much about what is happening in the far-east...however I can't help but wondering."

Chapter 4
Wilderness

In fact, everybody wondered what would happen next. The whole country seemed on pins and needles. It was as if Mary's anxiety exactly mirrored the nation's mood. And who better to analyze the nations mood than a newspaperman such as Bill Brydon. His natural curiosity and profession equipped him to at least report on the nervous tension that many people suffered during this prewar period. Perusing one of his competitor's newspapers Bill found such front-page stories about a union strike against a shipyard where half a billion dollars worth of government defense contracts was being held up. Next to that story there was one about the ridiculous escapade of Rudolf Hess and his parachuting into Great Britain in his weird attempt to end the war between Great Britain and Germany. On that same front-page Bill saw a report that 21 U.S. bombers had been sent to Hawaii as part of the continued military buildup there in response to the Japanese takeover of Indochina. The following story reported on the continued U.S. sales of machine tools to the Soviet Union. The same Soviet Union that had a treaty with the Nazi's, had taken 40% of Poland by aggressive conquest, and invaded Finland.[37] How schizophrenic could a country get? Strikes against our own defense industries, selling equipment to a country that was aligned with the Nazis, and the lack of support for Great Britain even as they stood alone against the Nazis; the United States seemed almost as weird and directionless as Rudolph Hess. No wonder Mary and others felt the pressure so acutely.

A slightly closer look at the Soviet machine tool situation shows just how confused and murky things had gotten by early 1941. An intrepid reporter confronted Roosevelt about it in October of 1940 asking about a relaxation of the Neutrality Act and the Export Control Act and whether the relaxation of those two laws had anything to do with the release of machine tools to the Russians. When asked about it directly Roosevelt responded, "I suppose so – yes; probably the same thing." Just to be certain the reporter asked the same question again about machine tool sales to the Soviet Union. Roosevelt answered, "In other words, the general idea is, if we don't need them for ourselves, we turn them over to a friendly power." That was something, implying the Soviet Union was a friendly power in October of

1940 when they were still an ally of the Nazi's and busy taking over nearly half of Poland and parts of Finland. The questions continued:

> Q: And Russia is a friendly power?
> The President's answer: I don't think Russia is the mainspring in that.
> Q: Just incidental?
> A: Yes.[38]

A few months later in January 1941 the Russians received further shipments of machine tools.

In contrast to the Russian situation Bill Brydon also read and reported on President Roosevelt's initial victory in the Lend-Lease legislative battle. Roosevelt wanted to help the British by sending them arms, which meant once again a modification of the Neutrality Act. The President had many enemies on that issue and his legislative victories were by no means assured. Whether Roosevelt gave a lot of thought to the concept that he was trying to help the British with Lend-Lease, at the very time he was helping the Russians, who were allies of the Germans, who in turn were the enemy of the British, is not well known.

Another local paper similar to Bill Brydon's carried a story at about the same time of yet another labor strike, this time at the Ryan Aircraft Company down in San Diego. That article is of particular interest in a tangential way.[39] Ryan Aircraft is the company that built the Spirit of St. Louis, the plane that carried Charles Lindbergh across the Atlantic Ocean and made him into a national hero and an international celebrity. But by 1941 Bill Brydon was criticizing Lindbergh in his own newspaper and reading headlines in other local papers such as, "Lindbergh Urges Cooperation with Nazis for Peace; Pooh-poohs Invasion Fear."[40] In fact no one more typified the American confusion of 1941 than Charles Lindbergh.

Charles and Anne Lindbergh left the United States in 1935 in response to the kidnapping and murder of there young son Charles Jr. At that time Charles Lindbergh became somewhat enamored with the Nazi's. His first encounters with the regime went well. Lindbergh was invited to tour facilities of the newly reborn Luftwaffe, the illegal German Air Force. Because of his status as an international celebrity Lindbergh was given nearly carte blanch in his weeklong tour of airfields, factories, and research facilities. He gave a speech to a host of dignitaries of the German Air Club in which he charged that aviators had a special responsibility to use aviation for peaceful purposes. The speech was favorably received. Later Lindbergh reported his findings to the United States government noting the advanced state of German factories, their aviation in general, and their excellent aircraft engines including the Ju-210 air-cooled engine.[41]

If Lindbergh's interaction with the Nazi's had ended there his work would have been hailed as a great help to the freedom loving peoples of the world. However, Hermann Goering, a fellow aviator and second in command in Nazi Germany, took a special interest in Lindbergh as he wined and dined his internationally known guest. A few weeks after his first visit to Nazi Germany Lindbergh wrote a friend that he had been impressed with Germany and favorably impressed with Adolph Hitler. Lindbergh's wife, Anne Morrow Lindbergh accompanied her husband Charles on the trip and wrote,

> "Hitler, I am beginning to feel, is a very great man, like an inspired religious leader – and as such rather fanatical – but not scheming, not selfish, not greedy for power, but a mystic, a visionary who really wants the best for his country and on the whole has rather a broad view."[42]

The Lindbergh's had been completely sucked in by Hitler and Goering. In 1938 Goering personally awarded to Charles Lindbergh the Service Cross of the Golden Eagle, a Nazi medal given in recognition of various fetes and services. Lindbergh considered living in Berlin and even acquired accommodations, but political problems caused him to abandon that idea. He came back to America in 1939 and then became the chief spokesman and supporter of the isolationist group called "America First." Lindbergh gave many speeches telling the public that the Americans should stay out of the European war at all costs. Lindbergh claimed that is was the Jews who were trying to drag America into the war. Anne Lindbergh's short book, "The Wave of the Future," argued that the governments of Italy, Russia, and Germany were the wave of the future. According to Anne Lindbergh the evils seen in those governments and countries were simply a small part of that future and would disappear just at the foam on top of a wave, "the wave of the future," also disappears. Anne wrote, "That it is futile to get into a hopeless 'crusade' to 'save' civilization," by getting involved in a European war against the Nazi's and other fascists.

In 1941 Lindbergh gave testimony in front of congress. This sample of some of the questions and answers are from A. Scott Berg's excellent biography of Charles Lindbergh.

> *You are not, the, in sympathy with England's efforts to defeat Hitler?* I am in sympathy with the people on both sides, but I think

that it would be disadvantageous for England herself, if a conclusive victory is sought.

> *You do not think that it is to the best interests of the United States economically as well as in the matter of defense for England to win?* No sir. I think that a complete victory, as I say, would mean prostration in Europe, and would be one of the worst things that could happen there and here...I believe we have an interest in the outcome of the war.
>
> *On which side?* In a negotiated peace, we have the greatest interest.
>
> *Which side would it be to our interest to win?* Neither.[43]

A view from our modern times with all of our knowledge of Nazi and Japanese crimes leaves us a little breathless. How could anyone entertain such thoughts? But to give some perspective, after one of Lindbergh's radio addresses espousing his support of isolationism, the editors of Readers Digest received a large volume of mail concerning the speech. About 94% of those letters were favorable to Lindbergh's views. Fifteen thousand people showed up to an America First Rally in St. Louis to hear Lindbergh speak. A few weeks later twenty-five thousand showed up to Madison Square Garden to listen and cheer his isolationist views. His largest speech was given at the Hollywood Bowl where the overflow crowd in the surrounding streets was estimated at eighty thousand.

The Roosevelt administration did not like what it was hearing. It went after Lindbergh employing the caustic efforts of Harold Ickes who pointed out that Lindbergh had actually been awarded a medal by Herman Goering. Ickes hammered Lindbergh stating,

> No, I have never heard Lindbergh utter a word of pity for Belgium or Holland or Norway or England. I have never heard him express a word of pity for the poles or the Jews who have been slaughtered by the hundreds of thousands by Hitler's savages.[44]

Even as the Roosevelt administration went after Lindbergh, he continued to enjoy wide support for his isolationism until September 11, 1941. That is when he gave a speech to eight thousand listeners at the Des Moines Coliseum and blamed Roosevelt, the British, and especially the Jews, for trying to drag the Americans into a war that the British were going to lose anyway. He singled out Jewish people saying,

> It is not difficult to understand why Jewish people desire the overthrow of Nazi Germany...But no person of honesty and vision can look on their pro-war policy here today without seeing the dangers involved in such a policy, both for us and for them...Instead of agitating for war, the Jewish groups in this country should be opposing it in every possible way...Tolerance is a virtue that depends upon peace and strength...Their greatest danger to this country lies in their large ownership and influence in our motion pictures, our press, our radio, and our Government...We cannot allow the natural passions and prejudices of other peoples to lead our country to destruction.[45]

The reaction against Lindbergh after the speech was almost indescribable. To claim that Jewish people were somehow pro-war was ridiculous. To claim that Jewish people living in the United States were somehow "other peoples" and not really Americans was beyond comprehension. Lindbergh's call for tolerance is laughable, tolerance for what? Nazi ideas?

In spite of the heavy criticism that Lindbergh endured after that speech he continued to be invited and to speak at America First rallies, an indication that at least his isolationist views remained popular even if his supposed anti-Semitism caused people to be terrifically disappointed. A couple of weeks later he spoke to a large audience and bitterly denounced the Roosevelt administration while not mentioning Jews. On October 30, 1941, he delivered his message to an audience of twenty thousand at yet another rally at Madison Square Garden. His next speech was scheduled for December 10, 1941. He never gave the speech.

Bill Brydon did not like what the Lindbergh's had to say or write. Nine months before the Empire of Japan attacked the United States at Pearl Harbor, Bill wrote to Fred,

> I'm hoping you'll blow the Japs out of the water. There isn't a fingernail left on the west coast. For Pete's sake tell the Navy Department to do something. A Navy doctor in Long Beach said to me that he expected half the navy wives to be in Las Campanas before it's all over."[46]

Bill Brydon's opinion was in line with an unlikely individual, the children's book author Theodor Geisel, better known as Dr. Seuss. Seuss was completely against the pacifists and "America First" types such as Charles Lindbergh. Soon after the war began in Europe Dr. Seuss started to draw editorial cartoons for the magazine, "PM." Seuss was avidly against the Nazi's and was highly critical of the isolationists in this country, especially the Lindbergh's. In one of his cartoons Seuss drew the "Lindbergh Quarter," which featured an ostrich with its head in the sand. In another he drew a Mt. Rushmore scene with Hitler and Hirohito in place of four great American Presidents, with the caption, "Don't let them carve those faces on our mountains!"

The United States seemed to suffer from Bewilderment, a loss of confidence, over-confidence, or just general confusion. Was Bill Brydon's perception the correct one, a perception shared by President Roosevelt and Dr. Suess, or was Lindbergh's and Robert McCormick's isolationist path the one to follow?

Indeed, Mary's unfortunate health problem seemed to correspond with America's lack of direction and decision. Mary had been stranded in Pomona with the responsibility of four children while her husband, whose life would be on the line the minute war broke out, was 6,000 miles away. Isolated from her family and from her husband she could not see the good that she could do at the moment, so she drifted. In the same way very few Americans could see the good they could do as the world fell deeper and deeper into the depressing depths of world war. America was drifting and not even the formidable powers of President Roosevelt could stop it.

Just as with America, Mary teetered on the edge as several people began to debate what was the best course for her and her family. Dr. Newhouse wanted Mary to stay at Las Campanas until she was 100% healed. Bill Brydon wanted to take Mary home as soon as possible. Fred Warder needed to take care of the Seawolf and was too far away to be of much help. During the last year of peace for the United States, people asked themselves, "What should we do?" Fred Warder's family asked the exact same question.

Bill thought he had the answer and took a calculated risk bringing Mary home early against the wishes of Dr. Newhouse. But Bill did not take Mary to his own house where maybe she could rest and get some help from Margaret. Instead, he took her to Mary's old duplex on Eleanor St. where she found her cherished desk from the Dennet house emptied and her papers "scattered about." Mary promptly fell apart and within three days she was right back in the hospital, just as Dr. Newhouse had predicted.

Wilderness

Bill decided that Dr. Newhouse was right after all and began to think of Mary's recovery in longer terms. Bill brought Fred Jr., Mary Jr., Grace, and Suzy back to his own house once again where he and Margaret could look after them. By this time the children were thoroughly scared over the condition of their mother. To help put their minds at ease Bill decided to take Mary Jr. and Fred Jr. to visit Mary at the Las Campanas hospital. Unfortunately, Mary was asleep when they arrived and the doctors would not allow Mary to be awakened. The aborted visit only added to the children's worry. Bill did assuage their disappointment by taking Fred Jr. and Mary B. for a pony ride. They enjoyed that very much and some smiles returned to their faces. The other two children, Grace and Suzy initially weathered the storm fairly well. Some neighbor children helped by inviting Grace to a birthday party. Grace was so excited about attending the party that she dressed up in her special party clothes two hours before she was to leave. Despite the ongoing problems the household calmed down, at least a little bit. A new housekeeper arrived who was a fine cook while Charles, Bill's son, and Suzy played at being newspaper reporters.

The need for Bill and Fred to exchange information increased during this tough period, but communications between the Philippine Islands and Pomona unfortunately remained poor. Fred successfully sent an amateur radiogram to Bill via a ham radio operator in San Diego. This was a system where private ham radio operators delivered messages for people cheaply. Bill found a guy in Pomona, Russell Hillen, who could do the same. While the two sent short messages they weren't able to talk to each other due to scheduling conflicts. This makeshift communications system did help a little but in the end it did not work well enough to satisfy the needs of Bill and Fred.

As if these problems were not enough the car situation added to Fred's worries. Mary inadvertently forgot to send the registration papers for the car to Manila along with the car. Without those papers Fred would have a hell of a time convincing the port authorities in Manila that the Ford at the dock was his. Bill gathered up the necessary papers and registration and sent them. Yet another disaster now loomed as he sent them by boat instead of airmail. Once the car arrived Fred would still be unable to take possession of it, because the papers would be several weeks behind on a boat. When the papers finally arrived, Fred figured that he would have to pay some significant storage fees to get the car released. If ever there was a time for Bill to splurge on a twenty-cent airmail stamp that was it!

However, Bill did have a good excuse for his rather flighty behavior. The corrosive pressure created by the tension of the pre-war months that caused so much bitterness in public debate and helped to undermined Mary's health, now creeped into Bill's life. Bill and his wife Margaret got into a lovers quarrel the day after Mary went into the hospital for the second time. Margaret left the house for a few days and fired the new housekeeper on the way out for good measure. This of course put Bill and the six kids into some turmoil. Simple things like getting three daily meals together for the now motherless family became somewhat of a challenge. The very next day the company that printed Bill's newspaper went bankrupt and would no longer be able to print his paper. Bill's livelihood now hung in the balance. But Bill Brydon's resourcefulness knew no bounds and he somehow got his papers printed, which of course saved his paycheck. Two days later Just as the dark clouds of despair seemed to dissipate, most of Bill's small staff quit. Looking after the kids became difficult without a housekeeper to cook meals. Looking after the two families while Bill wrestled with his business became understandably complicated for Bill.

The collapse of Mary and then the subsequent troubles experienced by Bill, left Fred's four children to fend for themselves. Bill worked fast and arranged for Mary Jr., Fred Jr., Grace, and Suzy to live at a boarding house on Sheridan Street in Pomona. Bill tried to soften the blow to Fred and described the place as, "An Orange grove with chickens, rabbits etc. You could look all year and never find a better place." Mary Jr. and Fred Jr. were able to stay enrolled at Lincoln Elementary School, so that much was good. Mrs. Ray Ingols, the woman who ran the boarding house, took them to school every morning and picked them up in the afternoon. In the evenings they all sat around and listened to the radio. It cost Fred $90 per month to board the children there, which Bill thought a real bargain. However, the unrest began to take a toll on the children. Even though Bill made the boarding house sound appealing, the children were basically lost without their parents. Young Grace, now seriously affected, spoke less and less until she became utterly mute.

Mary's medical costs meanwhile mounted. Las Campanas cost $225 per month, something Mary was acutely aware of and caused her great anxiety, the very thing the staff at Las Campanas was trying to treat. This did not however cause Fred any worries. He repeatedly wrote to Mary not to worry about the expenses or money. His only concern was for her to get better.

It had been a tough month for everybody concerned. Bill, did find some cheer though, writing Fred,

At the city election here today the mayor and one councilman, which I backed, Won! The publisher of the competition don't know which blood vessel to bust first. He's been running the town for the past four years. Now, I got something to say about it. The whole balance of power has been switched so things are rather lively along political row."[47]

Whether on the local level or the national level the loud debates went on about issues as great as world war, and as little as where to put a stop sign.

Mary had not written Fred for over a month, since her "female problems," as she called them, began. At long last Fred received a letter from Mary that explained a few things.

"From the first minute I have been in Pomona I've been terrified...I realized I made a dreadful mistake in uprooting the children from the home we loved [in York, Maine]. I have done little in the hospital except beg to go back to the children."[48]

Mary saw herself in a perpetual state of "fright" that would not end until she got away from the west coast and returned to West Virginia to be near her and Fred's family. The war in Europe caused Mary anxiety. She speculated that it would drag on through the summer. She lost all hope of seeing Fred before September 1941. The United States was not even in a war and yet it touched nearly every aspect of American life, at times the hold that world events had on America was so tight as to be suffocating, and yet few Americans even knew it.

Despite her unfortunate condition Mary never lost her ability to consider others. "The days must pass happily for you – I want them to," Mary wrote Fred. She loved her husband and loved her children. Even in these dark days, she remained confident that her problems would pass, while the people she loved remained. "I can count my blessings, all four," was her sweet sendoff remembering her and Fred's children. Mary had a lot of time to think in Las Campanas. She thought about the past and the mistake of leaving York and the Dennet house. She also thought about being reunited with her husband and children. This one desire became the focus of her life and she began to work very hard in order to achieve her goal.

Despite her clear vision and her determination to get better, Mary was getting worse. She tried to be a model patient and not complain but being separated from her children was almost too much to bear. The uncertainty in the international situation now meant a long separation for her and Fred.

Mary made many exhortations to Fred to do things such as, move to Grafton, quit the navy, get a command with new construction (as Seawolf had been), have Seawolf moved to New London, try to get onto a battleship, and even to buy the Dennet house, "so I can have my children there." But after all of that Mary decided that living in California might be the best unless she could get to Honolulu. In one of her rare bitter moments she said of York, "If the children cannot have a father they must have a mother, a home, and the friends that we loved and respected there in York Valley, and you my sweet must just plan to come there." It was a sad list of wants that would have strained the senses of most people. Fred requested an east coast duty so that Mary's dream of returning to York might be fulfilled. He thought that command of a submarine division in New London or command of a destroyer out of Boston or Bath was possible. Through it all Fred, at least in his letters, remained unflappable and supportive to Mary.

> Take care of yourself and keep your chin up. This won't last forever. I dreamed of you last night – you were prettier and happier than ever.[49]

Near Valentines Day Fred Wrote Mary,

> I would like to get you many many flowers. But failing in that please just know that I hope you'll always be my Valentine. I'm not getting any practice with bows and arrows or anything else in Cupid's line, but you can bet your bottom dollar that my heart will be always completely owned by the sweetest girl in all the world – my darling Mary. I'll come back one of these days with a gleam in my eye.

But the question of when would "one of these days" occur caused Mary many days and nights of worry. Mary needed to do something; however she was being pulled in different directions, and all of those directions consisted of clear uncertainties. First, where should she go? Fred said that he would definitely be back in the United States in January 1942. That was eight months away, a lifetime to somebody who was suffering as Mary was. And then, even if Fred received orders to come to the United States in January, his orders could change as they had before. Who knows what could happen during the last eight months of 1941?

Bill thought Mary should go home to West Virginia and the doctor Newhouse thought so too. The next question: how to get Mary and the family

Wilderness

to West Virginia with a minimum of expense and problems. A lengthy discussion ensued about air travel versus the train. To our modern ears this all sounds so absurd. We simply make a reservation and bounce across the country in a few hours. In the 1940's however a train trip across the country took four to five days, while an airplane, if everything went well, was at least a 24 hour proposition with refueling stops, slow air speeds, and bad weather restricting travel.

Fred wanted Mary to fly out to West Virginia. Flying was more expensive then the train, but in the long run he thought it would be cheaper. If Mary went east by train, Fred thought that his sister and Mary's mother would have to come out and help, thus increasing the travel expenses. Ever the realist Fred explained in a letter to Dr. Newhouse,

> I traveled with my children from San Francisco to Los Angeles about six months ago. I have almost recovered. A trans-continental train ride would probably result in there being three sanitarium cases on the east coast at the end of the journey."[50]

Mary departed for the east, leaving straight from the Las Campanas hospital to the airport. On the way to the airport she decided that West Virginia probably was not the place for her. She wanted to go to York again. Dr. Newhouse of course cautioned against this, saying that Mary's biggest need was a solid support structure.

What a confused awful ridiculous situation! The whole family, including Bill and a nurse, finally boarded the plane, which was equipped with Pullman style beds for sleeping during the long flight. They flew from Los Angeles to Cincinnati and then to Clarksburg, West Virginia. Fred's mother and sister met Mary and the children at the airport. Everyone loaded into two huge old-fashioned cars. In the darkness that surrounded the deep valley of the West Virginia coal country, little Grace's hand got slammed in a car door. She did not cry much as the car motors started and proceeded into the blackest night any of them could remember. Although the night was black there was hope in the air that a new beginning would now be upon them and that this would in fact be the end of their darkest days. After a long drive they at last made it to Bloomington, Maryland, where Fred's sister and Mary's mother lived.

Chapter 5
Endings

Mary and the four children reached West Virginia in May of 1941. During that time the Germans and the Japanese continued to enjoy military success, with the only exception being the German defeat in the air battles known as "The Battle of Britain." It would be some months after America entered the war and the British victory at El Alamein that Winston Churchill declared, "Now this is not the end. It is not even the beginning of the end. But it is, perhaps, the end of the beginning."[51] In the same sense Mary did not reach a new beginning upon her return to the east coast, but after a climactic struggle she finally put to an end to the most significant problems that confronted her.

While Mary settled into her new apartment in Baltimore the children were farmed out to various schools and relatives. Everybody thought this arrangement would serve Mary and the children best by bringing some stability to the situation and giving Mary a little time to rest. Grace and Suzy, stayed with Mary's mother at the Borderside mansion in Bloomington, Maryland. Fred Jr. lived down in the village with Sue Pattison, Mary's sister, and her husband Carroll. Later Fred Jr. went off to Camp Calvert, a summer camp run by Franciscan monks. Mary Jr. went to stay with Fred's mother in Grafton. Things were going well with the aunts and uncles very much enjoying having the nieces and nephew around. Hugh Robert Warder, "Uncle Bob," took a special liking to Mary Jr. after she moved out to Grafton, another uncle, Pat Moran, also helped out. (Pat's son Arthur served on the submarine U.S.S. Shark and visited Fred Warder in the Philippine Islands several times). Early on Sue Pattison took the lead in wrote some hopeful letters both on Mary's condition and the family situation in general. Things had now taken a turn for the better.

At first Mary and the children settled into their new situation fairly well. But after not too long a small trickle of discontent crept into Mary. She was upset with her brother Bill for no stated reason, and wrote, "Foolishly I asked Bill to come with me." A couple of days later Mary made it known that she should have stayed in Long Beach on the west coast. After a few days, a dazed Bill Brydon left, returning to the west coast and his own set of problems.

Endings

Things quickly deteriorated. In June Fred received Mary's letter written from the Athol clinic in Baltimore, Maryland, informing him that she had suffered a relapse. Mary was completely heart broken,

> I went down for the third time, I am in another hospital, and again it is hard for me to make an effort to get better. I told her [Sue] I was a terrible failure and wanted to curl up in a corner and forget I had lived. I did not run away from California, but from the family complications there. Sue is handling the finances of our family at the moment. You owe Bill nothing.[52]

Mary reiterated her desire to live in Long Beach, California, admitting that it must sound strange since she left there just a few weeks prior. Unfortunately, Mary and her brother Bill had quarreled over some insignificant thing and she ended up blaming him for her departure from the west coast. Mary and the children were right back at square one.[53]

What a strange situation confronting Fred, Mary, and the United States. Fred, confined to his submarine, trying to make sense of training regimens that at times didn't seem very realistic to submarine warfare. Mary, confined again to a hospital and feeling like a failure, desperately searched for a way back to tranquility. The people in America confined themselves to a proposition that the oceans could keep the problems of the world away. All three were confused and searching for answers, but would they find those answers before time ran out?

Fred didn't know that time was rapidly running out for him; soon he would be on the front lines of a new World War. Mary knew that time was running out for her, and over the next several months she produced an all-out effort to make herself better. Nobody in the United States ever knew or imagined that time had already run out for them, the Japanese were already training their aviators in anticipation of their unprovoked attack against the United States at Pearl Harbor.

* * *

Seawolf continued drills at sea and target practice with practice or "dummy" torpedoes. The warheads on those torpedoes were filled with water. After taking a shot, compressed air in the torpedo forced the water out of the torpedo and it floated to the surface. Later, after practice, Seawolf's crew retrieved them. Warder proved to be a superb shot, which was not an easy task before radar and "smart" weapons. In WW II shooting at the enemy required the crew to point the submarine in the direction of the target. It is true that WW II torpedoes did have a gyro to set its course after launching, but the torpedoes still had to travel in a straight line, and they still had to be aimed with the periscope.

The first step in the process consisted of establishing Seawolf's course and speed. Then Warder lined the "wire" in the periscope lens onto the target. As he did, Lt. Mercer read the relative bearing from the ring on the periscope. About five or ten minutes later another reading would be taken and from this, Ensign Casler would start to calculate the enemy's course and speed. While that was going on Warder tried to either identify the ship specifically or at least name the ship's class. If he did not know this from sight he could consult the several publications provided by the navy that presented photos of the various classes of ships, and also showed them in profile. This step was extremely important because from the identification Warder derived the range of the target. He did this by checking a reference or estimating the height of the enemy ships mast. A stadimeter in the prism of the periscope helped him in his calculation. From there Casler made a few easy trigonometric calculations that gave the range of the ship. All of this sounds pretty straightforward and scientific but in truth, with no computers and no reliable radar the whole operation was basically a series of guesses.

As the Seawolf got closer to attack position Warder called the "angle on the bow." This was the most critical part of the operation, on which the whole attack hinged. Unfortunately calling the angle on the bow had much more to do with art than science. Warder produced the angle on the bow by imagining a line calculated from the target's track, a difficult task as the target would more than likely be on a zig-zag course. From there, Mercer called a bearing from the submarine to the target, as Warder looked through the periscope. The angle formed by the intersection of those two lines at the target produced the angle on the bow. Believe it or not, with practice a good CO would regularly be less than 1° off the mark. Just before firing all the calculations would be gone through again. Just below the conning tower in the control room, Lt. Deragon put the final numbers into an analogue computer called a Torpedo Data Computer or (TDC). After a minute or so the solution light on the TDC came on indicating the final gyro angle for the torpedo had been solved. Deragon then turned a switch that sent those calculations directly to the gyro in the torpedo. After all of that the torpedo was fired. It must be remembered that unlike most of our modern ordinance, WW II era torpedoes had no electronic guidance. Once in the water the "fish," as the sailors called torpedoes, was on its own. It is a wonder that any ships were sunk with these rudimentary weapons. What is more impressive is that Warder rarely missed a shot.

Other systems that technology has all but done away with, such as the ship's compass, also needed scheduled maintenance. For this Warder "swung the ship." WW II era ships used gyrocompasses to find true north. As a backup, those ships, including submarines, had magnetic compasses too. Magnetic compasses always have a bit of deviation from true north making them a little bit inaccurate. Further, the readings they produce vary depending on where the compass is on the globe. The steel hull of a ship also causes problems with magnetic compasses. These problems are exacerbated in a submarine. For these reasons magnetic compasses must be calibrated by inserting or removing a series of small magnets located in its body. This process is referred to as, "swinging the ship."

Through the month of June life in the Philippines got into a pleasant routine. When he went ashore at Manila, Warder had a wide choice of entertainments. "Of course when we do go ashore golf is expensive, drinks are not cheap, we stay to dinner, go to a movie and generally manage to shoot 15 pesos rather easily." At least he didn't waste money on some of the more notorious sailor expenses. "I don't shoot craps or play roulette as do some, and I won't play the Jai Alai anymore."[54] Although he lost some money wagering on that game, Warder saved some money on drinks near the end of June. After coming in from a cruise he and a few friends tied one on pretty tight and caused some trouble. Warder decided enough was enough and went on the wagon, which was good for his health as well as his pocketbook.

Aside from those activities Warder got quite a bit of fishing in, his lifelong passion. He also began to take an interest in bridge. Being at sea for weeks at a time really encouraged sailors to play card games. Many, or even most, liked to play poker, but Warder's game was hearts, knowing that Mary was a bridge player Fred resolved to learn that game while in the Philippines. On occasion, when a game got together on Canopus, Fred went to watch, but did not feel confident enough to actually play. "I'll get in one of them [bridge games] one of these days but after all it will be more fun learning from you. My Seawolves and I get a lot of fun out of the hearts game – five of us can play it and it does require some skill," wrote Fred somewhat defensively. "I have attempted to work up a bridge tendency, but the reaction is very weak," as crewmembers preferred lighter forms of entertainment.

Fred continued to find the work on Seawolf rewarding. "If I were in another outfit I would be just as separated from you and my children as I am now, and the operations would not be so interesting and would be lots more punishing."[55] He did however suffer a few irritations; amongst them being his fitness report. Wilkes marked his fitness "excellent." Warder saw no reward in that. He considered his boat to be the best in the division, however all of the CO's received the same uniform "excellent" rating. Warder, thinking pragmatically, added, "It was the best I could hope for as I've tangled with him [Wilkes] more than the others." Warder already had a reputation for confronting his superior officers. He did have a solution to his problems though. "I'm sure I have the best boat in the division and so long as I keep her that way, he [Wilkes] can't treat me too badly." Despite the friction Wilkes complemented Warder a few times. Warder characterized each of those occasions as being, "Quite a concession."

One confrontation between Warder and Wilkes involved the safety of his men and the Seawolf. The rainy season came to the Philippines with a vengeance in June of 1941. During one of the typhoons Warder wanted to get the Seawolf away from the dock and anchor in deeper water where, if an emergency came up, he could simply dive the ship and escape the storm. To Warder anything that reduced the possibility of his ship being damaged should be done. He waited for orders.

Orders did finally come from Wilkes to get under way, but with no mention of an anchorage. Warder went to Wilkes's office to find out where Seawolf should anchor during the storm, only to find Wilkes still in his "Pj's" smoking a cigarette in his bunk! Warder had already been up for two hours sweating over the safety of the Seawolf. The situation irked him quite a bit. To make matters worse Wilkes told Warder they were not going to anchor at all, but rather go out for gun drill. Warder was incredulous. He knew he couldn't put men on deck during a typhoon let alone have some kind of meaningful practice with the deck gun. Wilkes replied that he wanted the Seawolf out on the ocean, and that the Seawolf crew could not just sit around doing nothing. One could almost see the smoke coming out of Warder's ears as he looked at Wilkes, nice and cozy in his pajamas pontificating on the need for more activity. "He damn well knows our engines and motors need work…but away we went for what was really a luau of a morning with mountainous seas and of course not able to put anyone on deck…I trust he [Wilkes] had a bellyful."

Other excitement in June included the arrival of the Deragon's new baby named Virginia Therese and a crewmember's appendicitis. A couple of accidents occurred, not unusual in a submarine. Torpedo Mate 3rd c. Chubbuck, fell down an open hatch while the Seawolf practiced surface torpedo tactics. Another crewmember named Bjerk was securing the three-inch deck gun when the ocean washed him against the barrel of the gun

Endings

cutting his forehead and nearly breaking his jaw. Six sutures later the seaman 1st class was back on duty.

In spite of Warder's sometime cantankerous nature, he and the crew got along very well. However, in late June two of his crew nearly cost him his command. Two Machinists Mates, John Street and J. Snyder, while on shore, went on a bender and got into serious trouble. After causing the usual problems in a local bar, shore patrol showed up. But for some reason the two sailors did not allow the shore patrol to gently lead them out of the bar and back to their ship. An officer came to lend a hand. An altercation ensued in which either Street or Snyder hit the shore patrol. A wrestling match began as the two sailors threatened the officer. Finally, the shore patrol subdued the two sailors and took them to the brig on Canopus.

Street and Snydor must have been excellent compliments to the Seawolf crew because Warder immediately came to their rescue. First, he brought them back to Seawolf, which was moored next to Canopus. Then on July 1st Warder quickly called a mast and charged both Street and Snyder with, 1) Resisting arrest, 2) Threatening a superior officer in the execution of the duties of his office, and 3) Using profane and obscene language.[56]

Deck Court quickly followed, presided over by Lt. Adkins, which was an oddity in itself. The third charge admittedly was not serious, in fact if ever fully enforced our Navy ships would be without crews. The first two charges, however, were very serious and should have warranted a full Court Martial, not Deck Court. Additionally, there was testimony during the Deck Court that one of the sailors actually hit the shore patrol, an offence that usually landed a person in Leavenworth. After their conviction on a plea of guilty, Street and Snydor were sentenced to ten days of solitary confinement on bread and water. Warder must have been playing a role behind the scenes because, considering the charges, the sentences were ridiculously light.

Admiral Thomas Hart certainly thought so. A few days later he called Warder over to his office at the Marsman building. Hart asked Warder a few questions about the case, a superfluous activity since Hart already knew everything about the case. Warder gave him some factual and courteous answers to the questions. Then Hart enquired as to how somebody who hit a shore patrol and threatened a superior officer is sentenced to only ten days of solitary confinement. Warder replied that it was his business and not the Admiral's. The conversation became heated. Hart demanded that Warder bust the men down completely. Warder refused. Some question might have come up between the Admiral and the Lieutenant Commander as to who ranked whom, and who gave the orders. Warder gave no ground. Finally the contest intensified into a short staring match. As Hart looked at Warder he thought, and then he thought some more. Warder was a good officer. Hart, maybe alone amongst high-ranking officers, thought a Japanese attack imminent. He continued to look at Warder. Then in a controlled voice Hart said to Warder, "You better sink a lot of Jap ships." With that, the interview ended. Warder saluted, turned, and walked out of the office.

Warder's crewmembers were ecstatic over their CO and his showdown with the Admiral. However, Warder knew that Hart, in the end, was right. He had better perform well if the war did come, or his career might be in jeopardy. In one of his few letters disparaging any crewmembers Warder wrote to his wife Mary,

> [I have] good men in the ship but their activity on the beach has been a bit trying on me – and no damn good on my service reputation.[57]

Later in the war Fred Warder was dubbed "Fearless Freddie." More than a few people recall that it was this encounter with Admiral Hart that caused him to be fit with that moniker.

As for Admiral Hart, he sincerely believed that war with Japan was nearly upon us, that is proved by the movement of ships under his command. Furthermore, he ordered special torpedo technicians from Virginia out to Manila to install a super-secret device in the nose of every torpedo. During the 1930's the Navy developed a special exploder/detonator for torpedoes called the Mark VI. After the development and manufacture of some several thousand exploders, the Navy locked them away in a vault to protect the secret. Only a handful of people even knew of their existence. In Adm. Hart's view the world situation had deteriorated to the point that the secret had to be let out. The technicians came out and installed the new "miracle" weapon giving the crews a great amount of confidence.

*   *   *

During the month of June Mary put in a terrific effort so that by the end of July she showed a remarkable improvement. She even recovered her sense of humor and sent Fred a funny newspaper clipping about how grown women were returning to live with their mothers and fathers while their husbands were away on military duty. The worst now seemed behind Mary. The rest of the family back east gave a lot of support and Fred's mother especially cheered Mary up with her letters. Looking on the bright side Mary now repeatedly said that the whole episode will probably "turn out for the best."

Endings

In addition to her returned sense of humor Mary had finally regained her faith in the future.

The children also did fairly well under the circumstances. Fred Jr., or Bubby as he was known in the family, won an archery contest at the summer camp. Susie and Grace both enjoyed living at the Borderside mansion with their Grandmother Grace Brydon. The house was big enough for good games of hide and go seek, and the surrounding acres made for fun outdoor games and adventure. The household help at Borderside allowed the two girls to assist in making biscuits while they all sang standards such as "Oh Susanna" and the like. When not helping to make biscuits in the kitchen Grace and Suzy enjoyed cooking up their own culinary surprises – mud pies. Grandmother Brydon might not have approved the messy dresses that the cooking of the mud pies created, but all in all the stay at Borderside was very enjoyable for the two girls.

Now that disaster had been averted and Mary returned to health, she and Fred could concentrate on the next problem; trying to explain Mary's recent problems to curious friends. In our modern times health problems such as depression are much better understood and are far more effectively treated than sixty years ago. There is not much of a stigma attached to it anymore. But in Mary's time depression to the point of hospitalization was thought to be a sign of a general unbalanced mental condition and was quite a shameful situation. Mary had not told anyone about it. Only a few wives of the crewmen, McDowell, and Watts, had seen her in Las Campanas hospital. Dotty Kinsella had come by to see her in the Athol hospital. Only a small group of people knew about the situation, none-the-less Mary knew of gossip, especially in New London where an important submarine base was located. Sue also took steps to try and keep the problems from the general public. Sue knew personally one of the tellers at the bank where she did business. Together they made sure checks going to the hospital and clearing from the bank would not become evidence for idle gossip. With careers and social standing at stake one could not be too careful arresting whispers.

However, the new cured and very rational Mary knew that "Bad news travels fast. One way or another it is generally known by now that I've been ill." Mary counseled Fred as to what they ought to do with enquiries of the last three months.

> Let's not play or trick about it. Nor do I think we need to broadcast. We have many good and kind friends in the Navy. When they ask about me, do not give them a short or mysterious answer. "Yes, Mary had some tough (or bad)

> luck in California. She is fine again, better than she has been in a long time." The whole story can be summed up as simply and truthfully and sincerely as that, in twenty words. All of us are curious for some reason. All of us have troubles, and all of us, find comfort it seems, in the misfortunes of another. We must not resent the inevitable questions that those who know us will feel they can ask. You were wise and right to keep your own counsel. We can keep it always about my "vacation." In a few years no one will ever remember. I, most of all, want to forget that it has been a long, lonely, and gruesome struggle at times.[58]

Mary understood people and society very well. As for her personal battle against her too active anxiety and worry, she had won. She had felt terrible during the dark days, letting down her family, causing worries for her husband, creating more money problems, and missing her children. So, it was especially satisfying to her that she had dug herself out of the depths. She topped it off with a question for Fred,

> Now three guesses how a woman starts to forget anything – yes – she buys a new hat! I bought the inevitable blue one yesterday.

Shopping as therapy, what a great idea, some things never go out of fashion. Since Mary's odyssey to the west coast, the war in Europe had taken many twists and turns. The battle of Britain had been fought and won by the good guys. In June of 1941, about the time that Mary and the children traveled to Baltimore, the Germans invaded Russia. For the next three years titanic battles took place on the eastern front between the armies from those two countries.

Closer to home, the Battle of the Atlantic raged between Germany and the United Kingdom. That ongoing struggle pitted the German submarines against allied merchant shipping and the few British destroyers sent to escort those convoys. The German submarine aces sank huge amounts of allied merchant shipping. The Germans sank so many British ships that the British became seriously concerned about their survival. That was the heyday of German submarine CO's. Gunther Prien of U47, who in addition to sinking scores of merchant ships, sank HMS Royal Oak in a daring attack at the British fleet's homeport of Scapa Flow. Otto Kretschemer, the "Tonnage King," sank 6 ships, all of them tankers, in one night for a total of nearly 70,000 tons. Joachim Shepke participated in one of the most successful

Endings

German submarine raids against a convoy in which twelve allied ships were tragically sunk.
But the allies answered back with improved tactics. In a span of ten days in March 1941, Prien and Shepke were killed in counter attacks against their submarines U47 and U100 respectively. As for Kretschemer, he survived the sinking of his submarine, but did not evade capture. The loss of those three famous, even celebrity German CO's, sent shock waves and depression through the German submarine ranks. Prien, "the Bull of Scapa Flow," was so famous that for months following his death, many Germans claimed "sightings" of him, much as today when people think they have seen Elvis Presley.

President Roosevelt, never one to shy away from the absolute strongest language possible, called the submariners "rattlesnakes." That did not sit too well with Mary. "Even the "thoughtful" words in an "historic speech" by a "great" President in a crisis becomes a part of yesterday," she wrote. The move between the west coast and the east coast did not mellow Mary's sarcastic attitude towards the President. She reassured herself on the issue of right and wrong saying, "The Seawolf – as the padre said when she was launched – is only a terror to those who do evil – a help to those who do good."

One's perspective is so important when judging good and evil. Mary's perspective never changed and turned out to be irrefutably, the proper perspective. War is an ugly business but at the very least the allies were fighting for a just cause, cutting short the Holocaust before its final conclusion, being an important part of that cause. As Winston Churchill said, "If we fail, then the whole world including the United States, including all that we have known and cared for will sink into the abyss of a new Dark Age made more sinister, and perhaps more protracted, by the lights of perverted science."[59] If some in the United States were confused at that time about right and wrong and the nature of the Germans and the Nazis, certainly Mary Warder was not confused; neither was the Prime Minister of the United Kingdom or the President of the United States, nor was the author of some soon to be famous children's books, Dr. Seuss.

With the coming of the school year and Mary still recuperating in Baltimore, it fell to Aunt Sue to look after school for the children. Upon returning from camp, Fred Jr. attended a Catholic boarding school called Leonard Town. Mary Jr. was to go to St. Augustine's, but transportation and money problems became an obstacle. Sue came up with about five different plans to get her into a good school. Judging by her deft handling of the negotiations amongst family members, Sue might have been able to become an important part of the State Department's international negotiating team. Everybody put their two cents in while trying to foist most of the effort onto some other person. Sue, always the last person standing, was able to organize the schooling effort with a minimum of damage to family feelings. She understood quite well that Mary's health was at stake when she wrote Fred,

> Your Mary is going to have all the chances possible to make a complete recovery, which she will in time, that is the main thing, and it will be done regardless of expense.

Fred could not have hoped for a better sister-in-law, and Mary could never have dreamed of having such a rock for a sister.

Through all of it Sue kept the social side of the family relations intact and she often had family dinners either at her house or sometimes at another relative's home. On one occasion however Sue's plans went completely awry when she bought a leg a lamb to be prepared at Fred's mother's house. As she loaded things in the car, Sue forgot something and went into the house for just a moment. Upon returning to finish loading the car she could see the leg of lamb firmly trapped in the jaws of the neighbor's dog as it ran away. Sue ran after the dog for a bit but realized that the treat in his mouth would be too motivating for Sue to ever catch him. She settled for a few choice words then calmly went and purchased another leg of lamb. Such are the day-to-day ups and downs of life, completely ignorant of extra efforts put forward by people like Sue.

Mary continued to improve through the month of October. In late November of 1941 she was discharged from the hospital and found a small apartment on Calvert Street in Baltimore near Johns Hopkins University. It was a very nice neighborhood with oak and maple trees lining both sides of the street. In the autumn chill of that dark November the leafless branches created harsh shadows on the ground. As she gazed up through the branches Mary looked forward to a bright and sunny springtime when those same branches would again be covered in leaves providing shade to people strolling up and down the sidewalks or playing in the yard. The apartment came furnished; a real bonus for Mary as hassling with her own furniture seemed unwise at the time. The ease of the move to Calvert Street suited Mary very well, as did the style of the apartment. Built of bricks with a nice backyard, the two-story dwelling had the kind of character that appealed to Mary's excellent taste.

On December 3rd she wrote to Fred describing her new place and promised that Christmas of 1941 would be happy after all. As she got the

Endings

apartment in order Mary, having learned well the hard lessons of the past eight months, did not overexert herself. When she got tired, she rested, which made her proud of herself. Mary had learned how to, "Make haste slowly." She also included very nice words for Anna Mary, Sue and Carroll Pattison, and the Gundry's, all of whom had given so much to help Mary get better. Mary proposed that they, "Should all be "decorated" as the "Committee-for-getting-Mary-well."" Very graciously Mary mentioned her brother and his wife,

> Of course Bill and Margaret and others in Pomona and Compton did their best. But you know so well what a "handful" I can be under ordinary circumstances – can you imagine how many handsfull I was out there (sic). Bill was wise to bring me East. I would have recovered out there but I am not sure the recovery would have been either complete or permanent. I am sure about both now. Quite quite sure. So, as I wrote before, when you do have time for a note to the Pomona family – give them a "hand."[60]

Mary had been a little concerned that she had not heard from Fred for most of October. Because of military secrecy she did not know of the Seawolf's movements to Zamboanga, Sulu, or Tawi Tawi. However, when Mary received the items Fred purchased for the family in Zamboanga, she filled in the blanks herself realizing he had been at sea. Fred intended those purchases to be Christmas gifts, sent out early to beat the busy Christmas mailing season. In her letter, Mary praised Fred, "Your shopping ability is excellent, and always has been." Mary suggested that they keep Fred's Christmas presents in Baltimore because, "you will be home so soon after Christmas," 1941.

Looking forward to the reunion Mary wrote,

> Making up is fun. Though I feel that my heart will be "soft like butter." I don't feel like Panama butter just around the heart – I'm afraid I feel that way all over (it's wonderful). Do you suppose I am in love?

Mary had once again found her happiness. Though separated by a continent and an ocean Mary and Fred could see their problems fading in the distance. Mary was recovered, things were quiet in the Pacific, and Fred's long anticipated return to the United States in January 1942 might yet happen.

Stavros

* * *

    While Adm. Hart was so convinced of an early war, others including Warder, were not. He wrote Mary, "I cannot discuss the international situation. I don't believe there are many who could intelligently." However, he might have had something else on his mind. He continued, "Let's hope for a good long quiet leave together and a leisurely shore duty." When confronted with a beautiful woman, which Mary certainly was, every sailor is entitled to a little wishful thinking, no matter how improbable. Much later, on November 12th, and maybe in a fit of denial he again wrote her, "I feel sure there is not going to be any war out here, so please don't fret on that score."[61] Only twenty-five days after Warder made that prediction his credentials as a prophet got shot full of holes, literally.

    And any thoughts of leisure in Manila came to an end rapidly. On July 9th Canopus and her submarines, including Pickerel and Seawolf, left for an intense training cruise. A few days after leaving Manila the small submarine fleet found itself in Cebu, a fairly large island in the Philippines next to the islands of Bohol and Leyte. The currents around Cebu are swift reaching speeds of over five knots at times. Traversing the seas in that area can be more like navigating in a river than the open ocean. Two days later Seawolf arrived in Davao, stopping for just a few hours. Unbeknownst to Warder and the crew, in just over a year Davao Gulf would be the place of their greatest triumph.

    Leaving Davao, Seawolf headed to Tawi Tawi for twenty-three days of concentrated drilling, devoting every day and many nights to intense torpedo practice. After nearly wearing themselves out, Seawolf left for Tutu Bay in Jolo for a few days of rest. Seawolf then split her training and berthing time between Zamboanga and Tutu, finally returning to Manila on August 24th. Their long sojourn away from their homeport, the equipping of the secret Mark VI exploders, and the intense training give good evidence to the critical political situation with Japan as Adm. Hart saw it. He continued to think war with Japan was immanent.

    The stay in Manila was a short one, just enough time for the crew to stretch their legs on shore and enjoy a few nights of revelry. Regrettably "Swede" Hanson had what amounted to his usual "liberty" problem. The good news is that he did not get a hold of any alcohol, which he sometimes drank to excess causing him to be absent beyond liberty on more than a few occasions. The bad news is that he and a buddy got a hold of some

Endings

Lambanog, a potion made from the nectar collected from the flower of the coconut tree. The "mangangarit," or sap collectors, climb a tall palm tree early in the morning and collect sap known as "Tuba." Once they climb the initial palm the mangangarit travels from tree to tree on bamboo bridges as high as twelve meters off the ground, collecting the Tuba. It is dangerous work. Falls are inevitable causing serious injury or death. After the Tuba is collected, it is distilled into the concoction known as Lambanog. People refer to it alternatively as coconut wine or vodka, of which it is neither. The American sailors knew it as Generbra Gin. It is potent and can cause hallucinations. When Hanson and his friend returned to the ship that night, loaded to the gills with the stuff, the rest of the crew knew that a long sleepless night lay ahead. Unlike alcohol Lambanog is not a depressant. Far from sleeping it off, the two crewmembers yelled and shouted at their hallucinations all night.

In spite of any high jinx some of the crew engaged in, Warder had a clear mental picture of what he wanted his crew to resemble. He wanted men who performed their jobs at the highest level of efficiency while on the Seawolf. That is why Warder defended men such as Hanson who performed his job to perfection and fit well with the rest of the ship's crew. Others, such as Vincent Munson, who was convicted of "treating his superior officer with contempt," Warder got rid of rapidly. The comparison is made even starker as one of Hanson's many convictions for absent over liberty came on the same day as Munson's single conviction for contempt. Munson was given confinement and immediately transferred while Hanson received a grade reduction; but Hanson's sentence was remitted on condition that he performed satisfactorily for the next six months. It was as if Hanson was not punished at all. It was also lucky that no one specified exactly what "satisfactory" meant. Good thing too, Hanson might have been planning his next lark, even as he received his so-called sentence.

In addition to keeping his "problem children" aboard Seawolf, Warder had to fight to keep non-trouble making crewmembers on his ship. To his benefit he had a multitude of highly motivated and qualified crew, undoubtedly a reflection of Warder himself. In June, Capece,[62] Enslin, Butler, Sandridge and Mocarskey, all made chief. At the time Warder had eleven chief petty officers on board his ship, which rated only three. "I will have to fight like hell to keep them aboard…and probably lose," was his opinion of the situation.[63] He already lost a favorite in Evan Watts, who appropriately was a Chief Electricians Mate, to the submarine Pike after a protracted struggle to keep him on the Seawolf. Watts and his wife were both personal friends Fred and Mary. Mrs. Watts had been on the scene in Pomona and very helpful to Mary and Bill Brydon during that crisis.

Warder suffered his greatest personnel loss though when Lt. William Kinsella, the engineer and electrical officer, received transfer orders. Kinsella was a personal friend of Warder's while Mary was a good friend of Bill Kinsella's wife Dotty. He was popular with the crew without pandering, and popular with his fellow officers because of his great competence. He went on to be X/O of Blackfish and then commanded his own ship, Ray. On his first patrol with Ray, he sank five enemy ships and participated in one of the great submarine battles of the pacific war at Paluan Bay, in August of 1944. By the end of the war he accounted for eight enemy ships sunk.

In all, four of the officers that served under Warder in the months prior to the war commanded their own ships; James "Catty" Adkins in Cod (four ships sunk), William Deragon in Pipefish (two ships sunk), Richard Holden in Gato (10 airmen rescued),[64] and William Kinsella in Ray. The success of those officers is a testament to Warder who gave them a good example of how to command a ship and lead men.

Commanding a fleet Submarine could, at times be glamorous. Exotic ports of call, roaming the high seas in rough and dangerous games, and of course all the other things associated with fun loving sailors. But sometimes the whole operation was simply a grind, which ate away at the crew's health. Warder himself had a few health problems in 1941 including his bum knee and an ongoing case of prickly heat. To make matters worse some bureaucrats "servicing" the government insurance policy Warder bought and paid for, decided to hassle him over his coverage. He was not the only one either; Wilkes, Reamey, and Adkins all reported similar problems with their government insurance. Aside from these problems Warder was trying to sell his car. For some reason he thought he could sell it for a better price in Manila, so he had it shipped the Philippines. But Warder, by his own assertion, was not a good salesman and the car lingered like an open sore for many months, as if he needed any more problems.

In late September Seawolf cruised back to Jolo. While there, Warder took some practice torpedo shots at the destroyer U.S.S. J.D. Edwards without missing once, proof that his marksmanship was getting even better. Good news is often coupled with bad. While in Jolo the ship's clock, a chronometer manufactured by John Bliss and Co., stopped working. To most people it is just a broken clock, but in the old days the ship's clock was one of the most important pieces of navigational equipment and the only means of locating the ship's position longitudinally on the globe.[65]

Endings

After exercises in Jolo, Seawolf returned to Manila and spent the rest of September, all of October, and some of November in that port. While there, Warder's good friend Hank Reamy's health deteriorated so rapidly that he was declared unfit for duty and removed from his command. In turn, this made him the only remaining original CO in the squadron. One unlucky CO lost his command when he was accidentally shot. Warder fervently hoped he would not "go the way of the other captains."[66]

During this time Warder expanded his training and went up in an airplane to observe submarine maneuvers. He came away with a much better "appreciation" of what aviators see and a better concept of the "submarine problem." Much of the submarine training before the war emphasized detection avoidance, which is good, but the high command went a little overboard on this, which in turn caused too much diffidence in most of the prewar submarine COs. During the early months of the war Warder and a few other COs displayed much more boldness than the majority of the submarine COs. It might be that as Warder flew over and observed those submarine maneuvers on September 20th, he began to formulate new ideas on tactics, understanding that Submarines were a lot harder to see from the air than he had been led to believe.

When not in training, Warder was able to enjoy his usual recreations of golf, bowling, fishing, and walking. He also attended mass at the church where his daughter was baptized. During the last weeks of November Warder had an opportunity, and took high mass with the Archbishop, then dined with him afterward, a real high point for Fred. Reassignments brought a bunch of his old submarine buddies – from the old "S" boat days – out to Manila. Mort Mumma, Lew Chappell, Ray Lamb, Casey Hurd, Ham Stone, Mick Irish, and Bull Wright, are a few of the people that Warder caught up with in the last weeks of November.

Late in November Warder's good fortunes briefly turned sour. Somehow his health turned bad for about a week. His prickly heat came back accompanied with a recurrence of his knee problems, a very bad earache, and for some reason he complained that his teeth were hurting him. Then he took a required yellow fever vaccine and landed in the hospital. Because of Warder's health problems Dick Voge, whose boat Sea Lion was in for a major overhaul, was ordered to take Seawolf if Warder did not recover rapidly. That "would have broken my heart," a thankful Warder wrote after his miraculous recovery.

While Fred was recovering from his health problems some excitement came to Mary back in Baltimore in the form of the Navy vs. Notre Dame football game. Fred Jr. was crazy about football and Mary was also a big fan.

She wanted to take Fred jr. to the game and somehow managed to get tickets to the sold-out contest. Attending the second most important game on Navy's schedule was quite a treat for Fred Jr. Notre Dame, under the legendary coach Frank Leahy, was having a great season and entered the game against undefeated. After a tough battle Notre Dame kept their perfect record and beat Navy 20-13.

These small family triumphs always came as good news to Fred. He loved to hear that everybody was healthy and having fun, but at the same time, the longer he stayed in Manila the lonelier and more morose he became. Most of the time he was able to put on a good show of happiness for his crew and fellow officers. Later he confided to Mary that, "I can't pretend that I have been exactly a beam of sunshine around the place." A few days later he wrote to Mary,

> I am sure that everything is for the best and that I have no need to worry about you. I am not worrying – my darling – so please don't fret on that score. The ship manages to keep by mind well occupied and I must be ready for the big chance. There are a lot of us out here with troubles and problems and it behooves us to stay cheerful. Sometimes it's a hell of a job to do so.[67]

The arrival of December saw Fred fully recovered, out of the hospital, and back on the bridge of the Seawolf. His position was ambivalent to say the least. He enjoyed his work on the Seawolf. He had been that ship's only Commanding Officer. But the situation with Mary, and his great love for her, superceded that. He wanted to get an assignment on the east coast of the United States to be with Mary and bring his family back together. As early as August he thought a transfer by the month of January possible. But as November turned to December those hopes became clouded.

With reassignment plans fading, Mary and Fred thought in simpler terms, such as a possible phone call in December. Both knew they probably had but one chance at a call, long distance telephone communication not being what it is today. Mary wrote Fred that they should try to call each other on Christmas day unless Fred thought he was going to be at sea. In that case, Mary instructed, they should try to call each other earlier than that on her birthday, December 17th, 1941.[68]

Chapter 6
Dark Days

The planned phone call from Fred to Mary on December 17 to celebrate Mary's birthday never happened. On the afternoon of December 7th, a message issued by the Chief of Naval Operations ordered personnel in the Philippines to "execute unrestricted air and submarine warfare against Japan."[69] For Frederick and Mary the sudden attack against the United States by the Empire of Japan put an end to one set of problems and concerns; namely Mary's health problems as well as keeping the family together and Frederick's grueling and dangerous training regimen. Unfortunately, the new set of problems, keeping the family together in wartime, dealing with housing shortages and rationing, as well as Fred's grueling and dangerous combat regimen, were of a magnitude exponentially greater than before.

The problems that occurred at Pearl Harbor are well documented and there is reason enough to at least mitigate the shortcomings of the commanders at Pearl Harbor. That is not the case in the Philippines though and it is of some amazement that the U.S. forces did so poorly there in the early hours of the war. This is especially puzzling since the early war warnings of November 24th and 27th, 1941 both explicitly named the Philippine Islands as a probable "surprise" target of the Japanese military "within the next few days." [70] This explains why reinforcements continued to leave Oahu for the Philippine Islands. Yet even under the emergency conditions the "sudden" U.S. military buildup in the Philippine Islands consisted of only 6,083 new army personnel between July and December 1941.[71]

Additionally, B-17 bombers were being transferred from Oahu to the Philippines. This is especially enlightening since those particular planes were considered a sort of "cure-all" to the problems facing the U.S. Military as war loomed with the Empire of Japan.[72] Indeed on August 20 of 1941 Colonel William Farthing sent a report to Washington that claimed, amongst its 10,000 prophetic words, that Oahu could be defended with just 180 B-17 bombers.[73] But reports are meaningless if they are not backed up with the actual planes. On December 7th the entire army stockpile of B-17s numbered only 109 planes. Previous to that time Roosevelt had generously given many B-17s to the British. Much to the chagrin of Secretary of War Henry Stimson, on September 12th, Roosevelt, in his airy way, gave five of the planes to a visiting Russian delegation. On December 1st the last of Pearl Harbor's B-17's, 12 in number, flew to the Philippine Islands. When the war began General Douglas MacArthur, who commanded the United States Army in the Philippines, had 74 bombers and a total of 207 airplanes of which only 35 were B-17s and 107 were modern P-40 fighter planes.[74] By contrast the Japanese navy alone had 2,274 warplanes.[75] Therein lay the crux of the problem.

While Warder and the crew of the Seawolf labored through countless hours of training with high morale, the numbers simply were not there for the Americans. At the beginning of hostilities, Adm. Hart's Asiatic command fielded just three cruisers, Houston, Marblehead, and Boise, 13 destroyers, some small gunboats, 6 PT-boats and 29 submarines with their three tenders plus the small rescue craft Pigeon.[76] Compare that to the Japanese forces of 10 battleships, 3 cruisers to every U.S. Asiatic Fleet Destroyer, 9 aircraft carriers, 113 destroyers, and 69 submarines. No matter how well the troops trained the situation on paper seemed hopeless. And it was.

The U.S. military simply did not have the wherewithal both in supplies and training to defend against a concerted and determined attack from Japan in late 1941. This is a bit perplexing because President Roosevelt could hardly be accused of not speaking to the Americans about the dangers of the Nazi's and the aggressive Empire of Japan. Plus, those two aggressive powers along with their Axis partner Italy, daily gave fodder to the news services about their latest atrocities.

Be that as it may some of Roosevelt's close advisers counseled that the U.S. should not have a Pacific perimeter of influence extending beyond Hawaii and Alaska. Harold Ickes and Senator Millard Tydings both had misgivings about our presence in the western Pacific, but the most vocal opponent of a U.S. Pacific presence was Attorney General Frank Murphy. This is a bit ironic since Murphy had been Governor-General and then High Commissioner of the Philippines beating Douglas MacArthur out for the job. One might think that he would cherish the Philippines, but Murphy was a pacifist who did not believe that the U.S. should have a defensive perimeter in the Pacific at all.[77] Murphy disliked MacArthur personally, which might have contributed to his lack of interest in defending the Philippines. He also had a cruel streak. One time when Treasury Secretary Henry Morgenthau Jr. sent a bill to Darryl Zanuck for back payment of taxes Murphy commented to Morgenthau, "Too bad you didn't send it on Christmas Eve."[78]

The murky political situation in the western Pacific, the pitiable amount of war material available, and Roosevelt's Europe first policy (even naming the destruction of the "Nazi Tyranny" as a goal in the Atlantic Charter in

Dark Days

August of 1941 four months before the attack at Pearl Harbor), sealed the fate of the men in the western Pacific. But the rust and rot of the U.S. military, which made the Japanese surprise attack possible, began eating away at the military long before the Roosevelt Administration even showed up. The American public is most responsible for the catastrophe of December 1941. In the end, if things go wrong in a democracy, the people have only themselves to blame. If America's fighting forces do not have the equipment to defend America's freedom, it can only mean that the people did not care enough to pay for that equipment.

* * *

As November rolled into December Admiral Thomas Hart saw the ominous signs of immanent war. On Monday December 1, and for the next four days, unidentified and identified Japanese planes were spotted near Clark Field and Iba Field. On Thursday December 4th American P-40 fighter planes began nightly patrols over Luzon and spotted some Japanese bombers over the Lingayen Gulf.[79] On December 6th Vice Admiral Tom Phillips flew to Manila from Singapore to discuss the situation with MacArthur and Hart. Phillips wanted Hart to give him 4 destroyers as escorts for the British capitol ships Repulse and Prince of Wales operating in the vicinity of the Malay Peninsula. As they conferred, a report came in that a large Japanese convoy had been sighted off the Siamese coast. Admiral Hart then asked Admiral Phillips when he was going back to Singapore. Phillips replied that he intended to leave the next morning to which Hart said, "If you want to be there when the war starts, I suggest you leave right now." At that time, Admiral Tom Phillips had 4 days left in his life.[80]

Unlike their attack on Pearl Harbor, the Japanese enjoyed no surprise when they launched their attack against the Philippine Islands, but they did enjoy an extraordinary amount of good luck. Admiral Kimmel, in Pearl Harbor, radioed Admiral Hart in the Philippines the famous message, "Air raid on Pearl Harbor this is no drill." But Admiral Hart did not relay the message to MacArthur. MacArthur did get his air force off the ground to avoid the problems suffered at Pearl Harbor; namely having our planes destroyed on the ground.

In another great twist of bad luck for the U.S., the main Japanese air assault against U.S. airfields in the Philippines was delayed due to bad weather. Foggy conditions forced Japanese pilots to take off from their bases in Formosa several hours later than planned. During this weather delay

American interceptors took to the air in search of the enemy. U.S. P-40 fighter planes flew in the direction of Lingayen Gulf, but when they arrived, the Japanese they planned to intercept were not there. It seemed like a false alarm. In fact, Japanese carrier-based planes had attacked Tarlac, Tutuegaraw, and Camp John Hay.[81] The U.S. pilots came back to Clark field and landed thoroughly convinced they were not under attack. In the meantime, the B-17's based at Clark had taken off but without bombs. They flew in the vicinity of Mount Arayat for the only purpose of not being caught on the ground by the Japanese.

Confusion reigned as General Lewis Brereton, in charge of MacArthur's air, and General Richard Sutherland, MacArthur's Chief of Staff, called each other repeatedly about what should be done. Brereton wanted to launch bombing attacks against Japanese bases at Formosa. That was a good idea. However, Brereton had no aerial photoreconnaissance, so he did not know what he wanted to hit. He ordered a B-17 outfitted to take pictures. Finally, at 11:00am, eight hours after the attack at Pearl Harbor, Brereton got authorization for the bombing missions. But by that time, the fog over Formosa cleared and 108 Japanese Bombers and 84 "Zeros" pounced on Clark field. With all of the P-40 fighters back on the ground, and all except one of the B-17 bombers on the ground, the Japanese easily destroyed the American planes. It was Pearl Harbor all over again with most of the Army air power wrecked in the first hours of the battle.[82]

The U.S. Navy avoided this incredible turn of bad luck. To the credit of Admiral Hart most of the U.S. ships were already at sea, safely away from air attack. The navy airplanes in the Philippines, consisting of 28 PBY seaplanes, could not be at sea and suffered a similar fate as their army brethren, being shot down and ruined one after another over the course of a month. By January 1, 1942, only 8 of the planes were left. (Upon making contact with the enemy one U.S. Navy Airman radioed, "Have sighted enemy planes please notify next of kin.")[83] This created yet another problem for the navy. Without air support, the Navy's ships were sitting ducks. Up to this point Navy doctrine said that air attacks against ships at sea would fail. The Japanese proved this wrong. The British finally learned this bitter lesson when the heavy cruisers Repulse and Prince of Wales were sunk near Singapore just three days after the beginning of the war.

* * *

With the cruisers and destroyers out to sea and the air force wiped out, all that remained around Manila were the infantry and the submarines with their tenders at Cavite Navy Yard. Nine submarines were already out to sea and eighteen more, including Frederick Warder's Seawolf, left on December 8th. That day proved to be hectic and dangerous. Men on the seaplane tender Langley manned guns to defend against air attack while Warder and the rest of the Commanding Officers attended a meeting on the Submarine tender Holland.[84] Orders were issued and the skippers were enjoined from acting too aggressively. Adm. John Wilkes wanted short "safe" patrols to gather information about enemy anti-submarine tactics, convoy formations, and other strategies employed by the Japanese. This seems incredible since the Japanese had been at war for several years already. One might think that the army and navy would have investigated these matters already. Furthermore, to call for "safe patrols" was redundant since all pre-war training emphasized timidity. But from the first war patrols, bold innovative commanders like Fred Warder and Wreford "Moon" Chapple shelved the timid approach, laying the groundwork for other successful skippers in the future.

Warder returned to the Seawolf at 9:00am with orders in hand. He limped slightly as he boarded Seawolf, his knee problems still unresolved. The crew quickly loaded fresh food and more torpedoes onto the Seawolf. By evening they were ready to leave on their first war patrol. As a last gesture the men threw all of their paint and metal polish overboard, harkening back to the days of sail when the order just before battle was, "clear for action," and everything not pertaining to fighting, such as livestock, chairs, and hammocks, were thrown overboard.[85] The crew ate a hearty dinner of steak, French fries, and asparagus cooked by Gus Wright; the Seawolf's chef; submariners had the best cooks and food in the navy. This time though the meal was a culinary waste. All of the men were antsy and wanted to get going so they choked down their food as fast as they could.

At precisely 5:00 pm the Seawolf left Cavite and steamed into the war. Langley, Pecos, Black Hawk, and the submarine Sculpin made up a small convoy that cleared the outer minefield by 9:30 pm. Problems began immediately as the army illuminated buoys and the Seawolf with a searchlight. While trying to be helpful it only had the effect of blinding the people on the bridge of Seawolf.[86] Warder later reported, "This practice must stop." This is another example showing that prewar training did not always give the best results once the war started.

As the small convoy gained the open ocean the ships began zigzagging, which slowed things down much to the annoyance of Warder. The very idea of being an escort in a convoy irked Warder and his crew. In the earliest hours of December 9 Warder pulled ahead of Sculpin in his eagerness to make contact with the enemy. When dawn came on that same day Seawolf submerged to 63 feet and headed for the San Bernardino Straits at a crawl of 2.5 knots.

As Seawolf proceeded through the Straits, Warder dutifully came to 55 feet for regular "radio skeds," times when they might receive messages and new orders. The radio operator only heard white noise static, probably due to the enemy's radio jamming efforts. For the moment the Seawolf operated alone in the sea without guidance from headquarters.

Later in the day rough seas compelled Seawolf to travel at a depth of 120 feet.[87] At 6:00pm Seawolf surfaced in complete darkness amidst rainsqualls. The crew began charging batteries, which thankfully ended by 10:30 pm so they could put all 4 diesel engines to the screws. Warder surmised that he could clear the San Bernardino Straits that night even though they were fighting an ebb tide. Upon diving in the early morning of December 10 the Seawolf cleared the Straits and found itself in open ocean headed for the northern part of Luzon to scout an anticipated Japanese landing near Aparri.

The Seawolf and her crew spent a relatively serene day December 10th; serene that is compared to the hell that Cavite and the men there endured. Only two submarines remained at Cavite Navy Yard when the Seawolf left on December 8th: Richard Voge's Sealion and William Ferrall's Seadragon. Undergoing overhaul, they could not be moved. The near destruction of the American air force meant that they could not be protected from Japanese air attack. That is just what the Japanese had in mind as they sent three groups of bombers, each group numbering 27 planes, to Del Carmen and Nichols air bases, and Cavite Naval Yard. 72 Japanese "Zero" fighters also joined the attack. The American air force could send only 20 P-40's and 15 obsolete P-35's against the Japanese who quickly overwhelmed them. At about 1:00 pm Japanese bombers made their first attack against Nichols field. Then Japanese fighters moved in with very effective strafing attacks.

The second group of Japanese bombers flew towards Del Carmen but abandoned that target for shipping in Manila Harbor.[88] Once again the Japanese attacked with great accuracy. The final group's destination was Cavite Naval Yard. As the bombs began to rain down on Cavite, Carl Mydans, a writer for Life magazine, and Mel Jacoby, a writer for Time, watched from the shores of Manila. Mydans commented on the incredible accuracy of the Japanese bombing, "Not a single bomb seemed to be wasted."[89] Admiral Hart himself watched the beginning of the slaughter from the Marsman building in Manila.

The Americans counter attacked with their battery of nine 3-inch anti-aircraft guns. But the shells that worked burst well below the high-flying

Japanese bombers. The unopposed Japanese flew back and forth over Cavite for the next two hours casually picking and choosing their targets until most of the base was in flames. To make matters worse the Japanese cleverly destroyed the powerhouse so that the fire fighting equipment did not work.

The men from the two stranded subs sitting at Machina Wharf, Sealion and Seadragon, also joined the counterattack using their shipboard .50-caliber machine guns. As the men blazed away at the Japanese, Commander Voge ordered them below. A few seconds later a bomb exploded sending metal fragments into both Sealion and Seadragon. Then a second bomb directly hit Sealion ending her career. She was later scuttled in Manila Bay. In all, five men died from those two Japanese bombs. Seadragon was able to stay afloat and later evacuated Admiral Hart and his staff from Manila to Corregidor. The shops of Cavite were wrecked, and the oil storage set on fire. The Japanese also managed to destroy 230 torpedoes. Most importantly and sadly 500 navy personnel were killed at Cavite on December 10th.

While Cavite went up in smoke the Seawolf traveled beneath the surface of the water for the rest of the day, coming to 63 feet every 15 minutes for periscope observation. When they came up for those observations the men swiftly scanned the sky 360° for airplanes. A submarine did not distinguish friend or enemy when it came to airplanes, always diving immediately upon sighting one. As for the aviators, they treated all submarine sightings as the enemy and tended to "shoot first and ask questions later." After looking for airplanes the person observing through the periscope did a quick look around with the low power setting and then if all was clear went to high power hoping to find an enemy ship. Failing that the ship proceeded to its cruising depth and 15 minutes later the whole process started again.

At 11:00 am on December 10th Paul Malay, then operating the sound sensing equipment, tracked down Eckberg, who was the senior radio operator, with a problem.[90] Maley was hearing strange noises all over the dial but could not make out what it was. The sounds also puzzled Eckberg. He did not hear the rhythmic cavitations "swish-swish-swish" that the screws of a ship make. Eckberg continued to listen to the confused and erratic sounds for several minutes and finally determined that the Seawolf had inadvertently come upon two Japanese ships, possibly submarines, and they were somehow communicating with each other. As his heartbeat began to race with excitement and additional sweat dripped from his face in the smothering heat, Eckberg reported his thoughts to the captain. Warder, while interested in what Eckberg had to say, discounted the report. After all they could hear no screws and they saw nothing while making periscope searches.

On a submarine during WWII discerning the sounds of the ocean was somewhat of an art form. Different propellers made different noises. Big ships sounded differently than little ships. This all had to be differentiated from the natural sounds of the ocean and ocean life. As Claude Conner put it in his book, "Nothing friendly in the Vicinity:"

> While listening a radio operator could easily identify snapping shrimp, croakers, and whales, but there were many other mysterious organic sounds that we were unable to identify. The sounds built up to a peak at sunrise and sunset, like those in a tropical jungle. It was a wonderful cacophony of discordant whistles, howls, hoots, rumbles, belches, snaps, crackles, and pops.[91]

Warder felt these "scanty contacts" by the radio operators were usually false alarms[92] and he did not want to slow down; getting to his patrol station was paramount.[93] On they went.

Then the troubles began. That afternoon Warder received a disturbing report from the engine room. The lubricating oil coolers were leaking. Manufactured by the Harrison Radiator Co. those coolers had already generated numerous letters and complaints from Warder. He vented his frustration in the War Patrol Report reminding whoever might read it that leaking oil coolers were not a new problem!

Luckily the Seawolf brought along some spare parts including some oil coolers. The crew in the engine room went into action. They disabled engines 2 and 4 and investigated the problems since Warder desperately wanted to have all four engines operational by nightfall for surface operations and full speed. Despite every effort the engines remained unfixed when Seawolf surfaced after sunset. As much as Warder wanted to put engines 1 and 3 to forward propulsion it was not in his nature to be reckless. The batteries, being depleted from the submerged daytime operations, needed to be recharged. If not then the ship and crew would not be able to dive if sighted by the enemy. The number 3 engine went to charging the batteries while the number 1 engine went to propulsion. With decks awash for added security the Seawolf crawled at 9 knots.

After three hours the battery charge was completed. Seawolf now had two engines on propulsion and her speed increased to 12 knots. It took the crew three more hours to complete repairs on engine number two and the speed increased to 13.5 knots. Finally, the 4th engine was repaired, and the ship cruised at 17 knots. Warder felt better and he retired to his bunk to catch a few hours of sleep before dawn and what he hoped would be an action filled day.

At 6:30 the next morning the sound operator reported ship contact and then another. Periscope observations proved disappointing again. Warder noted in the logs that the false alarms of this morning and previous day came from the same operator. Warder suspected that "yesterday's alarms were the result of men working in the torpedo room and this morning's alarms were the result of men working in the engine rooms and after torpedo rooms."[94] The rest of the day proved uneventful for the Seawolf.

The Seawolf reached its patrol area on the early morning of December 12th. As the crew hunted for the enemy, weather became an obstacle. Storm conditions brought the sea to condition of 6 and wind force to 5. Despite the thrashing the crew kept on the surface searching for the enemy. One can imagine the scene. Four men on lookout duty with, not just spray in their faces, but whole waves crashing over the conning tower soaking them in cold water as they were lashed by the wind. One man would be standing on the small platform high upon the periscope shears. As he searched for enemy ships, he might be able to distinguish the ocean from the sky while being pitched by what Warder reported as "mountainous" seas. But they had to try.

In calm seas the ship usually operated with decks "awash" to offer as small a target to the enemy as possible. But in heavy seas Seawolf needed to ride higher in the ocean. In order to achieve that position all remaining water had to be purged from the ballast tanks using the low-pressure blower. When activated the low-pressure blower made a hideous screaming noise nearly deafening to the men on the bridge. If that did not make lookout duty bad enough the continuous roar of the four huge diesel engines took away any thought of comfort on the bridge. One of the great ironies of submarine movies is that the action on the bridge is necessarily presented as being during the day, which of course is incorrect since most of the daytime operations of a submarine took place beneath the surface of the ocean.

As the sun came up on the 12th the Seawolf submerged. Warder reported that the ship was still uncontrollable at 55 feet, increasing the chance of broaching even as their patrol area became more infested with enemy ships. At 9:00 am they spotted the northern tip of Luzon and headed for the Babuyan Channel. At 4:36 pm sound reported pinging. The officer of the deck, Lt. Holden, ordered the Seawolf to periscope depth. A small electrical whirring noise signaled the rising of the periscope. Scanning the sea Lt. Holden found nothing. Less than a minute later the sound operator acquired the bearing of the ship 278° T. Lt. Holden ordered a coarse change hoping to find the ship. At 5:03 pm Holden made another periscope observation at a depth of 60 feet. This time Lt. Holden sighted a Japanese destroyer. He excitedly called for the captain.

Warder took a look and confirmed Holden's sighting, a Japanese Destroyer at a range of 6,500 yards. Immediately the ships intercom barked with the repeated order "battle stations, battle stations" as the ships general quarters alarm sounded "bong, bong, bong..."[95] They tracked the enemy ship for about 30 minutes. The sound operator listened to the "whish, whish" of the enemy's propeller. Every now and then the rhythmic sound skipped a beat; the sea being so rough during this encounter that the back end of the destroyer at times broached the surface causing its screws to spin wildly in the air.[96] The crew of the Seawolf also was being thrown around, some of the men getting quite seasick. Unable to close the range Warder decided to not pursue the Japanese warship and continued into the Babuyan Channel.

After submerging on the morning of December 13 Seawolf spotted another Japanese destroyer, which at 16,000 yards Warder initially mistook for a cruiser and tried to close the range for an attack. Seawolf got to within 12,000 yards when Warder realized his error and broke off the "chase." One of the most significant problems for a captain is properly identifying ships, as this case pointed out. Nothing else happened that day other than sighting a few broken down fishing trawlers in the harbor at Aparri.

At 5:00 am the Seawolf arrived at San Vicente and then submerged. As they crept into the harbor they began to hear the long range pinging of enemy ships sent to hunt and sink the Seawolf. In spite of that Warder kept the Seawolf moving forward, well inside the 30-fathom line, toward the port. As they proceeded the sound operator heard some short range pinging, which generally indicated that the Japanese had picked up a short-range target. The sound operator then reported a second set of pings as another enemy ship joined the hunt. Had the Seawolf been discovered? Warder ordered the crew to rig for silent running shutting down all blowers, fans, air conditioning, and refrigerator machinery. They "commenced avoiding tactics" and headed for the 100-fathom bank where 3 hours later the Japanese quit the search. Warder then led Seawolf right back into the port of San Vicente.[97]

By 12:30 pm the Seawolf was again deep in the harbor. Warder, looking through the periscope, reported a calm sea and beautiful bright sky. An hour later, as his search continued, his patience paid off. Warder spotted what he initially reported as a large seaplane tender at about 5,500 yards.[98] He called the men to battle stations. Henry Thomson, equipped with phones on his head and talking apparatus on his chest, repeated the orders on the intercom that echoed through the ship. The men ran to battle stations as the alarm sounded "*bong, bong, bong...*"

Dark Days

And now the real game was afoot. The fire control party consisting of Warder at the periscope, James Mercer the assistant fire control officer who read the relative bearing from the rings outside the periscope, James Casler the expert navigator at the plotting table, Rudy Gervas the helmsman, Henry Bringleman at the torpedo fire control panel, William Deragon at the Torpedo Data Computer (TDC), and Henry Thompson who stood just behind Warder and repeated his orders through the phone to the necessary compartments of the ship, mainly the people in the torpedo rooms and engine room. The crew spent the next hour covering just 1,700 feet as they made their way to the best firing position. Their quarry now floated in ten fathoms of water and moved slowly as if looking for an anchorage. There was little chance of missing such a slow moving ship in the calm waters of San Vicente harbor but Warder still ordered a spread of 4 torpedoes; 2 set to run at 40 feet and 2 set at 30 feet.

"Prepare torpedo tubes one, two, three, and four," ordered Warder.

"Prepare torpedo tubes one, two, three, and four," repeated Thomson.

"Target at 143°," called John Mercer reading the numbers on the outer ring of the periscope.

"Change course, 130°," ordered the captain getting into their final firing position. He spent the next few minutes coaxing the helmsman, "a little to the left Rudy…a little more…hold steady"[99]

"Open the outer doors," was the next order.

"Open outer doors," repeated Thomson.

One of the crewmembers in the forward torpedo room began turning a large wheel, which opened the outside doors exposing the smooth half domes of the torpedo heads.

"Bearing – Mark!" was his next order.

"Bearing 359°," Mercer immediately reported.

William Deragon the TDC operator turned the dials as the mechanical computer made its familiar coffee grinding sound; a few seconds later the green solution light flickered on confirming that the gyro angle had been solved.

"Ready to fire," reported Deragon as the TDC machine automatically sent the gyro angle electronically to the torpedoes now ready to leave on their one-way journey.

Henry Bringleman switched torpedo tube number one to the "on" position. A dim orange light then came on indicating the tube was ready to fire. Warder set up the first shot at the first smokestack on the ship. Patiently he waited as it moved toward the crosshairs or "wire" of the periscope. When the stack touched the "wire" he gave the order, "fire one!"

Bringleman hit the plunger with the palm of his hand and the torpedo left the Seawolf with a "swoosh." At that same moment Thomson repeated the order, "fire one," over the phones to the torpedo room. If the plunger did not fire the torpedo properly the men in the torpedo room could fire it at the same moment. As Bringleman fired the torpedo he clicked on a stopwatch to check their calculations for elapsed time to impact.

A small jolt went through Seawolf, now about 2,000 pounds lighter. The crew felt pressure in their ears as the poppet valve vented residual compressed air, which launched the torpedo, back into the boat. The well-trained crew quickly re-trimmed the ship in order to maintain a constant depth. Losing so much weight so suddenly could cause the boat to broach the surface, giving the enemy a precise area to counterattack.

Bringleman then switched on torpedo tube number two and the orange indicator light came on. When the enemy ship's forward kingpost touched the wire Warder ordered, "fire two." He waited a few more seconds until the mainmast touched the wire then ordered, "fire three," and then the fourth and final shot went to the last smokestack. Sound reported that all four torpedoes were running, "hot, straight, and normal." The actual torpedo firing, all four shots, took a total of about 24 seconds.

As Bringleman stared at his stopwatch the rest of the crew went into swift action.

"Full speed left full rudder," ordered Warder. The helmsman turned the wheel and set the enunciator, which signaled the men in the control room to put full power to the screws.

"Make the depth 90 feet, Warder ordered." The QM repeated the order through the phones to the diving officer in the control room just below the conning tower. The men in the control room adjusted the bow-planes and Seawolf gently descended. The men in the forward torpedo room worked feverishly to reload the torpedoes. That took seven minutes. In the meantime, Bringleman's stopwatch ran to twice the allotted time for impact and Warder concluded somehow they had missed.[100] Warder did not record any periscope observations of the misses.[101] He now set them up for a stern shot. Rudy steadied on a course of 270° and then Warder ordered a depth of 63 feet. With the periscope just protruding the surface of the water to where Warder "could only see the top of the stack," the firing bearing worked out to 178°, and the gyro angle set to 277°, four more torpedoes were let loose on what seemed to be a completely hapless enemy. But once again, notwithstanding reports from the engine room of four explosions, nothing happened.

Nothing, that is, except now the Japanese knew Seawolf's approximate position. The sound operator picked up and reported pinging to the captain. Warder decided to "run out of the area northward for the night and changed course to 323°." Three minutes after the course change the Japanese counterattack began. A depth charge detonated "well distant on the starboard quarter" as the men went to depth charge quarters. Seawolf descended to 200 feet and rigged for quiet running with all machinery turned off except the electric motors turning the propellers at full speed. After several more distant explosions the crew secured from depth charge quarters. The ship ascended to 120 feet, her regular daytime patrol depth, and at 5:24 pm went to periscope depth of 63 feet for observations. At 6:30 that night Seawolf surfaced in black darkness and began its battery charge as it cruised around the Babuyan Islands group. It had been an exciting yet disappointing day. Many problems needed to be solved and the officers and crew knew it.

For the next ten days Seawolf continued to patrol around northern Luzon. Hampered by incredibly bad weather the captain and crew made no contacts with the enemy and at one point could not accurately establish their own position as visibility sank to less than 300 yards. On December 26th the Seawolf cruised toward Manila Bay for some rest and repairs. The ship could not go to its usual place, the now destroyed Cavite Naval Yard. Instead, Seawolf anchored at Mariveles at the end of the Bataan peninsula. The crew wanted a little rest but the stay proved un-restful and frustrating. The Americans no longer had an effective air force to defend their ships. That forced Seawolf out into Manila Bay every day to lie safely on the bottom of the ocean until night when they could once again come in and dock.

Despite this discomfort and the inability to make a lot of use of daytime hours, Fred remained optimistic. To Mary he wrote, "Things aren't like they were in 1812 when Perry could write and say, "We have met the enemy and they are ours," but I will permit myself to say some things from which you may read between the lines to wit – we have had a splendid baptism and I have had good luck in the northern latitudes."[102]

Seawolf had many mechanical problems including leaking oil coolers, no submerged reception on the "loop," and poor water-making ability. Previously Warder had requested a vapor still and now he repeated it as a matter of survival. To make water the Seawolf needed to run at "load" but the engines tended to spark when running high, which could signal the Japanese of a U.S. submarine in the area. Warder again requested wet mufflers (good luck getting them). He also found that the pitometer log needed to be moved noting that with either one or two sound heads down the pitometer log had an error of 10% to 33% introducing corresponding errors into the position indicator and the data computer. The Seawolf also suffered from air leaks, which seemed to plague many boats throughout the war. Warder reported air leaks from the impulse piping, the sea chest, main ballast, safety, and bow buoyancy tank blows. In other words, the ship leaked just about everywhere.

The biggest problem though proved to be torpedo failures. As noted, Seawolf's first four shots of the war probably went under the ship it attacked. So there seemed to be a depth problem with the torpedoes. Tyrell Jacobs of the U.S.S. Sargo experienced similar problems. After taking a shot at a freighter sitting at anchor near Camranh Bay his own ship nearly blew up when the torpedo detonated only 18 seconds after he fired. Because of the danger to his own ship and his idea that the Japanese had developed a system that caused early detonation of torpedoes, Jacobs had the magnetic detonators removed off of his torpedoes and used only contact detonators. Ten days later he attacked two slow moving freighters at a range of only 1,000 yards with a spread of three torpedoes and all seemed to miss. He turned and fired two stern torpedoes at the same ships at 1,800 yards and they too did not explode. A couple of hours later he took two more shots at two more ships at a range of 900 yards and all missed. Thinking that the gyro angle might be off he set a new attack against two more ships with a zero-gyro angle. He double checked the periscope readings with the TDC readings and had his Executive Officer get his own readings and check them independently. After making sure that every bit of the equipment worked, the executive officer and Jacobs agreed on the firing solution and let a salvo of two torpedoes go. Nothing happened. In a last desperate move the crew adjusted the depth setting thinking the torpedoes might be running deep. To test their theory, they happened to find a slow-moving tanker, a rather big ship, took careful aim and fired. As they depressed the firing plunger and clicked on the stopwatch they waited anxiously. The time of estimated impact passed. Still they waited but in the end they heard no explosion. After firing thirteen torpedoes Jacobs concluded that the torpedoes simply did not work.[103] Other skippers reported similar results.

The problem with the U.S. torpedoes began in the 1930's during the design stage. Under the direction of Ralph Christie, the Newport Torpedo Station developed the Mark XIV torpedo, which became the standard torpedo for the United States through the first year and a half of the war. But the design did not work, which is not necessarily bad because after a few tests the design flaws would show themselves and be corrected. However, the Mark XIV was never tested from a submarine. All test shots had been made from a barge.

Dark Days

A new detonator was developed at roughly the same time called the Mark VI. In the past torpedoes simply hit the side of a ship and blew up on contact. This simply caused shipbuilders to line the hulls at the water line with extra armor to counteract the torpedoes. The Mark VI detonator was designed to explode a torpedo under a ship, where there was less armor, causing greater damage to the enemy. This was a great idea and a huge leap forward in torpedo technology except for one thing, the Mark VI also did not work. This again would not have been a problem except that no live tests were made with the new weapon. In defense of Christie, he asked for live tests on several occasions and even petitioned the Chief of Naval Operations to provide a ship for the tests. After the usual hassles the old destroyer Ericsson was made available for a live test of the new torpedo and detonator. There was only one hitch; the Newport Torpedo Station was told not to fire a loaded warhead against the ship, and also told that if any ship sank, they had to raise her.[104] With such ridiculous restrictions, the tests of course, did not go ahead. Later in October of 1941 just before the war broke out Warder also asked that two live tests take place out in the Philippines. That too was denied. Too many people had great faith in the magnetic detonator as a magic and infallible weapon that needed no testing.

This attitude is particularly peculiar considering that by 1941 the rest of the world had already been at war for nearly two years. Both the British and German navies developed magnetic detonators before the war. Both navies had found the new "miracle weapon" so faulty that after a short period of time they had them removed in favor of the old contact detonators. Two U.S. Navy observers in Britain, Lieutenant D.G. Irvine and George Crawford,* (later to command division 43 in Pearl Harbor), sent word to the U.S. that magnetic exploders did not work. The failures were reported to the Bureau of Ordinance.[105] In spite of this information the Bureau of Ordinance and the Newport Torpedo Station still did not attempt even one test of the new device.

After the dismal results of the first war patrols and the experience of Lt. Commander Jacobs, some skippers again asked for tests at Surabaya where,

---

* Later George Crawford, who had the nickname "turkey neck," was transported on the U.S.S. Seawolf. While aboard, the Seawolf had to make a crash dive and as people were racing down the stairs into the conning tower Henry Thompson, at the foot of the stairs, directed them to the second set of stairs that went to the control room below. Apparently Thomson was very energetic in his directing because Crawford ended up sprawled on the floor, which he did not appreciate.

after the latest retreat, the U.S. Navy resided. This time it was Adm. John Wilkes who turned down the request citing an extreme torpedo shortage. Of course, he did not reconcile the fact that without reworking, 70% of the torpedoes would not explode anyway! The Bureau of Ordinance was again contacted but as usual they blamed ship personnel for the problems. The Bureau finally sent Lieutenant Commander Walker out to the various submarine ports in the Pacific to go over torpedo maintenance and preparation for firing with the crews. After putting the crews through rigorous drills and checking everything they did, Walker found no problems with the crews' maintenance and preparation. In spite of the crews' perfect record Walker still insisted that the torpedoes ran at the correct depth.[106]

About this time George Crawford, after serving as an observer in the United Kingdom for the U.S. Navy, received new orders and reported to Pearl Harbor. This seemed to be a lucky break for the American's. Crawford knew firsthand the problems the British had with their magnetic exploders. When Crawford took command of division 43 at Pearl Harbor, he immediately ordered his CO's to switch to contact exploders. The sad stories of U.S. CO's blown opportunities because of defective torpedoes, and his own experience with the British made Crawford's decision easy. Unfortunately, his superior, Rear Adm. Thomas Withers, did not share his opinion and apparently did not think too much of Crawford's experiences in the U.K. Withers ordered Crawford to make sure all skippers in his division 43 used the magnetic exploder. In dressing down Crawford, Adm. Withers claimed to have been in Newport during testing of the torpedoes and exploders. As noted before no live tests had been done on the Mark VI magnetic exploder. Testing on the Mark XIV torpedo was from a barge not a submarine. Withers negated the golden opportunity Crawford offered to put an early end to the torpedo problem during the 4th month of the war.

Then John Wilkes, who had been a champion of the poor-quality torpedoes, was "rotated" back to the U.S. and took command of a cruiser, the U.S.S. Birmingham. Upon his exit he was awarded the Distinguished Service Medal. His accomplishments included tactical training that meant absolutely nothing when the war actually started and arguably hampered the success of the various submarines. His overall strategy produced very few enemy ships sunk, this despite the fact he could have learned from the experiences of both German's and the British and applied their experiences to enhance the success of U.S. submariners. His poor showing in those two areas contributed to the unbroken success of the Japanese fleet and the swift retreat of U.S. forces from the Philippines all the way down to Fremantle, Australia. And lastly,

Wilkes did not lift a finger to help correct the torpedo problem that plagued his forces.

Luckily for the submarine force, Charles Lockwood replaced Wilkes. Lockwood immediately enquired to the Bureau of Ordinance, now headed by William Blandy, of any recent tests that indicated the Mark XIV's ran deep. The Bureau of Ordinance gave their usual answer "the torpedoes are fine," and indicated that commanding officers should stop blaming the torpedoes and get to the real problem: poor marksmanship. Unlike Wilkes, Lockwood sided with his skippers and decided to do his own test. On June 20th, 1942, seven months after the war started and with the expenditure of about 300 torpedoes in combat that had accounted for 10 ships sunk by the Asiatic submarines, a controlled test of the Mark XIV torpedo finally took place. Lt. Commander John Coe commanding *Skipjack* fired three shots into a net at Frenchman's Bay. All three shots showed that the torpedoes ran about 10 feet deeper than their setting. On the 21st two more torpedoes were tested with the same results. On June the 22nd Lockwood sent a message to the Bureau of Ordinance with his test results. On June 30th he received a message back from the Bureau stating, "no reliable conclusions" could be drawn from the test citing "improper trim conditions." On July 18th Lockwood did another round of tests with the exact same results. The Chief of Navy Operations, Adm. Earnest King, now got into the act and ordered Blandy at the Bureau of Ordinance to do some real tests from a submarine. U.S.S. Herring fired the shots and proved what combat veterans knew all along; the torpedoes ran about 11 feet deeper than the setting.[107]

The Bureau of Ordinance sent out new instructions for depth settings. The problem seemed solved. Unfortunately, the depth problem hid the bigger problem; the magnetic exploder did not work. Here Charles Lockwood committed the same error as Wilkes. He did not call for tests of the exploder. He hoped the resolution of the depth problem also solved the failures of magnetic exploders. The tragedy is that Lockwood knew that the British and Germans had discontinued the use of their magnetic exploders but did not act to at least test the U.S. exploders.

So the officers, crews, and submarines continued to go into battle with defective ordinance. Not only did the torpedoes fail to detonate under enemy ships as designed but also, they had a tendency to prematurely explode shortly after leaving the submarines. It is not unusual to read in the various war patrol reports of expected torpedo runs of 40 seconds lasting only 18 to 20 seconds and then reporting violent explosions next to the submarine. These premature detonations many times were more violent than a depth charge counterattack by the enemy.

Nearly a year after Lockwood's simple tests, and because of the continuing failures, The Bureau of Ordinance issued new guidelines for the magnetic exploder. These guidelines included disabling the exploder in shots of less than 12 fathoms of water as the torpedoes tended to prematurely detonate (of course this went against the problem of deep running torpedoes), arming the torpedoes at 700 yards instead of 400, and a whole list of dos and don'ts depending on the submarine's position relative to 30° north magnetic latitude and 30° south magnetic. On June 24, 1943, Admiral Nimitz, the overall commander Navy commander in the Pacific, ordered that all magnetic exploders be deactivated. But on July 11 Admiral Ralph Christie, who had been on the original development team of the magnetic exploder and outside of Nimitz's area, directed that his command retain the magnetic exploder.[108] Incredibly the submarine crews of the South West Pacific Command continued to go into battle with the defective magnetic exploder all the way up to March of 1944, nearly two and a half years after the war started and over a year after even the Bureau of Ordinance had lost faith in the device they had created with Christie's help.

Except for Ralph Christie's command, the torpedo problems seemed solved. But incredibly results worsened after disengaging the magnetic exploder in favor of the contact exploder. It did not take long before the "brass hats" began hearing complaints from submarine skippers of a new torpedo phenomenon, the "dud." Lt. Commander L. R. Daspit experienced possibly the worst case of the soon to be infamous "duds." Daspit commanded U.S.S. Tinosa. In July of 1943 he caught the Japanese "supertanker" Tonan Maru No. 3, a 19,000-ton prize that virtually every submarine commander in the Pacific had drooled over and hoped to sink. As this monster came into periscope view one can only think of the exhilaration that the captain and crew must have felt. To make the deal even sweeter Tonan Maru lacked any escort whatsoever. Quickly and accurately, Daspit lined up and fired a spread of four torpedoes, two of which hit but raised only harmless water splashes. As the huge ship attempted to escape, Tinosa fired two more torpedoes both of which hit, one exploding violently. Tonan Maru lay dead in the water. Now Tinosa could sink the unescorted leviathan at its leisure. Daspit lined up a shot and fired. He watched the track go straight into the ship and then gasped when only a disappointing waterspout came up instead of the huge explosion and conflagration he expected. Undaunted he lined up another shot and another, all with the same results. He fired eight shots at the tanker with a zero-gyro angle with neither the submarine nor the tanker moving. All eight torpedoes hit but none exploded. Add to that the three "duds" in the initial attack and you have eleven torpedo "duds" out of twelve torpedoes fired.[109] And this after everybody thought the torpedo problem was solved.

When Daspit returned to Pearl Harbor, he carried his sorrowful tale and one last torpedo to Adm. Lockwood. By this time Lockwood knew better than to contact the Bureau of Ordinance and simply did his own tests. Firing two torpedoes at some submerged cliffs on Kahoolawe Island, just southwest of Maui, one torpedo exploded fine while the other sent up the familiar small waterspout of a dud. Salvage crews recovered the dud and upon inspection found that the pins that guide the firing pin to the detonator had been bent thus impeding the progress of the firing pin. This caused the firing pin to hit the detonator with insufficient force to ignite the torpedo. Lockwood organized further tests dropping torpedoes from a crane against a steel plate, which confirmed their findings as not one of the exploders worked. Interestingly when the steel impact plate was put at a 45° angle the exploder worked about 50% of the time. The angle reduced the force of the impact therefore the guide pins became less deformed, which in turn did not impede the firing pin's speed into the exploder. This explained why Daspit's shot at the fleeing tanker exploded while his set shots with a zero-gyro angle did nothing. With this information Lockwood contacted the Bureau of Ordinance and a redesign began. Also, COs were instructed to attack at acute angles, which once again went against all their pre-war training.

As noted, the British went through a short period of correcting torpedo problems that could have helped the U.S. One of the great ironies of the war is that the Germans went through an almost identical series of technological blunders that plagued the U.S. On April 16, 1940, Gunther Prien, one of Germany's most celebrated submarine commanders, attacked an eight-ship convoy sitting anchored at Bygdenfiord, Norway. All the ships overlapped each other and were at close range so there was no way to miss. Prien fired eight torpedoes at these sitting ducks, and nothing happened. On April 19th Prien found the British battleship Warspite and fired two torpedoes at close range. Both were duds. For his trouble he received a vicious counterattack from the British. It is no wonder that a day later when Prien found another British convoy, he refrained from attacking. Prien returned to base and bluntly reported that he could hardly be expected to fight with a dummy rifle.[110]

When the Germans switched to contact exploders, they also had a problem with duds as the exploder pins did not hit the detonator hard enough. Further the Germans found that depth control of their torpedoes was erratic due to leaks in the balance chambers.[111] It is almost as if the American's and the German's spied on each other so as to leave no stone unturned in their quest to make a faulty torpedo.

Chapter 7
Frustration

Between December 26th and December 29th the U.S.S. Seawolf spent the days submerged in Manila Bay escaping the Japanese bombs that rained down on the city of Manila and Corregidor. By night the ship docked at Corregidor Island, the headquarters of the U.S. Army, and for a time the home of Douglas MacArthur. During the day the crew had little rest or fresh air. They wanted to work on the ship, but obviously could not because of the enemy's relentless attacks. Despite the frustration and boredom, morale remained high as the Seawolf crew marked time. Then on the 30th they began to load stores for a voyage. The activity gave the crewmembers some hope that they would soon be returning to the fighting part of the war.

That early optimism just before Seawolf's second war patrol was soon replaced by another serious period of frustration. The men eagerly wanted to take the fight to the Japanese but just as the Seawolf shoved off several people, not in the crew, boarded the ship. The crewmembers found out at that time that this was to be another "special mission." Roughly translated that meant no combat.

The truth of the matter is that the navy by late December 1941 had written off the Philippine Islands. This of course brought Admiral Hart and General Douglas MacArthur into serious conflict. Amongst the problems was the Pensacola convoy. That convoy carrying planes, ammunition, guns, and men to Manila had been diverted back to Hawaii just as the war started. A few days later Chief of Staff George Marshall radioed MacArthur that the Pensacola convoy would get through to Manila by way of Brisbane, Australia. This of course pleased the aggressive and optimistic MacArthur. Adm. Hart however believed that the Japanese already had an effective blockade around the Philippines and therefore opposed the convoy's movement.[112] Two men could not have had a more different interpretation of the facts as they stood in December 1941.

What MacArthur termed as "defeatist" Thomas Hart thought of as pragmatic. The army however is different because unlike the navy the army can't pack up and leave when it is on an island. MacArthur therefore made plans to evacuate Manila, declare it an open city, set up his command post at Corregidor, and have the army retreat to its last stand area on the Bataan

Peninsula. He didn't communicate any of his plans to Adm. Hart, just as Hart had failed to tell MacArthur that the Japanese had bombed Pearl Harbor. Hart managed to find out about the evacuation of Manila on his own just two days before the army pulled out. He left that city for Corregidor on Christmas Eve. Then, in the early hours on the day after Christmas, Hart boarded the submarine U.S.S. Shark commanded by Louis Shane and left the Philippines altogether. Their destination: Surabaya, Java.

When Seawolf pushed off from Corregidor on December 30th, it probably did not surprise anybody that the "special mission" consisted of evacuating staff and personnel. Amongst the ten people officially coming aboard were Commander James Fife, Commander E.H. Bryant, and Lt. Commander Morton Mumma. On a personal level this had all the makings of a tension filled voyage. Being chased out of the Philippines did not make anybody happy, but the senior staff members having the higher positions of authority must have felt especially uncomfortable. At the time John Wilkes commanded Submarines Asiatic Fleet and Commander Fife was his Chief of Staff. But Wilkes was on the submarine Swordfish headed for Surabaya while Seawolf transported Fife to Darwin. Wilkes planned to direct submarine operations from the Malay Barrier while Fife directed the logistics base for submarines at Darwin. Only about 1200 miles separated the two. The Americans were reeling in the face of the Japanese onslaught and Fife could not help being frustrated.

Warder and Mort Mumma might be expected to have a genial time during the short trip to Darwin. The two attended Annapolis together, became good friends, and graduated together in 1925. Both took command of submarines at about the same time. Mumma commanded the Sailfish, which was an adventure in itself. Sailfish was the renamed Squalus that sank on the east coast two years before the war began with a loss of twenty-six lives. When Sailfish arrived fully repaired in the Philippines there was a morale problem. Seamen have been known at times to be somewhat superstitious and being a crewmember of a submarine that had sunk once already did not have a calming effect on those superstitions. Some of the crewmembers referred to the ship in a derogatory manner calling it the "Squalfish." That is when Mumma took command of the ship. He was a strict disciplinarian, and the ship eventually recovered its "spit-and-polish" to a certain degree.

That was in peacetime. Unfortunately, when the war started Mumma became the next tragedy of the Sailfish/Squalus saga. On December 13 his ship attacked a Japanese destroyer near Vigan on the northwest side of Luzon. Mumma followed prewar training exactly, which of course doomed his attack to failure from the beginning. He did a sonar approach at 100 feet and then

Frustration

fired at a range (who really knows under the circumstances) of 500 yards. The Sailfish was rocked by an incredible explosion just seconds after firing its torpedo. Mumma thought that the destroyer had launched a counterattack, but it is more probable that a premature torpedo detonation caused the explosion. Whatever the situation, the Japanese proceeded to drop 18 depth charges on Sailfish. Mumma could not stand the pressure and ordered himself locked into his cabin. The executive officer, Hiram Cassidy took command of the ship and Wilkes ordered him to bring it back to Manila.[113]

Wilkes relieved Mumma of command. But the problems did not end there. Mumma claimed credit for sinking a Japanese destroyer, which on the face of it seems incredible since the very ship he claimed to have sunk was the ship that supposedly counter attacked Sailfish. John Wilkes did not overrule Mumma and awarded him the Navy Cross for "extraordinary heroism…and inspiring leadership."[114] However, Mumma's morale had been broken and all the submariners and his fellow officers knew about his problem. Yet there was no way for him to get out of Manila because, of course, the Japanese had inconveniently shot down most of the U.S. aircraft. Mumma spent the next 15 or so days in Manila and on Corregidor having to face his fellow officers in complete humiliation.

Now Mumma found himself steaming towards Darwin with his friend Frederick Warder. However, Warder did not let Mumma get too comfortable. Plus, Commander Bryant, Mumma's former commanding officer, was also on the ship. The tight quarters of a submarine made this a prickly situation considering the failure of Mumma. At one-point Mumma decided to go up into the conning tower and look over some of the sea charts. Who can blame him for wanting to feel a part of the show or somehow demonstrate that as a Lt. Commander in the U.S. Navy he still equaled the other officers on the Seawolf? He probably should have laid low. When Warder got wind of Mumma's activities, Warder raced from his cabin, practically jumped up the ladder to the conning tower, and yelled at the top of his lungs for Mumma to get out of the conning tower. Warder screamed that Mumma should never look at Seawolf's charts again. He went on in a voice heard almost throughout the ship that Mumma had lost his boat and that he was a coward. Mumma steered clear of Warder and the conning tower after that.[115]

As for Warder by his own concession he had a bad temper that sometimes got the best of him, and this might have been one of those moments. At the same time Warder had an uncanny way of feeling the pulse of his crew. One crewmember claims that Warder used the moment to send a message to his crew that cowardness and slipshod work would not be tolerated. This probably better explains Warder turning on his friend in such a vicious manner.

It can be compared to another instance near Albany, Australia as Seawolf came in from a later patrol. One night an enlisted man on watch, (therefore armed with a .45 handgun), went to the captains' quarters. He pulled out the .45, put it to his head and said that he could not take the pressure of serving on a submarine anymore and demanded a transfer. Being at sea on a submarine Warder could hardly transfer him on the spot. Warder calmly assured the man of a future transfer and then disarmed him. Nothing further was heard about it during that patrol. Warder transferred the enlisted man without besmirching his record.[116]

Another time an enlisted man named Johnson got into a heated argument with an officer in the engine room. The confrontation quickly escalated and nearly turned to all out fisticuffs. Warder took Johnson aside and spoke with him calmly diffusing the situation. Johnson always remembered the incident recalling that Warder never set it down in his permanent record.*

That generally is the way Warder worked things out. However, on this particular patrol from Corregidor to Darwin things seemed somehow different. As Seawolf steamed south Warder reconnoitered several islands checking on enemy dispositions. One night, probably January 4th, Commander Fife was with Warder on the bridge when another full-scale shouting match took place. Fife wanted Warder to close on an Island called Halmahera. Warder didn't think very much of that idea. Fife pulled rank on Warder but should have known better. Admiral Hart had tried to interfere with Warder's crew prior to the war and Warder bested him on that occasion. Brass did not intimidate Warder when it came to his crew and his prerogative as the commanding officer of Seawolf. Finally, the shouts got so loud that the crew in the conning tower could hear it even above the din of the engines. Warder bawled something to the effect that the ship was his and he will say where it does and does not go. After that the visiting officers did not bother Warder anymore.

It is insightful that Warder saved much of his wrath for the brass above him and rarely got on enlisted men except for crewmembers that did not

---

* Johnson's father had died when he was young. He entered the navy at a fairly young age and always looked up to Frederick Warder as a sort of father figure. This action towards Johnson reinforces Warder's extra consideration toward enlisted men and the best example of this deferential treatment toward enlisted men being that of John Street.

perform their jobs well. In other words, Warder overlooked the spit and polish to a certain extent while emphasizing technical competency. It should also be noted that Warder and Fife remained personal friends during and after the war. Fife even attended the wedding of Warder's son out in Pomona, California after the war.

While the brass busied themselves with commanding the ship and blowing off steam to each other, disturbing thoughts haunted one of the humblest members of the crew. Pop Rosario, one of Gus Wright's mess helpers, agonized every mile the Seawolf went away from the Philippines. His wife and children lived on Luzon. He hadn't heard from them for some time. The Filipino knew what the Japanese did to civilian populations. Families with girls tried to hide them away. If the girls could not be hidden from the Japanese soldiers, the parents tried to make them look ugly to avoid the hideous Japanese practice of taking young women and raping them over and over as so-called "comfort girls." As Pop Rosario threw his lot in with the Americans, he could only hope that his family was okay. Pop was the man who brought sandwiches and hot coffee around to the crew during long stretches at battle stations. He was always a welcome sight. Additionally, he was the officer's steward making up their beds and taking care of their laundry, etc. His quiet, kind, and unassuming nature made the crew especially sad and sympathetic to him and his predicament.

Other men on this peculiar voyage of the Seawolf had problems too. They were the "unofficial" passengers. Just as Seawolf left Corregidor two stowaways boarded the ship. They were salvage divers from the ship Canopus, which had been heavily damaged from a Japanese bomb. Hidden in the torpedo room by sympathetic Seawolf crewmembers, they laid low hoping to escape death or imprisonment by the Japanese. Once out to sea Warder might have been informed. Hiding men on a submarine for longer than a day would be difficult, but Warder was the type of man who was sympathetic toward desperate people; submariners, like other servicemen, tended to look after their own. Crewmembers brought the stowaways some food and possibly felt some comfort with a wink and a nod from Warder. But one person who most certainly did not know about the stowaways was Fife. He and Wilkes were the people that drew up the list of submarine personnel to be evacuated from Corregidor. It is somewhat ironic that two of the men that Fife had slated to be left behind were now on the very ship that was taking Fife to safety.[117]

On the lighter side of the voyage Warder noted that 48 crewmembers became "shellbacks" on January 6th. This is the old maritime tradition of "crossing the line" (the equator). Those sailors that have not crossed the line are considered "pollywogs," those that have are called "shellbacks." There is a whole ritual that involves many characters including Neptune, in this case played by the Chief Petty Officer Edward Sousa, who usually organized this event. The ritual involves some light hazing including "kissing the babies butt." Of course, with no baby on board a man's folded arms somehow substitutes for the butt. What is most humorous is Warder's touch of solemnity in the War Patrol Report when he referred to this tomfoolery as "being initiated to the mysteries of the deep."

Despite the commotion and the disappointment on board Seawolf, Warder didn't loose his focus. The crew performed their regular periscope patrols every 15 minutes during their daytime submerged operations, but their southerly direction took them away from the enemy making it unlikely to find targets to engage in battle. But on January 9th, in the first hour of morning, the lookouts on the bridge spotted a ship. They attempted to challenge the ship but received no response so they considered it an enemy ship. The klaxon sounded for a crash dive.

"Clear the bridge," Shouted the OOD.

With that order the mad dash down the hatch ensued. After the last man came down the signalman pulled the lanyard slamming the hatch and then dogged it with the wheel. Seawolf slid into the depths of the ocean as the battle stations alarm sounded. The Sound crew listened intently for enemy propellers. One man operated the dials in the radio shack while another manually turned the JP sound head. But as they listened, they heard only silence. The officer of the deck enquired again, "Any indication of screws?"

"No," came the reply.

Six minutes later they came to 55 feet to receive their radio schedule. After making a periscope observation the Seawolf surfaced. The officer of the deck and the bridge personnel bolted through the hatch to find out if the mysterious ship still lurked about. They saw no ship. But they did see a small dark cloud at about the same bearing as the supposed ship, now lifting slightly off the surface of the ocean. The crew secured from battle stations.[118] Being fooled by a cloud wasn't quite as bad as being fooled by reef fish or men working on your own ship. But under the tense circumstances these incidents probably didn't help.

At about 3:30am Seawolf reached a rendezvous area about 18 miles from Darwin. They waited on the surface for an escort. And they waited. They waited some more. Finally, at about 6:30 that morning the Seawolf made contact with a British patrol vessel sent to lead them into port. As the small vessel came towards Seawolf, the impatient Warder nearly blew up. His description of the British vessel taking evasive actions at "various courses at various speeds" while the Seawolf lay stationary while waiting for him, dripped with sarcasm. The rest of the men on the bridge of the Seawolf must have been puzzled by this comical yet purposeful martial display by what amounted to a small tugboat. As they continued to watch Warder reported the speed of this amazing little boat as "9 knots." All of the zigzagging further decreased its real speed in the direction of the Seawolf. If the British boat did much more maneuvering, the last few miles of Seawolf's trip from the Philippines would take as long as the first 1000 miles.

Then, after that low-speed dash in broad daylight through a channel that the Japanese contested only a few weeks later, the British vessel broke down. The bridge personnel on Seawolf waited breathlessly for the next act of this vaudevillian folly to begin. Would the engines on the little boat get going again? Would the war be over before Seawolf got into port? Perhaps the crew of the Seawolf wished it would sink, and then they could be free of it.

Incredulously they watched as a belch of black smoke came out of the boat's smokestack. Somehow it got going again. Finally, to everyone's delight it broke down, for the last time. Warder by now had endured enough. He ordered the pilot to climb on board the Seawolf and guide her into port from Seawolf's bridge. Warder offered to tow the British vessel in, but the pilot declined, happy to be away from the tub. After that six-hour odyssey Seawolf found herself moored safely beside the tender U.S.S Holland in Darwin, Australia.[119]

After tying up, the crew eagerly waited for a launch to take them to dry land. Once in town they looked forward to a good time, ice-cold beer, fresh food, and some Australian hospitality. They only had to walk about a mile from the dock to reach the center of town. Too bad it was 110°. Too bad that the men had been in sandals during their cruise and now they wore heavy black shoes as they hiked to town. Too bad that when they got to town most of the buildings were boarded up. Too bad they couldn't find any beer, and too bad no pretty Aussie women stuck around to keep them company. Soon most of the crew gave up on the town and rejoined Seawolf at anchor.[120]

However, the executive officer William Deragon somehow scarred up some cases of beer over the next couple of days. The men played some baseball and generally got in some relaxation. After seven days it came to an end when orders arrived directing Seawolf to quickly get back to sea. The captain and crew, wanting to get into combat, anticipated a successful war patrol. But as the ship's stores went into one end of the Seawolf the men could see her torpedoes being pulled out of the other. As it turned out Warder had been assigned another "special" mission. He was seriously angry over the prospect of another "war" patrol with little prospect of successes against the enemy. A day before Seawolf's scheduled departure a group of motor launches came up beside her packed to the gunwales with small arms ammunition, .50 caliber machine gun ammunition, and 3-inch anti-aircraft shells. In all the Seawolf transported 72,585 pounds of ammunition to MacArthur's fighting men in Bataan and Corregidor.[121]

About midday on January 16th the Seawolf left Darwin never to return. Later, on February 19th, the Japanese bombed the allies right out of Darwin sinking about fifty ships in one air raid. At the early stages of the war the reach, or should we say over-reach, of the Japanese really was remarkable.

But that was in the future. As of January, one hour after leaving Darwin, Seawolf came to "point C" to wait for a rendezvous with an Australian ship Warrego for some joint exercises. And they waited. Finally, some thirty minutes later they received a radio signal stating that the exercise had been called off. In some disgust Warder ordered Seawolf to submerge. After surfacing that night, they listened intently to the radio tuned to an aircraft frequency. The captain and crew hoped to avoid any accidents with overly aggressive "friendly" airplanes let alone the enemy. They did not hear any airplanes but they did encounter an Australian sloop patrolling the channel, so they did a TDC drill on it. Later they surfaced and were challenged by another small Australian boat. Warder complained again that instead of a tube the Australians used an Aldis Lamp. He felt the enemy could easily see the Aldis Lamp from seaward. Warder hurried to clear the channel after he received a message of enemy submarines sightings from the U.S.S. Houston.

At daybreak Seawolf submerged but almost immediately ran into problems. The ship started to lose depth control after encountering water of inconsistent density. Then a little after 2:00pm on the 17th the Seawolf sank rapidly to 140 feet. The ship had a test depth of 250 feet, so the crew was in no danger. Unfortunately, they hit the bottom of the ocean and knocked out their QC-JP listening heads and once and for all destroyed their own pitometer log (it didn't work anyway). The chart guiding the crew affirmed that they were in 40 fathoms of water. However, since they hit bottom in 23 fathoms (140 feet) Warder concluded the chart was wrong. He made notes on the failure so that future charts could be corrected.[122] It seems almost ridiculous that such easily rectifiable problems could occur.

After four uneventful days at sea crewmembers sighted a couple of aircraft assumed to be the enemy. They could not accurately fix the position of the aircraft because of rain and clouds over the Celebs. But within two hours, at about 6:02 pm, the OOD sighted an enemy ship. Warder quickly came to the conning tower and identified an enemy destroyer at approximately 14,000 yards, way too distant to develop an attack. But in an instant, there appeared 3 other destroyers and the battle stations alarm sounded, "bong, bong, bong..." The crew made the mad dash to their stations. The approach party assumed their positions in the conning tower. Casler sat at the small chart table where he would navigate the approach upon the enemy. Ordinarily the responsibilities of navigation lay with the X/O, and in Seawolf's case that was William Deragon. However, Deragon assigned much of his navigation responsibilities to Casler who was somewhat of a genius in that field.[123] Casler entered the navy as an enlisted man but retired, because of his extraordinary skill, as a full captain, somewhat unusual even in a wartime navy.[124]

Warder took a few five second looks at the situation over the next two minutes. He noted that all four destroyers gave him port angles on the bow. He assumed they formed a screen so Warder came right to 039° in order to pass around the port screening ship. Warder observed the choppy seas and occasional rainsqualls and commented, "It's ideal for periscope [observations]." Then Warder changed his assessment. Now he felt that instead of 4 destroyers he had three destroyers and a cruiser. Warder decided to "pick him off," if that proved correct. The Japanese cruiser was bearing 004° T and had an angle on the bow 007° with a range of 5,900 yards, still a long shot.

The enemy ship moved fast, and Warder used this to his advantage. Six minutes later he closed the range to 2900 yards. Casler quickly plotted the moves of the four ships so Warder could get a clear picture of the developing attack on paper. The angle on the bow was now 30° to the port side. Warder ordered left full rudder and full speed in order to make a bow attack at about 1000 yards, a perfect range. The men worked rapidly as the attack developed in only seventeen minutes. Then in the 20th minute the target zigged away. Within one minute the cruiser was at a range of 5050 yards, rapidly increasing the distance between the Seawolf and safety. At this time Warder decided that the ship was not a cruiser but rather a destroyer. Warder noted that the "tripod mast and high fire control tower had fooled me."[125] It just goes to show the problems encountered by WW II submarines in identifying, tracking, and attacking ships with, by modern standards, fairly crude instruments.

Warder decided to hold his course hoping that targets could be developed astern of the destroyers. Then just thirteen minutes after the let down of the initial target zigging away, Warder spotted the real thing, a three-stack cruiser of the Kuma class. The disappointment of the earlier attack doubly motivated the crew even though the range was a distant 12,000 yards.

Warder ordered the ship to a "collision course" with the enemy cruiser.[126] Four minutes later they slowed to 1/3 speed. Then they hit the jackpot. In addition to the four destroyers and one cruiser already sighted they counted seven additional freighters in the convoy.

Now Warder and the rest of the crew silently cursed their primary mission; delivering ammunition to Bataan. They had removed all their "reloading" torpedoes so they could get more ammunition into the ship. Seawolf carried only eight torpedoes exactly the amount that could be carried in the eight tubes. What a time to stumble into such a rich target situation.

Warder began stalking the convoy searching for the best opportunity to attack. He wondered if these ships were "empties" heading for Palau or going to some new station. Such is the life of a submariner, always just a little out of touch with the surface world.

When night fell Warder could make out less and less of what was going on since the ships ran with no lights. The persistent rain squalls also "added to the confusion." Then he saw some lamp signaling between two ships. He headed to that location at full speed still submerged despite the darkened skies. Then at 7:18pm they heard a loud explosion. They rigged for depth charge attack and went to 150 feet, but sound reported that no propellers could be heard. The ever-aggressive Warder took only one minute to decide that the Japanese had simply done a practice drop. He secured from depth charge quarters and ordered the Seawolf back to 60 feet. At 7:36pm they came up and joined the chase on the surface. At 8:00pm he cleared his contact report hoping that he might receive new orders to pursue the convoy. Warder reversed course to 161° to stay in position to regain contact if Wilkes decided to modify Warder's orders and let him loose on the enemy convoy.

Warder increased Seawolf's speed to 17 knots and changed course to 180° in hopes, based on the Japanese cruiser's last known course, they might intercept it by midnight. That seemed very optimistic but just 20 minutes later they passed through an area that smelled distinctly of fuel oil. By 11:00 that night the jig was up. Warder did not receive any instructions modifying his mission, so he reversed course and headed for Bataan once again.

Five minutes into the early morning of January 22nd the OOD Ensign J. Mercer saw a light. Warder was immediately on the bridge in the poring rain trying to see a ship or anything for that matter. The crew lowered the sound shaft trying to hear what they could not see. Warder jumped up to the high platform on the shears above the bridge but still could not discern anything for sure. He toyed with the idea of a stern tube shot but on such scanty evidence as one blinking light decided not to. They secured from battle

Frustration

stations and at 6:00am dove and commenced with deep patrol with hourly observations.

Here again began a sort of lull in the action. Without orders to actively search out the enemy and doing somewhat of a milk run with the ammunition on board, the crew was almost killing time. Different crews did different things to ward off boredom. Most ships had card game tournaments and each ship tended to have its specific tournament game. Most ships played cribbage. Some played bridge. The Seawolf's game was hearts. The elimination brackets would be in the crew's mess and the excitement built until the ship's champion was crowned. On long cruises more than one tournament took place. Unfortunately for Warder there did not exist a "captain always wins" rule. When the men could not play cards, they resorted to old standby games such as "twenty questions," or having informal spelling bees. Then there is the classic too-much-time-on-your-hands antidote, the meaningless argument. One argument between the radioman Eckberg and a man named Sully lasted three days and turned on whether the phrase was, "Give me two spoonsful of sugar," or, "Give me two spoonfuls of sugar."[127] If only someone had brought a dictionary the argument could easily have been solved in a minute. Of course, nobody knows what the two men would have done for the next two days without a meaningless argument to pass the time.

Later that same day while still on submerged patrol Lt. Holden, the OOD at the time, spotted what he thought was a ship during his hourly observations. He called Warder immediately. Warder peering through the periscope thought he saw a large tripod mast. That indicated a cruiser or better. Despite the run of bad luck in their previous attacks the crew of the Seawolf did not become lackadaisical. The alarm sounded and the men went to their battle stations. The approach team started their work and the X/O Deragon began working solutions on the TDC. As they tracked the ship it suddenly turned to starboard rapidly on a course of 276°. Warder assumed the target zigged. But as Warder tracked the target in the periscope and the approach party worked through their solutions the idea grew in Warder's head that something was wrong. At 4:46pm, fully fifty minutes after calling battle stations and feverish work by the crew, Warder completed his examination of "a sunken schooner." In detail he described the deck of the "enemy" as being under water, the upper third of the mast broken and "two sea gulls sitting on projections from the hull giving a good imitation of [the] tops of [the] belled-out Jap smokestacks." Keeping his humor, Warder wrote, "Don Quixote and the windmills had nothing on us."

Warder and crew drove the Seawolf hard in the hopes of an early arrival to Corregidor. The sooner they got there, the sooner they could unload the ammunition and get a full compliment of torpedoes. Then they could hunt enemy shipping full time. On January 26th Eckberg sent message #261110 informing Adm. Wilkes the Commander of Submarines Asiatic Force (Comsubaf) that Seawolf expected to arrive one day early and unless otherwise ordered would spend the time patrolling. No orders calling them in early came so they headed for Bagac Bay.

*   *   *

While the Seawolf made its way toward Luzon the U.S. army battled ferociously on the Bataan Peninsula. Japanese General Nara had been making, in General Homma's opinion, slow progress down the eastern side of the peninsula. When the American General Jonathan Wainwright temporarily stopped the Japanese at Moron, Homma ordered General Kimura to leave Manila and attack on the 19th hoping for some sort of breakthrough on the coast. Wainwright however held his position, so the Japanese decided on a series of southward amphibious assaults to envelope him.[128] The Japanese launched the first of these assaults on the 22nd of January under the command of Lt. Colonel Nariyoshi Tsunehiro. 900 Japanese headed towards Bagac Bay in barges. Unfortunately for the Japanese an enterprising American Lieutenant named John D. Bulkeley showed up and ruined their plans. Bulkeley commanded a squadron of PT boats. As he cruised along near the shore in PT-34, he saw some blinking lights and investigated. It turned out to be some kind of boat. He called to the boat with a megaphone. The boat answered back with a stream of tracers. Bulkeley gunned the engines of his PT and charged in. As he got close he could make out a barge with machine guns on the bow and stern as well as a load of Japanese infantrymen. He fired away at the barge with his machine guns and sank it. Some time later he found another of the barges and attacked it. Before it sank, he boarded it, captured three Japanese, and confiscated a dispatch case with its documents still inside. Bulkeley's audacious attack dispersed the other Japanese barges, which landed in two groups instead of one. About 600 of the men landed five miles south of their objective at Quinauan Point while another 300 drifted almost to Marivelles itself landing at Longoskayan Pt. Three days later the Japanese reinforced that failure with another assault group on the 26th, which

Frustration

was turned away from Quinauan Point but did land further north at Canas Point.[129] One day later the Seawolf arrived.

At 4:00am Warder saw search light activity on Corregidor and rocket fire on the Peninsula itself. He also noticed searchlight activity in Bagac Bay while cruising several miles off the coast. At this point Warder could not chance a surface reconnoitering so an hour later they slowed the ship and flooded down gently sinking into the ocean. Then an hour later a mass of rockets around Bagac down to Luzon Pt. flashed. This turned out to be General Kimura's last drive to capture Bagac, which he did later that day. At about 6:00am dawn brought enough light for Warder to examine Bagac Bay with periscope observations. At that time, he found no shipping. Because of all the rocket activity Warder knew that a large action was taking place and he wanted to help in any way he could. Therefore, Seawolf proceeded up to Subic Bay. Maybe he could sink a troop ship or cause some other problem for the enemy in order to support the U.S. Army now desperately fighting for their survival on Bataan. He did find one barge at a range of 2000 yards. Warder questioned its seaworthiness and therefore found it to an unsuitable target. Seawolf proceeded north to Port Silanguin and Nazaso Bay but found no shipping. Unknown to him those areas had long ago been captured by the Japanese. He reversed course and went back to Bataan, surfaced, and waited for a rendezvous with the escort boat that would take them through the minefield.

The Seawolf moored to the starboard side of the south dock at Corregidor. The crew began unloading the ammunition. But in the middle of that they got a warning of a possible night air raid, so they battened down the hatches shoved off and moved east of the small island of Caballo. There they floated awash until the danger passed. At about midnight they received an "all clear" and went back to Corregidor. They could only dock during the night and Warder was especially anxious to get the ammunition unloaded. The men worked rapidly and had the ship unloaded at 5:45 just about sunrise. Seawolf then went into Manila Bay and lay on the bottom for the next twelve hours.

On the night of January 30th, as the crew completed loading extra torpedoes and spare parts, the radio operator Eckberg took a stroll around Corregidor. He visited Malinta Tunnel where everyone thought MacArthur and the U.S. army would make its last desperate stand against the Japanese. As Eckberg walked around the wind shifted and an especially sweet nauseating smell entered his nose. It became unbearable as he realized rotting human corpses caused the smell, yet the island fortress still impressed Eckberg. He went into the tunnel itself and was amazed by the bright lights and activity. As people bustled around others slept, too fatigued to be woken even in the unquiet chaos. Eckberg went to the communications room in the tunnel. When he tried to enter, a navy ensign shooed him away. Eckberg returned to the Seawolf and never laid eyes on Corregidor again.[130]

That night as the Seawolf prepared to shove off for the last time from the Philippines an army truck pulled up to the dock. About twenty-six men got out. Whispers went through the crew below. Then it became clear. It was another evacuation mission, which meant little to no combat for the crew of the Seawolf. This came as a blow to the crew. The passengers this time were mostly army aviators. You could almost see the sparks flying. Aviators, no matter what side they are on, tend to be the natural enemy of submariners since aviators tended to be very aggressive when confronting any submarine on the open sea. Submariners thought that "fly boys" too often shot and then asked questions later, so to speak. But then the crew of the Seawolf began to hear some of the pilots' stories. Some had been shot down several times. All had recently lost friends killed in action against the Japanese. Any animosity quickly disappeared.

Another situation though, arose between the two groups. Every time the chow bell rang the pilots crowded into the mess room. The mess room however was really designed for about 19 men fitting very close. The addition of twenty-six new people crashing the party every four hours really made the place seem small. But the pilots had been on short rations for several weeks taking in at most about 1,000 calories a day. They were permanently hungry and the Seawolf with its excellent food seemed like a sort of Shangri-La. The Seawolf crew overheard the pilots talking with amazement about getting coffee at any time and the great tasting food. After a few mess calls with the pilots lining up first, somebody politely informed them that it might be better to wait for the ship's crew to eat to relieve some of the crowding in the mess room. The pilots agreed and everything seemed fine until the next meal was served and they once again crowded into the mess room. After awhile the crew of the Seawolf gave up on the situation.

Even though the initial tension quickly dissipated nothing could change the cramped quarters of Seawolf. The ship now carried about 50% more men than it was designed for. It literally was sardines in a can as the men rotated sleeping times in the bunks and the pilots tried to stuff themselves into corners in order to stay out of the way of the Seawolf crew. One fellow, Maj. Wilkinson of the British Army, became somewhat of a favorite of Warder's. The two talked and played cards during the few moments that Warder could relax. Wilkinson had been on Corregidor for some time. He took his meals with Douglas MacArthur and his entourage. Much later in life Warder recalled with a laugh how Wilkinson, with a gleam in his eye, told how MacArthur always referred to Admiral Thomas Hart as "Tommy Fart." Apparently, relations between MacArthur and Hart had not mended.

The trip to Surabaya went smoothly with one exception. Rip tides caused the ship to lose depth control on a few occasions. What the airmen must have thought as the ship began to sink on those occasions they did not say. But remembering that in a submarine there is no "bailing out" or "hitting the silk" when something goes wrong it must have worried them. Seawolf arrived safely to Surabaya on February 7, 1942. The passengers thanked the crew for the safe, if cramped, voyage and gladly put their feet on dry ground.

Chapter — 8
Renewal

Fred's troubles corresponded generally in time to Mary's rebirth as she settled into her new apartment on Calvert Street. The move was easy for Mary because the apartment came furnished. Having settled into the two-story brown brick apartment Mary began to reassemble her family. The two young girls Grace and Suzy returned first. They had been living at the Borderside Mansion in the care of their grandmother Grace Brydon and the various maids and cooks. All the members of the household were sad to see the two girls leave. When Grace and Suzy first arrived at their grandmother's they brought quite a lot of life to her and the graceful mansion in which she lived. Whether playing on the wide marble steps in front of the house, that rose like a small mountain from the young girl's perspective, or pushing their baby carriages, or riding their tricycles, "Pudge" and "Suzy – Q" always had a smile to share with whomever came to visit. But every hello is an implied goodbye, and the people at Borderside accepted the departure with only a few tears. The sadness was tempered with the knowledge that Borderside and grandmother remained only a short car ride away and visits would be frequent. Sue and Carroll Pattison came and picked the two girls up and drove them to Calvert Street where Mary's open arms greeted them.

Later in November 1941 Fred Jr. came for Thanksgiving dinner. Even at the young age of ten Fred took care of himself to a certain extent and usually provided for his own bus transportation from his boarding school Leonard Town to Baltimore. The homecoming was so nice and warm that Fred Jr. decided that he wanted to leave Leonard Town and stay at Calvert Street with his family.

Mary Jr. showed up just before the family sat down to dinner completing the reunion, excepting for the father Fred Warder. Despite that, Mary enjoyed herself immensely. The family posed for the typical holiday picture to send to their father. Grace and Suzy wore "look-alike" dresses with Grace sporting a ribbon in her hair. Fred Jr. looked like a cherub with his blond hair creating a sort of hallow effect. He wore his navy cadet uniform from Leonard Town boarding school (it was just a coincidence that the school had nautical uniforms and not something that either Fred Jr. or Mary arranged). Mary Jr. was at what people refer to as an awkward age, however in less than a year she blossomed into a very beautiful young woman.

Renewal

As for Mary, the signs of strain on her face, so prevalent during her stay in Pomona, had vanished. The confident gaze from her friendly happy eyes had returned, an outward manifestation of her inner peace. The years between her marriage and this very special Thanksgiving had not diminished her great beauty as her luxurious auburn hair crowned her still pretty face. When Fred received the picture, he taped it to the bulkhead in his quarters on the Seawolf. There he looked at it from time to time, a reminder of his past and his future, should he survive the war.

After Thanksgiving the two older children returned to their schools to finish out their terms. Upon completion Fred Jr. and Mary Jr. returned to Baltimore with their mother and attended schools within walking distance of the new residence. Mary enjoyed the Calvert Street house very much and even sent Fred a small hand drawn map of the area. The children found one thing very curious about it though, it had a very wide screened porch in the back. When they asked their mother about it, she informed them that it was a "sleeping porch." Completely unaware of that novelty of architecture they enquired what it was used for generally. "Oh, wait until summer," Mary replied, "You will learn about it then."

To manage the new apartment filled with love and four kids, Mary wanted a little help. She hired a young woman named Dot to assist her in cooking and cleaning. The people that Mary hired for household help could all count their lucky stars. Mary never was the kind of taskmaster that handed a housekeeper a list of things to do and then direct them here and there. On the contrary Mary prepared meals for her family and on those occasions when she did not do all of the cooking, she assisted the housekeeper. The four children were also called upon to assist from time to time in cooking various meals throughout the day rather than just sitting around to be served. This "help" given by the kids at times might have been a hindrance. After a meal everybody contributed to the cleanup as well. Mary also assisted Dot in the housecleaning, taking special pride in a well kept home. When Mary went to the grocery store or ran other errands Dot stayed with one of the young girls while Mary took the other. Little things like that really helped Mary who was trying her very best to not overexert herself.

The children especially loved Dot. She was a very kindly country girl with a slim figure and fair skin. Her shoulder length sandy blond hair was often pulled back while working around the house but flowed loosely when she let it down. Dot was simple in her thoughts and opinions as might befit a girl from the hill country of West Virginia. Her homey ways and sweet disposition made everybody love her. When she served the children's meals, she would make up a song about the food she was dishing up. She organized the children into washing and drying relays to make cleaning the dishes fun.

With Dot around Mary had some freedom to visit a few friends from time to time. She took a quick trip to Annapolis to visit Harry and Helen Ingram, a couple she and Fred met during a cruise in the old China days. When Mary lived in Tsing Tao, she and Helen became good friends. Later they crossed paths in the Philippines enjoying tennis and golf every now and then at camp John Hay. The submariners were a tight fraternity whose members stayed in close touch through the mail and in person. Whenever they had a chance, they got together and updated each other on the news of their other fellow submariners. It truly was like a large extended family. Mary and the Ingram's met at the Army-Navy club for a cocktail and dinner. At the time Harry worked in one of the several navy bureaus and Mary thought he might have some inside knowledge concerning the possibility of Fred's return to the States. However, she was disappointed and wrote Fred, "Harry and I agree, not any of us can possibly know when you will be home."[131]

A few weeks later Mary took the train to Washington DC to meet Dorothy and Bob Folz, also submarine friends. Marjorie Carr showed up and the four of them had a great time. Soon after Mary wrote to Fred and reported everything stating, "I promised to bring you up to date on Navy wife news."[132] Mary kept in close touch with Betty Deragon and almost always had a nice story to tell Fred about her. Fred was very interested in Betty as she was the wife of William, the Executive Officer on board the Seawolf. After one visit Mary reported,

> Betty Deragon is at her mother's home as you probably know. I am as proud of her as you are of William. She tries so hard to keep a stiff upper lip – the going gets a little tough for her – as for all of us at times.[133]

The people touched personally by the war or the tensions just before the war, every now and again needed to rest on the shoulders of another. It seems that most Navy wives busied themselves trying to appear nonchalant about the war related separations from their husbands and the danger. In talking about each other they usually expressed the opinion that the other person was so strong, not knowing that the very person they were speaking about held the same opinion about them.

These scenes were typical of wartime America; Mary's husband in combat, Mary having to deal with emerging civilian pressures, but even so

Renewal

Mary, and people in general, continued to get out and enjoy the good company of their friends, the occasional ball game, and a show every now and then. In addition to short excursions around the Washington DC-Baltimore-Philadelphia area, Mary found time to meet here friend Dottie Kinsella in New York. As with many of Mary's friends, Dottie's husband also crewed on the Seawolf.

The two enjoyed living for a few days in the city that meant so much to Mary's early adult life. She made a nostalgic trip to the *New York Times* where she used to work. Dottie and Mary took in a few Broadway shows. Some of the shows that appeared on Broadway during the war were: Oklahoma, Carmen Jones, and a revival of Yankee Doodle Dandy, which was also released as a movie in late 1941 starring James Cagney. In addition to Broadway musicals and plays, Hollywood churned out plenty of movies to entertain the troops and civilians alike. Released in late 1942 Casablanca, starring Humphrey Bogart and Ingrid Bergman, became the quintessential wartime movie. Other movies with more obvious wartime themes were Dive Bomber, A Yank in the R.A.F., Bataan, and Sergeant York. The extremely popular movie Mrs. Miniver portrayed civilian life in wartime and had more than a few scenes that Mary Warder could relate to.

Mary left for home and soon filled another letter to Fred about her nice time in New York with Dottie. Fred was always grateful that Mary got out and lived a good and varied life. Mary kidded Fred a little about her recent excursions,

> You see – I'm being too good – not a flirtation on the horizon – out of practice I guess. Maybe time will take care of it – on account of how I love you.[134]

In addition to the happiness of having her family and friends back, Mary's Calvert Street apartment brought back memories of some of the happiest days in her life, the Goucher College days. The apartment was a few short blocks from the house where Mary stayed while attending Goucher College. Retracing some of those steps gave her much satisfaction. The memories of trips to nearby Annapolis while Fred courted Mary contributed to the pleasant reminiscing for Mary. As luck might have it, a reunion for her Goucher class took place not long after Mary moved to Calvert Street. Two friends of hers from Goucher, Francis Price and a woman named Victoria, met Mary and went to the Alumnae luncheon together. Despite Mary's short stay as a student at Goucher, her charming personality and spirit of adventure created long lasting friendships.

As Mary enjoyed time with friends and family the mail between she and Fred became more and more erratic. When he came into port some of Mary's letters might be waiting for him. Other of her letters traveled from port to port trying to catch up with the Seawolf. In so doing some of those letters probably traveled a distance equal to the circumnavigation of the globe. One of Mary's letters stated, "It is now nearly seven weeks since your last letter." She wanted to hear from Fred and wrote,

> Almost cable time again. There have been so many rumors of the possibility of your early return to the states that I haven't been able to take letter writing to you as seriously. I am optimistic enough to think that you will come riding in with Santa on his sleigh – if not before.[135]

Because of the communication problems Mary devised a plan to number the letters in a sequence so that both could better remember the contents when answering and check on how the mail service was working. However, this system did not help a lot. Fred's patrols became longer, therefore Mary sent out many letters without receiving any in return and delivery continued to be erratic. Coming in from his fifth patrol Fred wrote, "I spent half of the 2nd reading your wonderful letters, one from December 3rd, then nos. 27 to 36."

That December 3rd letter must have been nearly worn out from all its travels, one of the last letters the two wrote to each other in peacetime. Even when Fred got letters from Mary, he often was too busy to answer them writing, "I can't begin to answer them [the letters] until I get to sea. I will save them all then send them to you."

In spite of his promises, Fred spent most of his time on patrol avoiding or attacking the enemy as circumstances dictated, and always trying to keep his leaking ship afloat. This did not leave a lot of free time for Fred to write letters after all. Add to that his responsibility as commanding officer, which ground him down physically and mentally. Fred described his situation to Mary,

> As you may have guessed I was not well, a touch of flu and a great nervous tension due principally to an inability to relax at all well.[136]

Fred tried his best though, and in rare moments he retired to his quarters, which measured about 48 inches wide and 70 inches long, sat at his desk,

Renewal

looked at the pictures of his family taped to the bulkhead, and let his heart flow into his pen.

> I start thinking of you when I wake up in the morning and Bugawisan [Fred Warder's personal steward] brings me my coffee and I look at your picture and remember how good it used to taste and how I loved you when you used to bring it to me of a morning- with a kiss.[137]

And a little later,

> I have been busy as can be but got time last night to read all your letters again. They bring you so close to me and make me so happy and so proud of you and the children. Your love for me is the high light of my life. God knows how little I have done to deserve it – but I pray that I may always retain it.[138]

Fred's long patrols, the enemy's activities, and the difficulty associated with overseas mail, were not the only problems Mary and Fred encountered. The weather also conspired to separate themselves from the letters they wrote. On one occasion Fred was desperately waiting for word from Mary before he left port.

> The plane coming westward has been delayed for several days – right now we don't know when it will show up. There has been another typhoon and I've been fighting wind and rain most of the past week I don't believe there will be a plane bound your way until the one which I hope bears news of you gets out here.[139]

So Mary and Fred waited and fretted all the while trying to find a solution to their letter situation. Then a new government program in the form of "V-Mail" came into being with the hope of solving some of the mail problem. The Victory or V-Mail first originated in the United Kingdom as a way of reducing the weight of letters coming and going from the battlefronts. As the U.S. postal service began to get crushed by the weight of its own mail, they barrowed the system from the English.

A person participated in the program by purchasing the special V-Mail forms at a local stationary store. Then they typed a one-page letter directly onto the form and mailed it to the Navy Department for free. The letter was then censored, photographically reduced to the size of a thumbnail, put on a spool with other V-Mail, and sent overseas to a V-Mail center where it was blown back up and delivered. The post office claimed that 37 sacks of traditional mail containing 150,000 letters and weighing 2,575 pounds could be reduced to about one sack of V-Mail weighing 45 pounds. These were always sent airmail and consistently traveled faster than ship delivery even during typhoon season. That was the claim anyway. V-Mail proved to be a somewhat popular program and by April 1945 the military had delivered over 550 million pieces of V-Mail.

As with almost every other government program during the war, civilian companies doing war work pitched in with advertisements to promote the V-Mail program, as well as keep their brand names in front of the public. Hiram Walker & Sons, distillers of Canadian Club Whisky, ran full-page ads in newspapers and magazines explaining the system and quoted General Eisenhower, "The inauguration of V-Mail service is a vital forward step – we know and appreciate the value of the postal link that is our only connection with our parents, relatives, and friends." Despite these efforts regular mail continued to be the favorite choice of letter writers. In 1944 Navy personnel received 38 million V-Mails but received over 272 million pieces of regular first class mail.

Mary tried to "do her part" in the mail situation. She dutifully bought her V-Mail stationary and typed out her letters on the small forms and sent them to the Navy Department. Typing was the key to V-mail as the forms were so small that handwriting would be nearly illegible if one put more than fifty words in a letter. Mary thought that this new program offered some hope in solving her communication problems with Fred.

But this was not to be, as the "battle of the letters" took a new and unforeseen twist. The United States government took her typewriter, "recalled to be used for the war effort," as Mary put it when a typewriter shortage occurred in the United States in 1942. [140] This latest calamity came about through a string of circumstances and miscalculations instigated by the United States government that even the lowest rent fortune-teller could have predicted, but somehow eluded public officials.

The military began to grow rapidly, even as early as 1940. This in turn caused the military bureaucracy to grow from about seven thousand civilian employees in 1940 to about forty-one thousand in early 1942. This incredible growth in the military's bureaucracy in turn led to a shortage of office space. The Navy tried to solve its office space problem through hostile takeovers of other people's and company's offices and buildings. Nothing was sacred as the Navy sent "scouts" into Washington DC and its suburbs in its relentless search to find more office space for more Navy bureaucrats. And when the

Navy said, "nothing is sacred," they meant it. One of the buildings to fall into the Navy's mitts early in the war was the Mount Vernon Seminary, which was a girl's school located on Nebraska Ave. Of course, the gentlemen of the Navy waited until the girls attending the school went home for Christmas break before they took the building. The school administrators wondered where the girls would be housed and taught upon their return for the next school term. They were informed that was the school's problem, not the Navy's problem. Showing great determination, the school administrators located some space above Garfinckel's Department Store to conduct classes. The Navy never returned the property on Nebraska Ave. to the Mount Vernon Seminary, but in 1944 the school did receive "just compensation" for the property.

In the never-ending competition between the Army and the Navy, the Army decided that instead of taking other people's offices and buildings and shoving young women un-mercilessly into the streets, they would build their own office building. Construction on a new Army office building had already begun on Virginia Avenue in a place that Washingtonian's called "Foggy Bottom." However, Secretary of War Henry Stimson did not like the building or the area, so he gave it to Cordell Hull and the State Department. Harold Ickes, the Secretary of the Interior who thought that the State Department a befuddled organization and in a fog itself, could see sweet accuracy in locating the State Department at Foggy Bottom.

Stimson had bigger ideas. In the battle of the buildings only the biggest of the big could possibly suffice for the Army. The Army/Navy duel came to an end when Stimson settled for the creation of the world's largest office building later known as the Pentagon. That colossus had over three times the floor space as the Empire State Building and eventually 40,000 bureaucrats worked there. All those people in that bureaucracy, along with all the other growing bureaucracies in Washington DC, needed desks, chairs, water coolers, filing cabinets, and of course typewriters in order to fill out the massive amounts of paper forms that the bureaucracies themselves create.[141]

So out went Mary's cherished typewriter to some faceless bureaucracy. Some of those bureaucracies were so faceless that the people running them did not even know they existed. One day Ickes, who in addition to being Secretary of the Interior was also head of many other agencies, was answering questions at a press conference. One reporter asked him about certain policy of the OPC (Office of Petroleum Coordination). Ickes, who must have been perturbed over all of the "alphabet soup agencies" blurted out, "I can't speak for the OPC!" The stunned reporters looked at each other as one of Ickes' assistants came up and whispered in his ear that he (Ickes) was the director of the OPC. "I am all balled up with these initials," Ickes informed the reporters. No kidding, and so were a lot of people. Cordell Hull and others at the State Department must have enjoyed their chief critic getting in such a confusion. Perhaps they could lend Ickes an office at "Foggy Bottom" where he could work out his problems.

However, Ickes was not the only one tripping over his own tongue or red tape. If Ickes was director of the OPC, then who was the director of the OPA? What was the OPA? What did the OPA do? That agency, the Office of Price Administration, managed prices in the free capitalistic American economy. That would be a trick wouldn't it? As the new OPA got started the director Leon Henderson sensed a problem. They were unorganized and all mixed up, so Henderson hired some efficiency experts to help his OPA get better organized and more efficient. After studying the OPA for a few weeks these special efficiency consultants to the OPA issued Efficiency Memorandum #9808-1 if anybody was keeping track. That important war-winning memorandum directed how desk drawers in the government should be organized. Typists should have three drawers that should be numbered "1,2, and 3," and executives should have six drawers, which should be numbered "1,2,3,4,5 and 6." That was a real revelation. Thank goodness for the OPA and the efficiency experts they hired; we might never have won the war if that agency had not stepped into the breach to enlighten fellow members of the bureaucracy on the best way to number their desk drawers. And speaking of bureaucracy, just what was the PWPGSJSISIACWPB? Apparently that agency issued regulations for plumbers during wartime. One wonders if the director of the PWPGSJSISIACWPB knew what the letters stood for, or even if he knew that he was director of the PWPGSJSISIACWPB?[142]

With so many agencies needing so many forms typed, the demand for typists in Washington DC also soared. A nationwide campaign to lure typists, almost all female, to the capital proved very successful. The young women flooded the city. All that was required was a high school diploma and the ability to type, no tests required, and no questions asked. Beginning salary was $1,440 per year, pretty good pay in those times. Some of the women arrived at the train station, were immediately herded onto a bus, and then taken to a processing room located in a loft above a five and dime store in the city. There, amidst the noise and confusion, they were hired and given their assignments. Many women ended up at their desk's (drawers numbered 1,2, and 3) before they even found living quarters.[143]

Alas many of those desks, while being properly numbered, were devoid of typewriters. At the time that Mary's typewriter made the ultimate sacrifice

Renewal

to God and Country the government claimed a shortage of about 600,000 typewriters. How did this happen? The WPB (War Production Board) declared that typewriters were not essential to the war effort; therefore, the companies that produced typewriters now produced other items deemed more necessary to winning the war. When the typewriter crisis hit in mid 1942 the OWI (Office of War Information) swung into action with a nationwide publicity campaign urging people to donate or sell their typewriters to the government. "Send your typewriter to war," was one of the catchier slogans.[144] What a classic example of one bureaucracy feeding another. If the WPB had not stopped the manufacture of typewriters, the OWI would not have been able to come up with its' advertising campaign.

Mary's beautiful personality-intensive handwriting of the prewar and first six months of the war, had been replaced with her typewritten V-Mail forms. Now without the typewriter Mary once again rose to meet the challenge. As if she had been training all her life to write the names of circus patrons on a piece of rice, her handwriting became small and precise as she filled in the V-Mail forms without benefit of her typewriter. Fred did not wear glasses until later in life, however Mary was concerned about his eyesight as a later V-Mail stated, "My darling, this is V6 – a Victory Gram, I hope the writing is large enough – I'm afraid it has been too small on the others."[145]

Undaunted by the chaos of the paper and bureaucracy wars raging in nearby Washington DC, Mary remembered an old portable typewriter that she and Fred bought in New York during his leave from the U.S.S. Milwaukee. Mary had used that old portable typewriter while working at the *New York Times*. But where was it? So many boxes had gone to storage, things get "lost in the move," and who knows what else can happen. Mary started to look around and opened a few "lost" boxes. And then a miracle, she found the typewriter. Happily, she filled out her very next V-Mail form and sent it along to Fred, out in the Pacific somewhere.[146]

> Have forgotten how to use this portable that we bought in New York when you were on the Milwaukee. Will learn again in time. Use capital letters as hope they will make easier reading. Had no trouble with your handwriting, however (sic).[147] [All letters appeared in capitals in the original].

The mail wars had come to an end, or so it seemed, as long as Mary could keep the WPA away from her newly rediscovered portable typewriter. But the good times never last. By the time V-10 (Victory Mail #10 in Mary's numbering system) went out, the portable typewriter also left. Mary gave it to Peggy, a relative attending college at the time. Mary figured the next generation needed it more than her so off it went leaving Mary with only pen and paper and first-class mail once again. That was the end of the great typewriter saga, "for the duration." For that matter the V-Mail between Mary and Fred also died an unceremonious death. After Fred found several V-Mail letters taking longer to arrive than regular airmail he wrote to Mary that, "It is my understanding that it will be better for us to use the regular air mail for the time being."[148] And that, as they say, was the end of that.

While the bureaucracies fought each other in the Battle of Washington DC, fighting in the Pacific raged between the United States and Japan. From the first attacks on Pearl Harbor until June the Japanese success was astonishing. The taking of Guam and Wake happened early in the war. Indonesia fell, then the Bismarck Archipelago, along with that the northern side of Papua New Guinea. Singapore disappeared under the Rising Sun in February, Thailand was occupied, Rangoon evacuated in March, and all of Burma followed in the footsteps of those defeated areas a month later. Four of the most northern islands in the Solomon Islands archipelago were quickly captured to round out the bad news. The united forces of America, Great Britain, Holland, and Australia had effectively been pushed aside with only toeholds at Port Moresby and Midway Island.

The news could not have been much worse as Mary diligently followed the misfortunes of war on the radio and television. A few misfortunes also occurred for Mary and the kids back home. First a measles epidemic hit the Warder household. The girls succumbed to it while Fred Jr. somehow managed to escape the germ. He did his part in trying to cheer the girls up though. He strung a rubber band across a shoebox to make a sort of banjo that he played while singing. This delighted the sick girls to no end. Fred Jr. could be very sweet and helpful when he wanted to be sweet and helpful.

At other times Fred Jr. could be a terror, not too unusual for a boy of eleven years of age with too much energy and time on his hands. His pranks on the girls were common enough; a bag of flour over a door rigged to drop on an unsuspecting head, a tack on a chair, and other mischievous tricks. Mary Jr. and Suzy were the usual victims of Fred Jr.'s impish gags, often severely upsetting Mary Jr. Sometimes Grace entered the fray as an unwilling accomplice in the pranks, other times she too fell victim to the "Moriarty of Calvert Street." But Fred Jr.'s sweet and loveable nature was far more prominent than the prankster streak in him. He was quite cooperative around the house and helped with the usual chores such as emptying the trash

Renewal

or draining the icebox before the next ice delivery, a very important chore since the house had no refrigerator.

Even though the war brought a demand for sacrifice and the possibility of death for loved ones on distant battlefields, it also brought purpose and focus to the Americans, tempered with a good deal of self interest. Mary's frustration and tension left just as the war began. Fred Warder's frustrations and tension began at about the same time that Mary's ended. As their letters and thoughts followed each other around the globe, both hoped to be reunited soon, but both knew that duty came first. Mary fulfilled hers and kept the family together in the early days of the war. Fred's duty included sinking enemy ships. Bad torpedoes and "special missions" kept him from doing what he thought his duty ought to be. In saving herself and her family Mary had experienced a breakthrough and was a living testament to the powers of the human spirit triumphing over misfortune. Fred Warder needed some of that same human spirit to overcome his bad luck, as he too searched for his own breakthrough.

Clockwise: Fred jr., Susan, Mary, Grace, Mary jr.

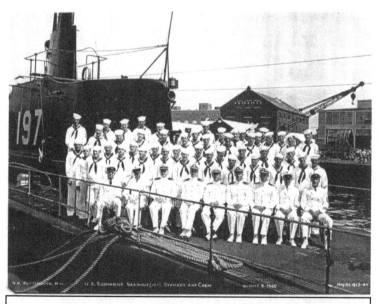

U.S.S Seawolf Officers and crew August 1940

Meeting a Japanese supply ship in the Davao Gulf

Mary and a moment of peace

Fred Warder receives his first Navy Cross

Seawolf

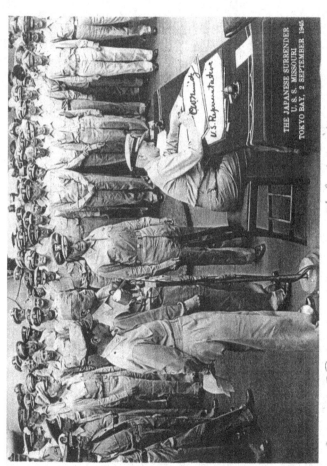

Chapter 9
Breakthrough

With Seawolf docked at Surabaya on February 7, 1942, the crew could take a little rest. Meanwhile the Japanese began their southern thrust taking control of Macassar Straits and then the oil rich area of Balikpapan by January 24th. As an example of the completely overwhelming firepower brought by the Japanese during the early phases of the war, they were attacked while landing at Balikpapan by four U.S. Destroyers, had five ships sunk, and didn't loose one minute from their invasion "schedule." Next the Japanese solidified their gains on the other side of Borneo in the South China Sea. Surabaya became the next step target of Japanese coming under aerial attack starting on February 3rd. The Seawolf crew "rested" in Surabaya amidst daily bombing raids.

But military people have a knack for making something livable out of a bad situation. Considering the conditions they generally work under it is a sort of unwritten job requirement. Gus Wright scared up a five-gallon can of fresh milk that the crew quickly ingested. Strolling around the open-air shops later that first day, the men bought and ate plentiful amounts of fresh fruits. The street scene itself was exotic and represented every kind of people in the world. Brown skinned Javanese, Blacks, Whites, and turbaned Orientals browsed around together. Almost every allied uniform could be seen from Dutch, British, Australian, and even a few Chinese soldiers milled about.

At Malang, about fifty miles south of Surabaya, Adm. Wilkes established a rest area for the crew. Half of the Seawolf crew went there for three days while the other half worked on the ship doing what they could to repair her under bad circumstances. Later the two groups swapped places. An open-air train took the men up the mountain making it easy to view the colorful birds and the rich foliage. A Dutch garrison hosted the Seawolf crew at Malang where they ate well and relaxed. Their Dutch hosts had some horses that the crewmembers rode breathing in the fresh mountain air; so different from the stench of diesel in the Seawolf. Their mountain perch had a clear view of the harbor at Surabaya. The men witnessed the daily bombing raids by the Japanese. Those raids forced Seawolf and the remaining crew to rest on the bottom of the ocean for much of the time during the day.

Seawolf herself was in some pain. The QC-JK sound head and the pitometer log were all damaged from the grounding a couple of weeks earlier. The Fathometer shorted out so they could not tell their depth with any accuracy. Worse yet the gasket on the negative flood valve cover broke so they had to run with the negative flood tank fully loaded at all times. A diver from the submarine tender Pigeon could not repair it at Surabaya. If the crew of the Seawolf ever needed to dive rapidly to evade a counterattacking ship "flooding negative" was not an option; a dangerous situation in combat to say the least. Also, the forward battery room was flooded with saltwater from a leak in the forward trim line. This was the second trim line section found defective in less than a month. Further investigation proved that aside from the hole in the trim line the battery room deck leaked salt water into the battery tank in "several places." Add to that the propeller shafts that leaked so much that they resembled an ornamental fountain or as Warder put it, "This condition of leaks is apparently general." Having a leaky ship is one thing but a leaky submarine is quite another!

After chronicling the many problems of Seawolf, Warder reserved his last and most ferocious blast on port entry procedures. He pointedly wrote that Seawolf arrived at the established rendezvous point "three minutes in advance of the appointed time," exactly 03:32, yet they were made to wait another two hours and seven minutes before they finally spotted some Dutch patrol vessel and were escorted into Surabaya. When similar problems occurred in front of Darwin a few weeks earlier, perhaps the frustration was alleviated by the pathetic sight of the broken patrol boat, but not in the present case. From the blistering sarcasm and criticism in the War Patrol Report, which is supposed to be fairly devoid of editorializing, one can only imagine the pyrotechnics set off by Warder's sometimes-noteworthy temper.

Warder had been told that the minefield in front of Surabaya was especially dangerous. The time spent waiting for an escort and the change in conditions obscured landmarks making a positive check of their position impossible after about an hour. Drifting around in such a situation caused his ship to be "unnecessarily hazarded," according to Warder. He advised that the patrol vessel "performed no useful task…and the employing of such a vessel for this purpose appears doubtful to me." Again, some prewar exercises involving the navies of the several countries now fighting as allies would have solved that problem. Just to put the icing on the cake Warder pointed out that chart HO3045 was completely useless since it did not have the location or identification of mountain peaks around Cape William.[149]

The badly needed repairs also did not come easily. Warder estimated that the leaks required at least 10 days of dock time to fix. He also thought that a team of skilled laborers from sheet metal workers to electricians, plumbers, and coppersmiths would be needed. While native shipyard workers and the few Dutch technicians did good work on Dutch ships they were of little value to the American ships. Wilkes, realizing his mistake in having his tenders and maintenance crews in Darwin, quickly hustled them over to Surabaya, but too late to help the Seawolf. She steamed into battle, for the most part in disrepair bringing an extra amount of danger to her crew.

As the crew did what they could to get under way the Japanese continued their progress south. It now became somewhat imperative that Seawolf get away from Surabaya and the relentless Japanese attacks. By February 10th the Japanese had Macassar in the Celebes and a day later Banjarmasin on the southern end of Borneo. On the 14th of that same month Palembang fell and the Japanese dominated Sumatra. Java was plainly in the cross hairs of the Japanese and a huge sea battle was in the making.

The military crisis caused a command crisis. In the East the British had failed and the Americans had not done much better. The Dutch however were determined to fight it out. As these national forces converged on Java, a command structure was set up hopefully to coordinate all the military assets of the Australians, British, Dutch, and Americans (ABDA). At the head of ABDA was the British Field Marshall Archibald Wavell, with Admiral Thomas Hart commanding all the navy forces. But Hart and the Dutch commander Admiral Helfrich did not share the same views on strategy let alone tactics. Hart for the most part did not want to commit the navy to battle as he thought the defense of Java already lost.[150] This is defeatist thinking, but to take Hart's side the Japanese did have overwhelming forces against the ABDA.

In the end Helfrich probably was right; military people must fight it out. If Douglas MacArthur used Hart's logic, Bataan and Corregidor would have surrendered long before it finally fell in May, possibly damaging the American war effort. Plus, the Americans did win a tactical victory when the four Destroyers, Ford, Pope, Parrott, and Paul Jones, successfully attacked a superior Japanese force during the battle of Balikpapan on the night of January 24th. True, that one action did not stop the Japanese, but the U.S. did sink five Japanese ships with no losses for the U.S. An enterprising, energetic, and creative commander could probably have repeated that with great effect. One last note: the allies realized much too late the importance of air power. Without air support navy operations are very difficult to say the least. The Japanese had air supremacy throughout the struggle in the

Philippine Islands and Indonesia. Even with creative energetic leadership the going would have been tough for the allies.

President Roosevelt finally relieved Hart on February 15th. The reason given was health. Hart might have been burnt out from the strain of three months of unbroken defeats, but nobody questioned his health.[151] Politics probably played the biggest role. The Dutch wanted a Dutchman in charge, so Hart was recalled to Washington DC. Helfrich took over all navy operational duties in Indonesia. On the same day Singapore surrendered to the Japanese.[152]

With trouble behind them in the form of a nearly broken command structure and another defeat at the hands of the enemy, Seawolf got under way on the 15th taking a full load of twenty-four torpedoes with them. Despite the maintenance problems morale remained high on the Seawolf and the crew anticipated their fighting role in stopping the Japanese. Seawolf left the "safe" harbor of Surabaya in the afternoon. The pilot left Seawolf at about 4:30 pm. Warder noted that Seawolf cleared the "danger area," which wasn't very dangerous, about thirty minutes later and dove to periscope depth. Whether the sarcastic remark, (he wrote the words in all capitals), showed his continued displeasure at the lack of organization or frustration about the failure of the allies to mount much resistance against the Japanese is not known.

The first day out of Surabaya proved uneventful, but for some reason the X/O continued to have problems navigating and could not fix their exact position. When the airmen had been on board a few weeks earlier they helped the crew with the use of the octant because sextant use was limited on account of light on the horizon at that time of the year.[153] Even after the coaching by the airmen, the X/O who was in charge of navigation still had significant difficulties navigating and for some reason Ensign Casler was unavailable to help out.[154] Warder once again had to note that the fix was doubtful so they changed course slightly to err on the side of safety. To modern readers used to the near perfection of satellite navigation where one simply presses a button and your location is fixed anywhere on the globe to a few inches, it must seem humorous imagining these crew members looking through an octant on the deck of a swaying ship trying to find out where they were. Back in the old days there was still plenty of "art" in the science of navigation.

Upon Seawolf's next foray into action in early December, mechanical trouble started immediately. This must have been especially disheartening considering they had just left port where they got in at least a few repairs. Just before 10:00 am on the 16th they discovered saltwater in the lubricating oil of the starboard main motor. That's all they needed; one of the main motors to wreck itself due to lack of oil because of another leak! The crew took that motor off propulsion and proceeded, of course at a slower rate. But then the same thing happened to a second motor. The crew began to alternate between the motors until they could get all of the contaminated oil out. Then they removed both oil coolers, which had been put in new at Surabaya, and replaced them with the original oil coolers – the very coolers that Warder had been railing about at the end of the first patrol!

While all of this was going on they limped their way north toward their station in the Macassar Straits. Periscope observations proved difficult due to heavy rain as visibility dropped to about 1000 yards. Then at 9:34pm they received a message from Wilkes to turn around and go to Lombok Strait, which separates Bali from the Island of Lombok. By dawn of the 17th they had traveled about 400 miles to Lombok Strait, which was about 150 miles from their point of departure, Surabaya.

After arriving at the southern entrance to the strait they began looking around. In the first few hours at the new station the crew could find no shipping and weather remained a problem with heavy rainsqualls. They nosed around Nusa Besar and sighted some fires near Benoa on Bali.[155] Warder figured the Japanese had bombed some gas and oil facilities in preparation to a landing in the area. Warder had guessed correctly, the Japanese were landing on Bali at that exact moment. Concerned that the fires silhouetted the Seawolf, Warder ordered a course change to 90° and headed east.

Then thirty minutes before midnight they received another message from Wilkes directing them to close in and attack shipping in the Badung Strait, which is the narrow body of water that separates Nusa Besar from the eastern side of Bali. Strong currents in the Strait made operations tricky. While wrestling with the Seawolf the crew completed the battery charge for the night, cut out two main engines, and gently flooded down creeping around Badung at between 5 and 10 knots. At 2:12am sound reported high noise levels and then three minutes later the cavitation sound of the enemy propellers, or "screws" as they are sometimes referred to in the Navy. In the first hours of February 19th at least three Japanese ships were in Badung Strait; the transport Sasago Maru, which by the time Seawolf arrived already had landed its troops and supplies, and two destroyers Asashio and Oshio.[156] Those two destroyers now passed directly over Seawolf. Sound picked up pinging from both destroyers as they searched for the submerged Seawolf. After about 20 minutes Warder decided to take a peek and ordered the periscope up. He spotted one destroyer at only 1,000 yards. The orders came quickly:

"Down periscope," Warder ordered. Bringleman standing next to Warder pushed a button and the periscope quietly slid down.

"Left full rudder, full ahead," was Warder's next order.

"Left full rudder," The helmsman repeated as he turned the wheel. While he did that, he clicked the enunciator to "full ahead," which repeated down in the maneuvering room where the crew there adjusted the controls and the Seawolf surged forward.

Three minutes later Seawolf began evasive maneuvers. Now the earlier problems of correctly fixing Seawolf's position posed a threat. Uncertain of his position, therefore uncertain of the water depth, Warder stayed at periscope depth, just 63 feet. Being nighttime, the hazard was small, but they would not be able to do that during daylight hours only three hours away. Warder decided to head away from Bali and fifteen minutes later Sound reported no more pinging. Not aware that the Japanese troops were already ashore Warder guided Seawolf to "likely landing places" to stop the Japanese. As they got close to the beach, they retracted the sound shaft and the pitometer log not wanting to lose those in case of an accidental grounding, which temporarily destroyed both instruments a month prior.

At dawn the men were called to battle stations. Seawolf circled waiting for an opportunity but then it started to rain heavily, and visibility became very low. Still they waited, circling left full rudder. Until finally they made contact with an enemy destroyer, bearing 126°. Warder now thought they had successfully penetrated the destroyer screen. Then a loud crash came as Seawolf hit the bottom. Again, the orders came rapidly

"Emergency back," Warder ordered in an elevated voice.

"Emergency back," repeated the signalman into the phones as the men in the maneuvering room quickly reversed the motors.

"All back full,"

"All back full."

"All back 2/3."

They worked themselves out of the jam. Because of the shallow water Warder switched to the periscope in the control room and tried to stay at 55 feet as they continued working themselves into deeper water. Warder gave the orders calmly and with confidence.

"Starboard ahead standard."

"Left full rudder."

"All ahead 2/3."

"Steady on 090°."

Breakthrough

The crew worked smoothly and all seemed right again. Then suddenly a violent crash rocked the Seawolf as she slammed into the sea floor again. The crew tossed about inside the ship as the lights flickered. Coral scraped the bottom of the ship and a grating noise reverberated throughout.

"Blow safety," Warder immediately ordered. In less than a minute Seawolf surfaced. Seconds now counted an eternity as the Seawolf floated helplessly on the surface within close proximity of the enemy, which only 40 minutes earlier Warder himself observed through the periscope at a range of only 1,000 yards.

Even before the Seawolf completely broke the surface the hatch in the conning tower was opened. Amidst a shower of residual water on the bridge Warder raced up the ladder to look. Almost magically they had surfaced in a severe rainsquall that reduced visibility to about 500 yards.

"I went to the bridge and found myself well fenced in with coral patches and discolored water, [I] picked myself a hole and went ahead," Warder later wrote.[157] It took eleven minutes for Warder to visually guide the Seawolf clear of all shoal water. Then he spotted a Japanese destroyer about six miles away. Thinking that the enemy could not see him because of bad visibility and the land background Warder continued on the surface and even coolly ordered a battery charge.

The four-man watch team came up to the bridge. During the daylight surface operations, those four sets of eyes were the only defense Seawolf had. As each man went atop the QM (signalman) counted the people going up the ladder to the bridge to keep track of those outside the ship. Everything continued smoothly but unfortunately about thirty minutes later a four engine Japanese plane flew over at about 2000 feet, a low enough elevation to easily spot a submarine.

"Dive, Dive" yelled Warder. The QM slammed the klaxon, "Ahooga ahooga," sounded throughout the ship. The men on the bridge slid down the ladder as the QM counted and checked off their names. The QM then grabbed the lanyard and yanked. The hatch slammed shut. Mounting the first couple of steps on the ladder he spun the wheel, which dogged the hatch shut. Now the crew waited. Had they been seen? Twelve minutes later a quick turn of the periscope showed no planes in the sky and no ships in the area. They headed back to Badung Strait.

By 8:30am on the 19th the crew had already been involved in plenty of excitement but no combat. The weather finally began to clear greatly increasing visibility; Warder could now clearly identify the area where they earlier grounded at Serangan Island. Twenty-five minutes later he spotted some smoke and headed towards it. After cruising for ten more minutes

Warder made another periscope observation. At a range of 14,000 yards, he spotted one of the Japanese destroyers. The battle stations alarm sounded, "bong bong bong," as the crew hustled to their assigned areas and prepared for action. Fifteen minutes later they found the second destroyer, but they began to experience problems tracking the enemy ships.

Seawolf had been traveling towards the targets at the slow speed of about 2 knots. With the weather cleared the seas became perfectly smooth and glassy making it easier for the enemy to spot Seawolf's periscope because it tended to create a little wake when raised for observations. At the same time severe currents, rip tides, and the occasional whirlpool moved southward through the strait pushing Seawolf in the opposite direction Warder wanted to go. He decided to take a small risk and increase speed to 4.5 knots, slowing for observations.

At 1:30pm, after spending six hours traveling just a few miles, Warder could see the whole scene open up. Two destroyers, one at 12,000 yards bearing 335° and the other at 16,000 yards bearing 352° with an angle on the bow at 90°; a good setup except for the extreme range involved. Additionally, he sighted two transports similar to Akagi Maru and Kinai Maru, which he looked up in Booth's Merchant Ships and matched it to #36 and #55.

As Warder began to develop his attack sound reported 4 enemy destroyers in the area (there were in fact only two as Warder observed). The enemy destroyers started to get nervous, and sound soon picked up one of them pinging as it searched for Seawolf. At the next observation the range to the two transports, Warder's primary targets, narrowed to 8,000 yards. Warder ordered 90 feet and an increase of speed. Two distant depth charge explosions reminded the crew of the incredible risk involved in this attack. Sound reported screws bearing 295.5° as Warder ordered to 63 feet, slow to 2 knots, and raised the periscope.

One enemy destroyer was now in range, 1,800 yards. Warder clearly saw the ship's gun crews at the anti-aircraft batteries, their attention focused shoreward. Warder wanted to get at the transports but as he said, "He [the destroyer] looked too good so I turned left at full speed to give him [a] straight bow attack."[158] Four minutes later the Japanese commenced firing with their anti-aircraft batteries, aiming towards the shoreline. With the Japanese engaged supporting their infantry on land, Seawolf could move with quite a bit of confidence in spite of continued distant depth charge explosions.

However, the Japanese destroyer began moving rapidly to get a better position for its action ashore. It rapidly stretched the range from Seawolf to about 2,800 yards. Warder switched his attention back to the transports both with their gangways down and anchor chains perpendicular to the water. To get at those transports Seawolf once again had to get into shallow water. Warder again ordered that the sound head and pitometer log be retracted due to the shallow water. One can admire the coolness and the bravery of the captain and crew going into such shallow water after being violently grounded twice just nine hours before.

Warder increased speed to 6 knots as he closed on the targets. Another string of depth charges exploded. The crew noticed the increased volume of the explosions as the Japanese hunted them. By 3:36pm Seawolf was in position. Earlier, as the attack against the destroyers developed, Warder had ordered tubes one and two ready with doors open. Subsequent to that of course they had gone to 90 feet and experienced some depth charging. Warder decided to shoot torpedoes 1 and 3 at the first transport and 2 and 4 at the second just in case something had happened to torpedoes 1 and 2 during the dive.

At 3:36:50 Warder gave the order to commence firing. 38 seconds later the attack was over. Sound reported that the shots were, "Hot, straight, and normal." But Warder could not see any wakes or explosions. He did see one of the destroyers turn rapidly towards the Seawolf's position, so he ordered 90 feet but was very worried as there was "considerable uncertainty as to just how much water there is here. The beach looked very close."[159]

Warder ordered evasive maneuvers as the ship came to 155° T. Then suddenly Seawolf slowed for no apparent reason. About one minute later two strings of three depth charges blew up "forward of starboard, fairly close." Warder noted that if the Seawolf had left their firing area at full speed they would have been killed by that string of charges. The approach team abandoned the conning tower for the control room below. Seawolf rigged for silent running, which meant turning off air conditioning and other machinery including the bilge pumps. Bilge water accumulated weighing Seawolf down. A few minutes later they hit a freshwater stream moving at 5 knots.[160] Seawolf suddenly accelerated away from the depth charges. Before they new it Seawolf descended to 170 feet. Warder noted this stroke of good luck as the charges had been "going off right over us."

After ten minutes of the intense counterattack the crew hoped for a reprieve but far from letting up the Japanese depth charges intensified. Warder ordered flank speed in an attempt to outrun the Japanese to deep water. All of a sudden the Seawolf stopped. Henry Thompson shouted into the phone to the Chief Electrician's Mate asking what the problem was. The main relay to the electric motors had tripped off due to an especially close depth charge. It would be impossible to get the relay switched back on in a hurry as they were located behind a large steel mesh cabinet as a safety measure against electrocution. Seawolf glided "dead in the water" and unless somebody got the relay connected Seawolf and everybody in her would really be *dead* in the water.

Luckily the Chief Electrician's Mate, Ed Capace, had some clairvoyance. Prior to the Seawolf's fourth war patrol he had packed a long 2x4 piece of wood. He figured if the relays ever tripped off a person could rapidly fit a long piece of wood through the handle hole of the steel mesh door, reach the breaker, and then flip it on. The wood acted as insulation while manipulating the giant breaker. Even before Thompson could relay to the captain the report from the maneuvering room that the breaker had tripped off, Capace took his 2x4 and turned the breaker back on. The Seawolf began to move forward again at flank speed after losing power for only about 18 seconds. That planning by Capace, and then his subsequent quick work during the crisis saved the Seawolf and its crew. For that he received the Silver Star. Yet, knowing that the crewmembers survived because of his actions was truly reward enough.[161]

During a depth charge counterattack a submariner can do very little but wait out the storm of depth charges. At least on land an infantryman can run or dig a hole but, in a submarine, they wait and wonder if this will be the one that will drown them. Under these circumstances the crew looks to the officers and mainly the captain to guide them through psychologically. Any show of fear or even greater than normal concern could send the crew into a panic under the strain. As for Warder he sat calmly in the control room. Only incredible composure and self-control can explain this. Warder described this depth charging this way:

> My face was stung with flying cork and paint chips, my ears were deafened and my eyes were kept busy watching the gauges and manifolds dance. On one blast the overhead appeared to come in 6 inches. This ship is strong.

Each exploding depth charge compressed the interior walls of the Seawolf blowing a sort of eerie fog off the walls, giving the inside of Seawolf a surreal dreamlike appearance. Despite the pounding the crew never lost control of the ship even though at one point the bow planes went out. The savagery of the depth charge attack can be understood when Warder reported the hatch between the conning tower and the control room got so contorted from the blasts that it "showed open" and could not be properly closed. The Japanese counterattack lasted 18 minutes and dropped at least 43 depth charges on them. As another crewmember remembered, "It was really rough."

At 4:18pm Seawolf came to periscope depth and observed three Japanese destroyers and one troop carrier. Warder reported that one transport seemed to be down at the stern and listing. He presumed the listing ship to be the one he attacked earlier. As Warder looked through the periscope one of the destroyers fired a broadside in his direction but Warder paid little attention to that action. He did however turn Seawolf around and headed for the open sea to surface and charge batteries.

At about 8:00 pm that night Warder reported a flash of light. It was probably a searchlight or a signal of some kind and not gunfire. As Warder patrolled on the surface, he was unaware that Dutch and American surface ships were about ready to make what they hoped to be a major strike against the Japanese in the Badung Strait. Unfortunately, the allied fleet came a day late to prevent Japanese landings on either Bali or Java. Admiral Doorman, commanding from his Dutch flagship De Ruyter, had huge problems in planning the operation. The ships he wanted to use were at three different locations: Tjilatjap, Surabaya and Ratai Bay and he could not concentrate them all at once. He therefore planned to strike the Japanese in three different waves throughout the night of the 19th and the early morning of the 20th. In total Doorman had 3 cruisers and 11 destroyers to face only two Japanese destroyers and one troop transport. The allies should have crushed this small force.

In the meantime, Seawolf continued to cruise just five miles south of Nusa Besar on an east/west patrol right where the allies planned their attack at Badung Strait. Then at 10:13 pm they received a radio message from the Commander of U.S. Submarine forces of the Asiatic Fleet. Sent in code the message took about 45 minutes to decode. The orders directed Seawolf to vacate the area and proceed beyond the southern entrance of Badung Strait. At 10:55pm the message was decoded and Seawolf changed course and headed out of the Strait. Considering that Adm. Doorman's fleet passed into the strait at about the same time and the action opened with gunfire from the cruiser *Java* at 10:25pm, one could reasonably say that the overall commanders cut things a bit close. The danger of Seawolf being depth charged by U.S. destroyers was quite real. Or suppose that Seawolf got a good look at the Dutch cruisers and attacked them with torpedoes mistaking them for the enemy in the dark night. Of course, in that case the Dutch ships would have been safe since the U.S. torpedoes probably would not have exploded.

Other things also did not pan out for the allied forces. When the U.S. and Dutch destroyers left Tjilatjap prior to the attack, the Dutch destroyer Kortenaer ran aground.[162] Communication amongst the several allied ships in the three different waves was nearly nonexistent. In fact, the two U.S. destroyers in the first wave, Ford and Pope, did not even exit Badung Strait to the north as planned but broke off their action and headed south passing Seawolf in the night. The Japanese had their own problems. Two of their destroyers, Oshio and Asashio, mistakenly fired several rounds at each other but unfortunately for the allies they chose this time to fire inaccurately. After all was said and done the allies lost one destroyer and the Japanese had one destroyer damaged.

As for Seawolf the bridge personnel watched the flashing light of the battle for about two and a half hours. They had one scare when a ship illuminated them with a searchlight at 11:01 pm (this was probably either Pope or Ford heading south away from the battle). The OOD called the crew to battle stations and prepared to dive but the ships kept moving apparently not noticing the Seawolf. Three minutes later the crew secured from battle stations. In a couple more hours they finished charging batteries, changed course, and headed toward Badung Strait to enter by morning.

As the Seawolf patrolled the strait submerged during the daylight hours of the 20[th.], Warder noted the difficulty handling the ship.

> Currents are swift, erratic; tide rips and whirlpools make this strait a very difficult place in which to steer a submerged submarine or to control its depth. On one occasion observed ship to swing to starboard with left full rudder, requiring standard speed to straighten her out.[163]

Later that morning the crew of the Seawolf observed a plane being shot down and at least one aviator bailed out. They watched the person floating down to Nusa Besar and noted that he "hit hard." Then another plane made a low pass over the area and about an hour after that the OOD saw a small raft being paddled rapidly by four men. But were the men friendly? How about the guy that landed hard on Nusa Besar? Despite being so close the man at the periscope could not ascertain the nationality of anybody on the surface. It would be a huge risk to attempt any rescue during the day even if they knew who the men in the boat were. Such are the misfortunes of war.

Cruising in roughly the same area over the next five days proved to be uneventful. Then on the morning of the 25th enemy activity started to intensify. Seawolf tracked a few transports and a destroyer. Seawolf entered the narrowest part of the strait where maneuvering space became very tight and due to short-range one attack against a destroyer had to be aborted. While setting up another shot Warder realized, just in time, that they were on a collision course with the target and steered away as they closed to only 200 yards. Finally, at about 5:40 am he spotted a transport he decided to shoot at a range of only 750 yards. They shot tubes 5, 6, and 7 at the bow, stern, and "goalposts." Warder saw "one torpedo hit just forward of [the] bridge, throwing up a sheet of water to [the] top of the bridge."[164] Good reports of solid hits came from the sound operator and personnel in the engine room and the after-torpedo room. Warder himself reported a "distinct thud with the deck [of Seawolf] moving out from under me."[165] But even after all of that reassurance Warder stated, "There is not enough of a bang out of these fish [torpedoes] to suit me."

The Japanese did not counterattack so Warder worked Seawolf back into position to attack another ship in the group. He picked out a destroyer at 1500 yards. They fired three torpedoes but Warder did not observe their tracks due to insufficient periscope exposure. With three other destroyers around who can blame him for trying to keep a low profile. Sound reported two hits and a few seconds later the crew heard two loud explosions. The following evening Warder noticed a radio broadcast that reported the sinking of 4 ships in the area. He had attacked a multiple ship formation with a total of six torpedoes expended so mathematically it was possible to have sunk four ships. However, Warder discounted that report believing Seawolf sank two ships. Postwar analysis gave him no credit for enemy ships sunk in that engagement.

After the attack the Japanese destroyers dropped a few depth charges that hit close. Warder, along with the rest of the men in the conning tower, abandoned that position and went to depth charge quarters. Warder's report shows the crew received a serious test from the Japanese.

> There followed a pretty bad four and one half hours. Every time we would start a pump to get down the bilge water, or run up a periscope to take a look, or start the hydraulic plant to hold out the sound head, a destroyer would start for us. They were more sparing of charges than were the gang on the 19th but the charges appeared to be heavier and deeper and more accurately dropped.[166]

Warder had made an important discovery here. The Japanese depth charges tended to be lighter than the American depth charges. Also, the

Japanese depth charges seemed to generally explode no lower than about 150 feet. During this counterattack by the Japanese Warder only reported problems when Seawolf tried to get within 63 feet of the surface for periscope observations. When the ship was at a depth of 200 feet things seemed to be smoother.

Believe it or not Warder still thought about going in again for another attack. The Japanese thought the same thing, so they stationed two destroyers in the eastern approaches to Badung Strait to try and keep him out. During one of Warder's periscope observations a fairly large feather temporarily blocked the periscope. So down went the periscope hopefully to rinse the feather away and any other marine life that chose to make the periscope its temporary home. On the next observation Warder counted 10 lookouts on an enemy destroyer all looking at Seawolf. He ordered a deep dive and rigged for silent running. Three times the enemy destroyer passed overhead but did not drop a thing on the Seawolf. Damage to the Seawolf during the entire five-hour ordeal consisted of a leaking battery ventilation pipe and bilge water flooding in the gyro setting motor in the forward torpedo room. During the counterattack the men counted 21 depth charges.

By 11:00am Seawolf stood safely out of Lombok Strait. At 4:00pm they radioed Surabaya with a contact report. By 7:30pm they received a receipt for the message plus orders to vacate the straits towards the south because the allies were planning a major surface strike against the Japanese for the night of the 25th. The Seawolf surfaced and headed south charging batteries on the way. While the lookouts on the bridge searched for shipping other crew repaired the leaking battery ventilation system. They used the same materials for this leak and the many prior leaks: wicking, white lead, tape, and marlin. If crewmembers of the Seawolf had known how many leaks their ship would spring they might have bought large blocks of stock in companies that produced marlin and tape. All levity aside Warder reported the next day that the repairs did *slow down* the leaks.

Just before midnight on the 25th Warder changed course and headed again for Badung Strait. Seawolf spotted several planes in the area, Japanese bombers wreaking havoc on Surabaya and other targets. After spending about 24 hours in the area they spotted a ship. Having a low battery charge Warder exercised caution and did not pursue it. He also thought that they might be part of another allied striking force. Such is the optimism that carried America through these early dark days of World War II; as everyone knew, apparently with the exception of submariners, there weren't any allied ships going north at that time. In another day the battle of Java Sea would take place and by March 1st the oceans around the Malay Barrier were cleared of allied shipping.

The battle of Java Sea took place on February 27, 1942. In short, it can be characterized as a last desperate chance or a gamble with the odds stacked against the allies. Even though on paper the Japanese fleet and the combined ABDA forces were fairly equal, the ABDA had no air cover either to fight the enemy or to scout and spot the enemy. Plus, they had units from three different navies that, owing to no pre-war training together, could not communicate with each other. Even if the Japanese fleet had been defeated on the 27th, and that is a big if, within a short period of time they would have been able to swing their aircraft carriers into the battle for Java and win anyway.

The ABDA lost three destroyers and two light cruisers during the battle. Two days later they lost five more ships. The Japanese landed their ground troops on Java and the allies had to escape any way they could. Unlike the Philippines a little later, there would be little if any guerrilla warfare in Indonesia. The native people did not necessarily like the Dutch, unlike the Filipinos who liked the Americans and mounted a very effective guerrilla war, along with many Americans who escaped into the jungle.

The loss of the ships did not stop the Americans. In a sort of last ditch gasp the United States decided to send 59 more P-40 fighter planes to Java. The Langley carried 32 assembled planes and the Seawitch carried 27 crated planes. The two ships left Fremantle, Australia on February 22nd headed towards Tjilatjap. The personnel at Tjilatjap worked hard to widen the road from the harbor to the airfield to accommodate the wingspan of the arriving planes. The great urgency to get the planes to Java caused Admiral Helfrich to order the ships to make an unescorted run toward Tjilatjap. Unfortunately, the Japanese caught them on February 27th and sank Langley and all the planes on board. Even if the planes had landed, they would not be ready to take flight until March 1st at the earliest and that still would have been one day too late to make a difference at the battle of Java Sea. Things seemed to look better for the Americans when the oilier Pecos was able to rescue all but 16 of the Langley crew. That turned out to be a curse in disguise as the Japanese then sank Pecos. The destroyer U.S.S. Whipple came to pick up the 232 survivors of that ship but tragically had to leave the rest in the ocean to eventually drown.[167]Things couldn't get much worse, or could they?

The Seawitch, under the command of Lt. Commander J. M. Hatfield, managed to get through and unload her airplanes at Tjilatjap.[168] The men ashore who came to meet the Seawitch laughed at the whole venture. Apparently there had been rumors that hundreds of planes were arriving on board the Queen Mary. They looked with incredulity on this pathetically small offering knowing the air armada they were up against. Everything seemed to work at cross-purposes as the pilots for the planes were leaving for Australia anyway. After all that effort the 27 planes, still in their crates, were pushed into the bay just a day later.[169]

During this time Seawolf continued patrolling around Lombok Strait. The only excitement was provided late at night on the 27th when the OOD sighted a ship, and the crew went to battle stations. Warder speculated that it was the Spearfish but more than likely it was one of the four American destroyers that had been involved in the battle of Java Sea and was now escaping to the south. On March 1st orders came directing Seawolf to the southern area of Java around Tjilatjap right where the Langley and Seawitch would be. As they left the area, they again encountered a rush of cold water, which sent the Seawolf plunging nearly out of control. Quickly Warder ordered 10,000 pounds of water flooded into the damaged negative tank. He then ordered the slow venting of that tank as they got into warmer water.[170] Once again creativity and fast thinking, combined with a well-trained crew, saved the Seawolf, but how many more times could only the sheer will of the men keep the Seawolf afloat?

Late on March the 2nd the OOD spotted a ship, but Warder elected to not pursue it. "Investigation would necessitate my losing considerable time...away from my assigned area and I believed that I might be wanted to Tjilatjap very soon account [sic] evacuation of personnel or resistance to Jap bombardment."[171] Notwithstanding being in a submarine Warder had an uncanny way of knowing the situation on the surface. When Seawolf arrived at Tjilatjap Warder noticed large fires burning. The Dutch were determined to leave nothing for the Japanese. When Warder received a message on March 7th to go to Sunda Strait between Sumatra and Java the fires at Tjilatjap still burned. It must have been a great blow being chased out of the Philippines only two months before and now saying good-bye to a burning Indonesia.

By March the 11th they had made no contact with the enemy in the Sunda Strait except for a wrecked Japanese plane. At 6:30am the lookouts started to get ashes in their eyes. A volcano erupted on the island of Krakatoa between Verlaten and Lang Islands.* Huge plumes of white smoke (probably

---

* In 1883 a German Imperial Cruiser was in the area and witnessed the creation of the new island of Kracatoa. Apparently, the volcano blew up from 1,000 feet below the surface of the ocean to a height of 1,500 above the surface of the ocean in a matter of minuets. The tsunami created by the

steam) rose into the sky. Occasionally black streaks could be seen outside the white. Huge rainsqualls darkened the sky one minute and then were gone the next. Spectacular gas explosions occurred, and an electrical storm broke out making night as day as fire from the sea volcano met the bolts of lightning coming from the sky. But the show put on by nature was, for the most part, lost on the crew. Warder only noted that the Great Channel of the Sunda Strait was a poor place for patrolling because the light from the volcano silhouetted the submarine.

As the crew searched in vain day after day in the Sunda Strait the ship threw the usual assortment of mechanical problems at the crew. The oil cooler on the number four engine started leaking, no surprise there. Right after they fixed that the oil cooler on the number two engine went out, at least there was comfort in consistency. A few days later crewmembers discovered three inches of water in the after-battery room. That problem put the ship in peril. The batteries could short out and ground themselves into the ship; or worse yet, the batteries could leak chlorine gas swiftly killing everybody aboard. The crew immediately "pulled the after battery clear of load." They cleared the deck of water and began tracking down the cause of the flooding. They spent an hour ripping out lockers, clothes, provisions, and decking until they found the culprit, a leak in the riser to the trim line hose connection in the galley store room. At least the batteries were not ruined. They applied the usual leak treatment of marlin, white lead, tape, and even threw some shellac on it for good measure this time. The next day the forward battery room became flooded. The crew began their usual search routine removing some clothes lockers where, to everyone's astonishment and surprise, a new area of the trim line was leaking. According to Warder the crew applied "another baling wire fix." Seawolf was quickly becoming a big ball of yarn.[172]

Day stretched into day. The crew at the time seemed a bit edgy. The Seawolf had not had a serious approach for several weeks let alone an attack. By March 27th, the 40th day of the patrol, several of the crewmembers weren't speaking anymore. Most of the crew had not seen the sun or even had a breath of fresh air that whole time. Cigarettes were running low, the pipe tobacco was finished, and the cigars had long since run out. When loading provisions at Surabaya they took on local Indonesian coffee. Despite hype to the contrary the crew did not like the taste. Bad coffee, nicotine fits, and no approaches or attacks; tempers could not have been stretched any further.

---

eruption killed about 36,000 people, which considering the sparse island population in the south pacific is quite a lot.

Then deliverance! At 8:23 pm on the 27th they received a coded message CSWP 270815 directing Seawolf South toward a small speck in the South Pacific called Christmas Island. That is not what got the crew excited. The orders said they were to investigate Christmas Island *on the way* to Fremantle where a new base was being set up for the U.S. Navy in Australia. Crewmembers wanted to get some rest on dry land with some fresh air.

Right as the clocked ticked from midnight on the 28th to early morning on the 29th they sighted Christmas Island. Seawolf poked its nose into a docking area of Christmas Island called Flying Fish Cove. They patrolled uneventfully for the next two days. Warder and Deragon planned to have Seawolf cruising on a line 11 miles long 124°-304° "in order to command approaches from either Lombok or Sunda Straits." It made sense that any Japanese landing on Christmas Island had to come from those two areas and that any landing would be at Flying Fish Cove. At 5:30am on the 31st Warder noted fairly nice weather with light rainsqualls. A few moments later the moon set into the sea. When they reached the center of their patrol line Warder ordered the engines secured and they lay-to waiting and listening. As if by a miracle they picked up a slight ping to the port side of the ship. "No check that it is to starboard," came a correction about a minute later.

Then seven minutes later near panic on the bridge. A searchlight from a Japanese ship "fully illuminated" Seawolf. Warder shouted, "Dive, Dive," and the QM hit he klaxon as the men on the bridge leaped down the stairs. The hatch slammed shut, the QM spun the wheel, which dogged the hatch tight. On most boats the captain might be expected to clear the area to avoid a punishing depth charge attack by the enemy. But instead, Warder ordered, "Left full rudder," which brought them to a course of 290° in order to close the enemy formation. Eckberg in the radio shack reported, "pinging all over the dial." After a few seconds of thought Warder "realized that [the] ship that picked us up was leading [the] port screen so [we] came left again to close the Cove on 215°."

The approach party got to their stations in the conning tower as Warder ordered evasive tactics attempting to shake the Japanese destroyer. Casler at the plotting table worked his dividers in order to dodge the enemy destroyer while somehow keeping Seawolf on the base course of 215° in order to cut off the other ships at the entrance of the Flying Fish Cove. At 6:27:30am the crew heard two depth charges. Warder, now very experienced in Japanese depth charge attacks, ordered negative flood and a depth of 200 feet. Everyone in the crew must have crossed their fingers at that point wondering if the trim lines would hold as the water rushed to the front of the ship. Over

Breakthrough

the next 15 minutes Seawolf was crisscrossed by pinging and the screws of the enemy.

About thirty minutes later Warder came to periscope depth, 63 feet. He looked around. As if by magic the whole scene opened up: one destroyer, two transports, and two cruisers. Quickly the approach team worked through the problems to get a clear picture of the attack.

Warder lined up the periscope wire on the destroyer and directed, "Mark." Immediately Rudy, at the helm, reported, "211.5°." Mercer, the assistant attack officer reading the rings on the side of the scope reported at the same time, "Relative bearing, 230°."

After that Casler quickly worked the problem in his head as he plotted on the table. It only took a few seconds for him to report, "True bearing 081.5°, on a course of 161°."

While Casler worked Warder used the statometer on the periscope lens to estimate the height of the mast. It only took about a second to call out 15'.

Immediately Mercer looked at the corresponding scale on the periscope and called out the range, "6,000 yards."

Warder then estimated the all-important angle on the bow and called out, "Angle on the bow 150°." This information was relayed by the signalman Henry Thompson, standing right next to Casler at the plotting table, then to the X/O Deragon at the TDC below them in the control room. Deragon started working the TDC, which made the familiar coffee grinding sounds. Whenever the green solution light came on all of the figures were crosschecked.

The whole process took about thirty seconds. Warder then whipped the scope around to view the other ships (the destroyer was trailing the formation). They worked through the same sequence with the rest of the enemy ships coming to the solutions:

> 1 AP (transport) bearing 315° T, 8,000 yards, angle on the bow 75° port.
> 1 AP bearing 308° T, 8,000 yards, angle on the bow 90° port.
> 1 CL (cruiser) 257° T, 7,000 yards, angle on the bow 15° port.
> 1 CL 212° T, 8,000 yards, angle on the bow 115° starboard.

Initially Warder wanted to get the transports. A few minutes later he noted that the cruisers seemed to be "just milling around." Maybe he could get a good shot on them. A few minutes after that the transports again looked favorable but then they moved too far west.

One can imagine Casler working feverishly at the plotting table sandwiched between Henry Thomson with the headphones and Rudy Gervais at the wheel. Working in such close quarters Casler might be bumped on occasion messing up his nice strait plotting lines. While Mercer stood next to Warder reading the bearing numbers off of the periscope, he would brace himself against the wall and the #2 scope trying to stay out of Warder's and Thomson's way. As the approach party worked the temperature crept up to 95°. Despite being clothed in only shorts and sandals the crew quickly became uncomfortable. Then they switched off the air conditioning and other nonessential machinery. And as the heat began to rise past 100°, perspiration trickled down their faces. A few minutes later their shorts were soaked with sweat. The six men stuffed into the close quarters of the conning tower quickly began to give an unpleasant odor. But after 40 days in a submarine they didn't notice it so much anymore.

The attack continued to develop quickly. Just thirty minutes after the two depth charges and about eight minutes after sighting the Japanese cruiser Seawolf found herself in the middle of a substantial Japanese movement to capture Christmas Island. One destroyer stood to the starboard side of Seawolf, two transport ships held a course crossing her bow at just over 8,000 yards and then the two cruisers made a sharp turn ending up on the port side of Seawolf. What a stroke of luck! The cruisers brought themselves into firing range of the Seawolf. Warder ordered right full rudder to line up for a stern tube shot. They closed to within 1,300 yards, perfect range. Abruptly the two Japanese cruisers changed course and within a matter of seconds Seawolf's perfect setup disappeared. By necessity Warder turned his attention back to the transports. After a quick look he knew he could not get them.

But the cruisers continued going back and forth across the opening of the harbor and Warder realized that he could get the cruisers only if he got into Flying Fish Cove. The back-and-forth patrolling track of the Japanese ships should give him enough time to set up for the shot. Warder identified a Jintsu type Cruiser as the flagship. He noted that particular ship hoisted flag signals first and tended to be out of any formation with the other ships. Also, he could clearly see a full color Chrysanthemum and Rising Sun on the clipper bow therefore he pressed his attack against it.

Then just as they got into their final firing position the cruiser turned away. The approach party must have been getting frustrated by now. The crew doggedly continued to work Seawolf into position for a good shot. Warder noted that the water was "nicely rumpled with occasional whitecaps," which helped conceal the periscope. Then they heard a distant depth charge from one of the destroyers. But the Japanese were shooting blind and had guessed on that one. With some dread Warder spotted a pair of Japanese Seaplanes at an elevation of about 1,500 feet. If the ocean had been flat the planes would easily have spotted Seawolf through the clear tropical water. As it was, the whitecaps kept Seawolf safe.

They heard another depth charge explosion. Had they been spotted? Regardless Warder pressed home the attack. Another 15 minutes passed and Seawolf still could not get into a good firing position. Patiently they kept at it. Finally, at 8:47:25, the approach party took their final observation and made their final calculations on the cruiser. 206.6° T, 60° port, 1,400 yards, with the cruisers speed at a casual 15 knots. The green solution light flickered on the TDC and Deragon gave his usual, "Ready to fire." At 8:48:15 they commenced firing four torpedoes, one each at the bow, stern, foremast, and mainmast. That took about one minute. Warder watched the torpedoes for about 30 seconds and gave this narrative.

> [I] observed men to be running and shouting on the cruiser quarterdeck and measured range at 700 yards. I am still forward of the CL [cruiser] beam and he is turning towards me. I can see smoke from [the] torpedo tracks drifting across [the] field of vision.[173]

Warder did not wait to watch the impact of the torpedo. He ordered Seawolf to 120 feet with right full rudder. The planesmen dipped the controls forward and Seawolf went down. Some of the crew reported that they heard two explosions. Warder insisted it was only one. The chief of the boat watching a clock in the control room reported one explosion at an elapsed time of one minute and ten seconds from firing. Warder later said, "It seemed like a year to me." Sound reported 30-40 minor explosions as Seawolf turned away. Warder heard none of these, which is important because when a ship is torpedoed and sinks to a certain depth it begins to make "breaking up" noises audible to the entire crew. Maybe the Japanese cruiser sank and maybe it didn't. Warder didn't claim a sinking, although he did not see the ship again.

Before they could claim any enemy ships sunk Seawolf and her crew would have to survive the most determined counterattack yet by the enemy on the surface. They did not have to wait long as eight huge explosions rocked the Seawolf within a minute. The men bounced around like rag dolls. Warder ordered a depth of 200 feet to escape the worst of the barrage. They tried to use the negative tank to take them to safety, but the flood valve did not open against the sea pressure. They shifted to "hand power" and were able to get the valve open but then the gasket blew. Would they be able to seal the valve? As Warder said, "We're going to have one helluva time."

The next set of depth charges put the radio operators Eckberg and Maley on the deck with glass, paint, paper, pencils, and cork flying around. Just as those depth charges faded, Eckberg, now struggling back into his seat in front of the sound equipment, picked up another set of screws and pinging of a destroyer hunting them. Another eight well-placed depth charges hit close to Seawolf. After the attack on their cruiser the Japanese seemed very motivated to sink the Seawolf and for the next seven and a half hours the Japanese searched and dropped depth charges.

As the counterattack worsened the Seawolf literally began to fall apart. First the oil cooler sprung a leak, the ninth to go bad on that patrol. Salt water started to fill the engine sumps due to leaky overboard circulating water valves. Two gyro repeaters went out, which meant that two torpedo tubes could not be used. The radio transmitter "went haywire" and finally gave up. One torpedo tube leaked "more than it should," as Warder optimistically put it. But the thing that became very unnerving is their inability to run the very loud bilge pumps. Every time they started the pumps the Japanese immediately homed in on them and worked over Seawolf. The submarine bilges filled to overflowing with water endangering the electrical equipment and raising concern over a possible electrical short. To meet this latest emergency the crew formed a sort of "bucket brigade" carrying bilge water to the sanitary tanks where they were emptied. All the while the Seawolf was being bounced up and down like a rubber ball from the depth charges with Warder noting, "the depth gauge needles whipped 16 feet."[174]

As the depth charges fell the crew heard a loud thud on top of their own ship like a heavy metal object. What was it? The object began to slowly role down the deck towards the back of the ship. Quickly the men surmised that it was an unexploded depth charge on top of them. Once it rolled off of the deck and fell to its preprogrammed detonation depth, it would explode blowing The Seawolf into a million pieces. The crew waited wondering if this would be their last few minutes on earth. As long as the depth charge stayed on top of Seawolf they were safe. The men in the engine room could clearly hear the object rolling around. They started to inform the approach party in the conning tower the whereabouts of the object. It rolled and slowly rolled. The crew was transfixed by the eerie sound. Then there was silence. Everybody braced but nothing happened. Did the depth charge roll off and misfire? Was it lodged somewhere on top of Seawolf's superstructure? Everyone remained quiet. An hour later they slowly came to the surface, made another observation at 63 feet, and found all shipping gone. But

Breakthrough

because of Seawolf's close proximity to Christmas Island and the daylight hour Warder could not surface. The temperature continued to rise inside the Seawolf, and the men dripped perspiration all over the decking. Warder decided to play safe for a moment and the Seawolf headed for open ocean to take stock of the situation.

By 1:00pm the Seawolf was sufficiently out to sea to avoid the Japanese destroyers for the most part. But the sinking of a single Japanese cruiser did not satisfy Warder or the crew; after all there was a war to win. He wanted to make an attempt at the other cruiser not to mention the transports unloading troops onto Christmas Island. However, the Seawolf could not be controlled very well as the trim line leaked. It leaked so badly that any attempt to use the trim tank could lead to disaster.

Most captains would have given up by now, and rightfully so, but the always resourceful and energetic Warder devised a scheme whereas they used the torpedo room bilges as a trim tank pumping water out of them with the drain pump and line. He instructed the torpedo room personnel in blowing and flooding the trim tanks to and from the sea using a torpedo tube drain and vent. All this patchwork seemed okay in theory. Now the crew had to test their ideas in combat in the close quarters of Flying Fish Cove.

At 2:40pm Seawolf got into proper trim. But just as they were going to do a periscope observation the trim line (what else could go wrong) burst in three places in the torpedo room. The crew pulled out the string and did a quick patch job. Warder felt like this was his day and the rigged-up patch job on the trim line would have to hold for this entire encounter, there was no turning back. About a half hour later Seawolf came to 63 feet for a periscope observation. Warder saw one cruiser and one destroyer. He wanted that cruiser, but the destroyer came over and decided to drop a few more depth charges in the area forcing Seawolf to run quiet.

Seawolf surfaced 7:49pm that night. As they opened the hatches the cool night air came rushing into the ship. As the bridge personnel came up the hatch they noticed, much to their horror, the deck shelter light burning brightly. That's one sure way to tip the enemy to their position. Warder immediately ordered all topside lighting "de-fused for the duration." Knowing that action might be imminent they put in a quick charge on the batteries. As the men on lookout duty scanned the ocean with their binoculars, one of them noticed the ships bell lying on the deck broken. Somehow one of the depth charges had dismantled the bell, which made a perfect landing on the submerged deck, and then rolled around causing the men all of that worry during the depth charge counterattack. What a relief! Or was it. For normal people this incident might inspire some melancholy for the damaged bell, or someone might simply fix the bell. But for a submariner (or any sailor) with a heightened sense of superstition, it could be a bad omen.

The radio room sent out a message of the day's action to headquarters, now in Fremantle, Australia. But just as the men were getting comfortable after the long day of combat, the OOD reported two torpedo tracks headed towards the Seawolf. The order "dive, dive" was shouted and the signalman hit the klaxon alarm and in less than a minute the Seawolf slid beneath the sea. Sound heard nothing overhead. Warder was skeptical about the tracks as he "had observed similar phenomena the night before in the general area; definite streaks of refuse material probably washed off the island by the spring tide and drifting to the northwest in the prevailing current."[175] Ten minutes later the Seawolf surfaced and continued the night patrol. About an hour later the Commander of Submarine Asiatic Forces radioed the Seawolf with congratulations for the days action. Warder posted the message to the bulletin board for the crew to read. "It helped a lot," noted Warder. He continued saying, "We were feeling pretty well beaten down."

At about 1:50am on April 1st Warder was able to get into his "stateroom" and finally get some sleep. At 1:51am the OOD woke him up, so much for sleep on a submarine. A destroyer had been sighted. Warder looked at the enemy with his 16-power telescope and a few minutes later the ship turned away. Warder's original plan had been to get within 10 miles of Northwest Point and then dive at about 5:00am. Now he modified that to put them about 15 miles out. Then at 3:00am they sighted another ship, which Warder took to be a cruiser. That got everybody's interest up again. The enemy ship appeared to be heading right for Seawolf, so they dove. This could be trouble as a WW II submarine's atmosphere deteriorated greatly after about 10 hours under water. For that reason, most captains wanted to stay on the surface as long as possible before daylight. At the very least Seawolf would probably have to remain under water for about 16 hours; that is if nothing went wrong.

As soon as Seawolf submerged Warder called for a course to 335° to bring the stern tubes to bear, as they had no more torpedoes in the forward torpedo room. They tracked the ship for the next hour but could get no closer than 6,000 yards. Even at this early stage of the battle Warder realized that battery power would play a critical role in their survival, so he kept his speed to standard and did his maneuvers using only the outboard screw for turns.

At 4:37am the Seawolf closed the cruiser to about 3,000 yards; the steady progress pleased the approach team very much. One minute later Warder ordered full speed to course 345° in order to fire the stern torpedoes with a 90° track. Unbeknownst to Warder this angle of attack, which all their pre-war training called for, was of course the worst due to the bad torpedoes. One minute later Warder made all his final pre-firing observations.

"Enemy cruiser bearing 151.2°T, course 261°, at a range of 1,900 yards," Warder said in his elevated voice.

Deragon, down in the control room, fed the information into the TDC and when the green solution light came on, he reported, "Ready to fire."

Bringleman at the torpedo firing control panel flicked a switch and the orange light came on indicating tube five was ready. Just before Warder ordered, "commence firing," the torpedo room reported that the anti-circular run device, which he had ordered deactivated, was causing problems on the torpedo in tube eight. With no time to make an adjustment Warder settled for a three-torpedo spread. Ever steady Warder watched as the cruiser's middle smokestack crossed the wire on the periscope. As it did, he ordered, "Fire." Thompson repeated the order to the torpedo room as Bringleman hit the plunger and the torpedo left the ship. The crew's ears felt the usual popping as the residual compressed air came into the ship. Eckberg, on the sound equipment, reported "Hot, Straight, and normal," as the first torpedo headed for the cruiser. 15 seconds later they fired the torpedo in tube six, but it left the ship off course. Apparently the Seawolf yawed a bit after firing the first torpedo. Nobody knew the course of torpedo six. 15 seconds later they fired the third torpedo from tube seven. "Hot, Straight, and normal," reported Eckberg.

Then they waited, but not for long as only about 20 seconds after firing the last torpedo Warder reported a violent explosion. The men wondered, was that the first torpedo hitting the cruiser or a dangerous predetonation of the third torpedo? Warder ordered, "Up periscope," and chanced a peek. He saw a huge amount of smoke coming from the enemy ship but no flames. Just then clouds covered the moon making observations difficult. Warder really wanted to see at least one ship that Seawolf attacked go down, so they increased to 4.7 knots and went towards the cruiser. Warder searched on the same bearing but could find nothing. He felt sure the ship had sunk. Just then Eckberg reported screws heading their way. Everybody on Seawolf knew what that meant; the Japanese counterattack was about to begin. To make matters worse Seawolf's oxygen was nearly depleted due to its extended submergence. If the Japanese were persistent, they could literally suffocate the crew of the Seawolf.

About a minute later Warder took one more look and instead of a destroyer coming after Seawolf it was another cruiser. He decided immediately to attack as events dictated strategy and tactics. Sound estimated the enemy's speed at thirty knots. Warder knew that was ridiculous but none the less the ship was moving quickly. The range reduced to 1,500 yards within about 40 seconds. The crew in the torpedo room already had tube seven reloaded. Unfortunately, the torpedo in tube eight continued to give them problems.

Warder had ordered the circular running device deactivated, but the securing nut was stuck. Feverishly the torpedo men partially extricated the 2200-pound torpedo from the firing tube to get a wrench on the securing nut. But when they replaced the torpedo into tube eight the gyro setting spindle slipped. They tried several times to reengage the spindle but failed. They once again took the huge torpedo out of the tube and finally recalibrated the gyro.

All of that took time and after about five more minutes the target seemed to wander away. Warder began getting fidgety and frustrated. He criticized himself saying, "I am losing an attack waiting on tube eight, due to my own lack of foresight." The attack on the Japanese cruiser slipped through Warder's fingers. He decided not to shoot stating, "[There] is no sense in shooting without [a] spread." Helplessly he watched the Japanese cruiser's range increase to 7,000 yards and then disappear all together. The morning twilight had begun. The crew secured from battle stations and began plotting a course to Fremantle.

Just before departure Warder decided to take one last look into Flying Fish Cove. The Japanese apparently took this time to make one last effort to find Seawolf. Suddenly the sound equipment picked up pinging "all over the dial." Warder took a quick look. Indeed, there were several destroyers but much to Warder's surprise out came another cruiser. The crew came back to battle stations and the whole process started over again. Only now the approach party had been up for about twelve hours and if there was significant daytime action, they could count on at least another twelve hours without sleep. If required, the crew could overcome their lack of sleep. But being submerged since 3:00am and looking at the possibility of another thirteen hours submerged, the crew would not be able to overcome the increasingly toxic environment inside the Seawolf.

As Warder made his observations and the approach party worked away in the conning tower, nerves became frazzled. They tracked a cruiser, while trying to avoid the four destroyers deployed by the Japanese. Then another cruiser showed up. But even counting the now fixed torpedo in tube eight, Seawolf still only had two torpedoes left; yet another frustration. The second cruiser had an airplane catapult that was empty. Warder surmised correctly that the Japanese had commenced an aggressive air search for Seawolf. The

Breakthrough

smooth water in Flying Fish Cove gave a further advantage to the Japanese looking down into the water hunting the Seawolf.

While Warder worried about the plane overhead, maneuvering for a final shot became a real problem. "As we would close one of them [the cruisers] for attack, they would move somewhere else. It was most maddening," he later wrote. Then the approach periscope fogged up. Only a day before he sang praises for that device – one of the few pieces of equipment on Seawolf that had so far worked perfectly. Warder was determined, if nothing else, and he moved to the second scope based below in the control room.

Several times over the next few hours all the Japanese ships formed up indicating that they were about to "sweep out," but each time they split up. Warder did not want to return to base with two unexpended torpedoes but on the other hand he didn't have the luxury of time; he knew at some point the build up of carbon dioxide would incapacitate the crew making any operation difficult. As the Japanese continued to do everything right Warder's frustration grew.

As for the crew they continued to slow down. By 4:00pm the atmosphere in the Seawolf was so thick that a sort of misty fog floated throughout the compartments. Crewmembers not on duty lay in their bunks trying to not use up valuable oxygen. Speaking itself became a chore so the ship fell into a silent stupor. As the approach continued the men became more depleted while Warder made his way through the ship to give encouragement. He stopped by the radio shack to check in with Eckberg.

"How are you doing?" asked Warder.

Eckberg couldn't hear him and enquired, "what?"

Warder repeated the question and Eckberg wondered why the captain was whispering.

Eckberg replied in a robust voice, "I'm Fine," but he noticed that his words seemed to stop dead in the air. The air pressure inside Seawolf had grown so much that it was difficult to hear anymore.

As the Japanese searched above, they listened for any sound the Seawolf might make so Warder ordered all machinery turned off including the air conditioning. This caused the temperature to rise to about 110 degrees with about 98% humidity. Sweat dripped off of the crewmen onto the floor making them moist and slick. The Chief Pharmacist's Mate groped through the passageways passing out saline tablets. Some men took them, and some didn't. They tended to make a person very nauseated even if they supposedly helped retain body fluids.

But even under these oppressive conditions every crewmember hoped to get one more chance at sinking one of those Japanese ships in the Cove. At 4:30pm Warder observed one of the cruisers at about 8,000 yards – a far too distant shot. It then zigged away increasing the range. Warder, hoping for a miracle, maneuvered Seawolf to 180°, where maybe he could close the enemy's track and then swing around for a stern shot where his last two torpedoes waited to be released. By 4:44:45 Seawolf closed to within 4,500 yards, still too far for a shot but at least they were making progress. And then at 4:54:45 the miracle happened. The ship zigged back or as Warder put it, "That is when he made his mistake."

The adrenaline pumped as the orders flowed.

"Mark."

"Bearing 289°," called Mercer.

"45° starboard, course 070°," Casler reported.

Then Warder, in his excited elevated voice gave the figure on the statometer, which Mercer converted from the scale at the side of the periscope and called "2,200 yards."

Then the final call came at 5:01:35.

"Bearing 312°, 45° starboard, course 086°."

Mercer called the range, "1,300 yards," and lastly Warder estimated the angle on the bow, "75°."

Below in the control room Deragon worked the TDC, "Ready to fire," he reported up to the conning tower.

Warder looked through the periscope and when the wire bisected the two front gun turrets of the Japanese ship he shouted "Fire."

While Bringleman hit the plunger sending the torpedo on its way Henry Thompson repeated the order to fire in the telephone to the torpedo room. Six seconds later when the Japanese ship's mainmast crossed the wire Warder gave the order again and Bringleman happily pressed the plunger that fired the troubling torpedo in tube number 8 into the sea toward the enemy.

With no more torpedoes it was definitely time for Seawolf to go to a friendly base. Warder ordered, "Right full rudder, all ahead full, and 200 feet." As they turned Sound picked up "one violent explosion" and three depth charges. Sound did not hear any propeller sounds from the cruiser and Warder thought for sure it sank. With a very weary cheer from the crew all seemed right. As Seawolf sped (8 knots!) submerged to safety the effects of the poisoned interior of the Seawolf seemed less. The crew anticipated surfacing, which meant breathing clean air again soon.

About two hours later Warder asked for a report from the Sound, which confirmed no propeller noise in the area. Warder ordered the diving officer to bring the ship to 63 feet for a quick periscope observation just prior to surfacing. In just a few minutes the whole trial would be over. Then suddenly something went wrong. Instead of gently rising to 63 feet for a quick look, the Seawolf shot up like an over inflated rubber ball and in fact broached the surface. Alerted to the presence of the hated submarine the Japanese raced to the area.

What happened? During the action of the previous day the trim lines became so bad that the trim tanks really could not be used therefore, Warder devised a system using the torpedo room bilge water as a sort of trim tank. The crew pumped water in or out of the bilge using the drain pump and drain line. The water then went to the torpedo tube drain then to the torpedo tube vent and blown into the sea.

This jerry-rigged system actually worked for a day. But in the critical maneuver at 7:00pm on April 1st things went awry. The diving officer ordered 1,500 pounds of water blown from the forward bilge via a forward torpedo tube. The crew in the forward torpedo room opened the master tube drain valve preparing to blow water out via the torpedo tube. When Warder gave the order to blow the torpedo tube the men opened the torpedo drain tube and 15,000 pounds of water left the bilge and the trim tank. The Seawolf, suddenly so much lighter, shot to the surface. The torpedo men should have opened the master tube drain valve last as instructed by Warder. As usual though Warder was most critical of himself.

> My instruction was not sufficiently thorough. A crew should be drilled in this operation as a damage control feature (in shallow water but at considerable depth).[176]

Once Warder figured out what happened he ordered full speed with the diving planes at a maximum angle for diving. It took only three minutes to get back to a depth of 80 feet, but the damage had been done and as Warder put it, "The party was back on again." Within 10 minutes the Japanese were overhead dropping depth charges.

The depth charging itself was not so bad. But the men had been down for 18 hours already with no end in sight. The gravity reading reached 1.150 with a hydrogen level of 1.4%. This meant that the ship's batteries were all but dead. The crew could tough it out a little while longer but in a short period of time the batteries would go into reversal and leak chlorine gas or even explode outright. The air pressure was 6 ½ % causing the interior of the Seawolf to appear as a misty nightmare, and the carbon dioxide buildup made every movement by the crew a major task. The men had little choice but to droop wherever they were in the ship, leaning on machinery or with heads flat on desks and work areas. Sweat ran down their bodies in streams as they slowly succumbed to the poisoned atmosphere. Warder probably made the understatement of the day when he reported that, "The ship is most uncomfortable."

In the first hour of April 2nd, an unbelievable five hours after Warder's last desperate report and with the crew near death, sound still reported pinging on the surface as the Japanese continued their relentless search for the hated Seawolf. Knowing that the end was near Warder took Seawolf to 63 feet to chance a periscope observation. He didn't see anything. Maybe the Seawolf and crew could have one more piece of luck. Warder ordered the lookout crew to the conning tower. They waited with red goggles on for ten minutes to let their eyes adjust to nighttime conditions. After taking another look around through the periscope Warder ordered the Seawolf to the surface. Water blew out of the tanks and the submarine shot up. The hatches opened as the bridge personnel raced up the ladders amidst a flood of water poring down on them. Just as soon as the air intake valves could be opened three of the four diesel engines were put to the screws. (One of the engines had been ruined by salt water). Seawolf began a desperate dash to safety. The crew on the bridge searched the water behind them, no Japanese could be found. Unbelievably they had endured nearly 21 hours beneath the surface of the ocean while being depth charged nearly one hundred times. As Seawolf sped away from Christmas Island the crew not on the bridge, stood beneath the open hatches reviving themselves as the cool night air streamed in.

The trip to Fremantle took six days. But it was a comfortable six days. The trim line was so bad that Warder decided to run the last three days entirely on the surface. That meant plenty of good air for the crew below, but increased vulnerability from the above. Seawolf's division commander sent congratulations. Warder posted it on the bulletin board along with a personal note thanking the crew for their efforts. During that breakthrough voyage Seawolf was credited with sinking one transport, one destroyer, one cruiser, and damaging two other cruisers. After the war, studies of Japanese records reduced that score to one damaged cruiser. Regardless Warder and the crew had shown how patients, coupled with boldness along with fortitude, could get a U.S. Submarine close to the enemy and help bring the war to a quicker end. Now all that was needed were a few good torpedoes.

Chapter – 10
Hunting

Springtime in Baltimore proved to be pleasant for Mary, Mary Jr., Fred Jr., Grace, and Suzy. No more overcoats or mittens, and no precautions against the occasional snowstorm. Mary was very well settled and entered into a comfortable routine of school schedules and visiting with friends. Her quiet life was pleasantly disturbed when word about her husband's battle at Christmas Island started to filter around the United States. It was the first time she had heard about Fred in over a month, which was pleasing enough. Then on April 13th the Associated Press ran a story about the battle, and by the 14th nearly everybody in the country knew the name of Fred Warder. Letters of congratulations poured into Mary's mailbox. Old friends from the York days such as Adm. Henry Ingram and his wife Helen sent letters of congratulations. Mathew Neely, the Governor of West Virginia, Made Fred a Colonel in the West Virginia State Guard. Fred accepted the commission gratefully, however thinking ahead he might not know which team to root for when Army next played Navy. His friend Dr. Pracht, who had been nicknamed "tubby" in his youth, also sent a note, and thought it a bit amusing that Fred was now a Colonel in the Army as well as a Commander in the Navy.

The publisher Henry Luce ran a story in his magazine *Life* on Warder and his crew. Luce was the husband of Clare Booth Luce, the woman whom Warder had so graciously given a personal tour of the Seawolf only eight months prior. After the publication of Warder's story in Life hit the newsstands a whole new round of letters came in. One letter came from Wade Williams, who worked for the Justice Department at Alcatraz Island. Wade remembered Fred from their days at Berkeley, where other newly anointed heroes, Chet Smith and Ken Hurd, had completed their master's degrees along with Fred. Wade kidded Fred saying, "That it must have been that wonderful education that they [and you] received at Cal."[177] The members of the Grafton post of the Veterans of Foreign Wars sent Warder a "paid in full" membership to their post.

H. R. Greenlee who currently worked for the Houston Shipbuilding Corp and previously managed the shipyard where Seawolf was constructed, sent congratulations and a little advertising, "I am glad that I had something small to do in connection with the placing in your hands of such a fine piece of equipment as the Seawolf."[178] Mr. Greenlee might have been a bit embarrassed if he ever saw the litany of complaints Warder made about the machinery on the Seawolf. M. A. Barrett from the Portsmouth, New Hampshire Navy Yard also sent congratulations and repeated their slogan, "We are doing our best to build them, knowing full well that you fellows will do a good job fighting them." Mrs. Kalbfus, the sponsor of Seawolf, sent a nice note and newspaper clipping.

Fred Warder's fellow submarine commanders also chimed in with many letters of congratulations, most notably from Charles Brindupke, who tragically had only a few months left to live when his own submarine, the U.S.S. Tullibee was destroyed by its own torpedo. Excluding Fred's family members, perhaps the most telling of congratulations came from B.F. Irwin who served under Fred on S-38 during the China Station days.

> Dear Commander: Attached hereto please find new-photo of my former Skipper on S-38 and article in explanation of the gallant deeds credited to him.
> It is the belief of the writer that the above is merely daily routine to the Captain Warder I once knew. Yet, to me, this is more than justification for the esteem I held for you.
> Keep up the good work and, to you and all your men, here's hoping for a not-too-distant Sail Hypo William.[179]

In addition to all of the written accolades Charles King, the Mayor of Grafton, proclaimed April 28th to be "Fred Warder Day." In announcing this King asked that special lessons be taught in school extolling the brave deeds of Fred Warder and that "the flag of our country be prominently displayed." Later that evening a parade led by the Grafton drum and bugle corps, supported by two high school marching bands, marched down the main street of Grafton to the B. & O. train station square. Nearly 3,000 people lined the parade route, which is saying something considering Grafton's population approximated 7,000 persons. Mary sat in for Fred and received in his absence the respect and adoration of the citizens of Grafton as she was driven through streets waving to the crowds. Other honored guests that day included Fred's mother, his sister Peggy, and his brother Charlie.

State Supreme Court Judge Ira Robinson gave the principle oration. That was fitting because Fred's deceased father Hugh Warder and Judge

Hunting

Robinson had been law-partners with one of their clients being the B & O Railroad.

Apparently Judge Robinson thought some of the citizens of the United States were not as committed to the war effort as they should be.

"There is too much nonsense in America in the fight for liberty," punctuated his opening remarks. Robinson continued saying, "The enemy cares not for our philosophies of life." That must have struck Mary as a little funny since it was those exact philosophies that her husband was fighting for.

Judge Robinson thought that the Americans had become apathetic towards the war effort. From Mary's viewpoint there did not seem to be a whole lot of apathy, of course her husband Fred and his friends were on the front lines of the war. Was Judge Robinson correct in his assessment or was Mary? Maybe both – most Americans look back and think that most everybody worked hard and consistently at home and aboard, to defeat the enemy, which is how Mary saw it. Mary and her family had committed everything to the war effort.

However, in defense of Judge Robinson's remarks, a look at labor relations might prove his point. President Roosevelt understood that a healthy American economy was as much a weapon pointing at the Axis as a gun. He wanted to make sure the economy stayed strong and accordingly tried to clamp down on wage inflation. Early in the war organized labor agreed to a "no-strike pledge," but far from pitching in to the war effort, organized labor was deeply distrustful of the administration. Confirmation of their suspicions occurred when the President organized the National War Labor Board and tasked it with controlling wages. The board proved to be extremely unpopular, or at least very misunderstood. When the war finally ended, labor counted at least 14,471 strikes of various lengths against war industries.[180] Blame could easily be apportioned between workers and management for the problems, which in no-way changed the fact that somehow not everybody agreed on the best way to Victory, thus confirming some of Robinson's points in his speech.

Mary sat on the stage and listened politely to Judge Robinson's remarks, which were well received by the audience. The next speaker was Ward Lantham, a World War I veteran. He gave a vivid firsthand account of the trench warfare that he engaged in as a soldier in Europe. The Americans were well aware of the sacrifices of that war, which explains why they had been so reluctant to get entangled into another European mess. Indeed, most Americans were weary of the war almost before it started. There is a difference though between being tired and still doing what you must do, and doing nothing at all. And Americans, as usual, rose to their ordained duty of once again trying to save the world from itself. Lantham concluded by saying that, "Warder's spectacular successes against the Japanese vessels would serve as an example to other units of our armed services." After Lantham finished speaking some patriotic songs were sung including God Bless America. The evening ended when the two Mrs. Warders, Mary and Fred's mother, received flower bouquets from the auxiliary of the Veterans of Foreign Wars.[181]

Fred Warder Day in Grafton was a huge success. Mary and Fred were both pleased that even though the day was named after him, all the men and women from Taylor County serving in the armed forces were honored. The Grafton display of patriotism would be repeated in towns across America and is the snapshot most people think about when looking back on the World War II era.

After the festivities Mary returned to her small apartment in Baltimore feeling like, "Cinderella after the ball."[182] She was very happy about the celebration at Grafton and reported all the details to Fred. For some time afterward newspaper and magazine clippings continued to come to her house. Most of those clippings described Fred Warder as a man with a slight build. As the clippings continued to pour in Mary wondered more and more whether Fred had been misidentified, she had never thought of her husband as "slight." The Fred Warder she knew measured nearly six feet in height, was broad shouldered and muscled as befitted his chosen recreational sport of boxing. Then Mary received a clipping from a Seattle newspaper that somehow acquired a recent picture of Fred out in the Pacific. After viewing his hollow cheeks and the shadows around his worried sunken eyes Mary understood the description. Fred's days at sea and in combat had taken an unhealthy toll on his body and facial features. Mary was shocked when saw the picture and admonished Fred to drink more beer to gain some weight back.

Fred and Mary did not mind some of the sincere gestures during the initial euphoria surrounding Seawolf's success at Christmas Island, but soon they were turning down many interviews and invitations to attend various functions organized either in their honor or to help with the selling of something. Just when both thought the hoopla had died down, it would be reincarnated in some other form.

In one of the worst instances of hero worship gone awry, Fred received a book written by Lowell Thomas entitled, "These Men Shall Never Die." In the book Thomas wrote short sketches about certain actions by U.S. Military personnel including a rendition of Seawolf's encounter with the enemy at Christmas Island. The section of the book that dealt with the Seawolf roughly coincided with a fairly lurid account also given by Thomas on his nationally broadcast radio news show. During one broadcast Thomas quoted Warder as saying, "We had the pleasure of seeing a Japanese cruiser sink," and other such remarks. Thomas attributed the account to a chief electrician's mate named Sherman. Lowell Thomas was so proud of his effort that he sent a copy of the book to Warder.

Fred looked through the book and just could not believe what he was reading, mainly because what he read never happened. Fred had been at the events portrayed in, "These Men Shall Never Die," and thought it was a marvelous bit of fiction. He quickly called his secretary in to his office and began to dictate a response to Mr. Thomas and his gift of the book.

> This is to acknowledge your kind letter offering me one of your books inscribed to Mrs. Warder. The inaccuracy of that part of the book having to do with me prevents my acceptance of your kind offer. In the first place, I have never had the pleasure of seeing a Japanese cruiser sink: although the ship which I had the honor to command was credited with sinking one on somewhat strong circumstantial evidence in the early part of the war. This claimed sinking took place during a patrol on which Electrician's Mate Sherman (who is quoted in the narrative) was not on board.
>
> Secondly, Electrician's Mate Sherman was only on board the ship which I commanded during one patrol. During this patrol we were able to witness the destruction of one freighter and two transports. It is apparent that Sherman either had words placed in his mouth, which he did not relate, or was badly confused as to the nature of the targets which we sank during his stay on board.[183]

Obviously Fred Warder had reached his tolerance limit concerning his "hero" status. Earlier he and Mary simply laughed off such things but now they were simply tired of it. As for the "newsman" Lowell Thomas, he certainly was not going to take that kind of a tongue-lashing lying down. He dashed off his own letter to Fred,

> I have delayed answering your letter while trying to find a copy of the news broadcast in which I related about the Seawolf. I wanted to verify the memory I have of the source of the information. Unfortunately, I can't find the script, but my memory is definite that

the story came from the United Press, was on the regular U.P news wire, and consisted of an interview with Electrician's Mate Sherman.

We take these things as they are given to us by the news services, which in turn accept the stories of soldiers and sailors who have been at the war fronts. I suppose there are some of these latter who dream up things, and perhaps we are too credulous in passing along their thrillers.

I am exceedingly sorry that the story about you turns out to be false – it was a good yarn. At the same time I hope you will consider the position of us newsmen who deal with what are sometimes perhaps over-heated war recitals.[184]

Warder must have gotten a real laugh out of Thomas' explanation, which passed the blame of inaccuracies off to the sailor Sherman as well as Lowell Thomas' fellow reporters at United Press. When Fred received Thomas' ridiculous letter, he could only shake his head; Lowell Thomas addressed his letter to: "Commander F. B. Warder, Submarine Division 121." At the time Fred commanded Submarine Division 122, which was clearly emblazoned on his stationary. The poor man Thomas could not remember Warder's unit number, or even copy the numbers correctly from one page to another, however his "memory was definite" about the source of his story.

Fred Warder was not the only military man who disliked the excesses of the press. Robert Sherrod who fought at Tarawa complained, "Early in the war one news story gave the impression that we were bowling over the enemy every time our handful of bombers dropped a few pitiful tons from 3,000 feet...The stories which deceived people back home were rewritten by reporters who were nowhere near the battle."[185] Bill Mauldin said the newspapers should "Clamp down on their rewrite men who love to describe smashing armored columns and ground forces sweeping ahead." Robert Kelly, who was the CO of a PT boat in the Philippines at the beginning of the war said, "The news commentators had us all winning the war. It made me very sore. We were out here where we could see these victories...They were all Japanese...Yet if even at one point we are able to check and attack, the silly headlines chatter of a victory."[186]

The newsmen did exaggerate and did make up a lot of stuff with Lowell Thomas probably one of the worst offenders. However, later in the war, Fred Warder was confronted with a genuine horror story in the form of, "U.S.S. Seawolf: Submarine Raider of the Pacific." In late 1943, after Fred's days with the Seawolf were over, he started to hear whispers that his former radioman Eckberg was writing a book about the Seawolf's first seven war patrols. Some of the other former crewmembers also heard about it. "It couldn't be true," Fred thought. Then in 1944 he received a letter from Commander Walter Karig who was in the "book section" of the Navy. The Book Section oversaw censorship. Sure enough a book had shown up at his office needing to be passed by Navy censors. Upon closer inspection the book turned out to be authored by Gerold Frank and James Horan, two newspaper reporters, in an "as told to by" format with the guy telling the story being the former Seawolf crewmember Joe Eckberg.

Karig sent over the galley proofs and Fred Warder just about died. He seriously could not believe what he was reading. He quickly sent Eckberg and Karig a list of objections.

> This book is written with considerable artistry in the description of a submarine's internal and external activity...it is extravagant, overdone, contains too much profanity, contains too much of the commanding officer in contrast to the space devoted to the officers and crew.
>
> The title is cheapening to the name of a gallant ship, which fought hard but turned in little more than an average performance during the first year of the war. I would prefer that the title be "A submarine Raider o the Pacific" and that the name of the ship not appear in the narrative. Our ship has not been awarded the Presidential Unit Citation and many others have.[*]
>
> Should this book be published, I sincerely desire that my name appear nowhere in this narrative. "The Captain," "The Skipper" and similar substitutions could well take the place of my name.
>
> A close study of the submarine war to date convinces me that the publication of this book would be in poor taste, when one considers the accomplishments of other submarines, many of which have been lost in enemy action and of which the story has not yet been told. I strongly recommend that this book not be published.

---

[*] Later the Seawolf was given the Presidential Unit Citation for the fourth war patrol.

Right when Fred thought he had stamped out that fire another story appeared, he lamented to one of his fellow submariners,

> I think Joe Grenfell was responsible for that "Time" baloney. The other stuff I have not seen, which is probably just as well for my state of mind. It would be better for the service and all of us personally if it did not appear, I feel sure.

Fred probably regretted ever giving Henry's wife Clare Booth Luce that tour of the Seawolf in the Philippines way back before the war started. Some of Fred's friends thought the whole thing to be humorous and nothing to get excited about, but he continued to be peeved over the whole thing writing,

> Submarines are getting very publicity minded as you inferred and we are getting photographers and movie people here by the dozens [too]. Eckberg's book is a bunch of drivel, which fact I communicated to him and to the officer in the Navy Dept. who has had these books in his custody together with a request that the book not be published, but apparently they're letting loose of all such stuff.[187]

If only the "Silent Service," as the submarine section of the United States Navy refers to itself, could be a little more silent, Fred Warder thought. Much to his chagrin the Navy also got in on the act by putting out its own book called "Battle Report," authored by none other that Karig of the book division. In Karig's defense Battle Report is really just that, a report on what some of the various Navy units had done up to that point in the war. It was a dry rendition much different than Eckberg's sensational book. Fred liked it but sent Karig a note that an action he ascribed to Seawolf near Hainan should have been credited to Swordfish.

* * *

As Spring melted into summer the people in Baltimore melted in hot and humid Baltimore weather. The children finally learned all about the "sleeping porch" at the back of the Calvert Street Apartment. It was so hot that Mary decided that a move somewhere else should at least be investigated. Also, with the entire family there, the Calvert Street house began to shrink, or at least it seemed that way. The hunt for a cooler bigger house began.

Hunting

Mary wanted to get a place a little to the west of Baltimore in the suburbs, possibly in Catonsville, but Annapolis was also a possibility. Her idea was to change houses before the new school year began so that the children could remain together with her and be settled in for the upcoming school year. Mary wrote Fred of her plan but warned that it would be difficult finding a place, as landlords generally did not like renting to women with small children or wives whose husbands were in active combat, even during the crisis of World War II.

What started out as a plan to escape the heat of Baltimore, soon turned into a necessity of survival. The owner of the Calvert Street house decided he wanted it back. Did he discover that in addition to Mary her four children also lived there? The landlord told Mary that his impending nuptials caused his decision to take back the house. Mary, who always preferred a positive approach to problem solving, did not contest his decision. Besides, Mrs. Kloffel who owned the furniture in the house, wanted that back. In the end Mary wrote Fred that, "We were so lucky to find this – and to have it for nine months."[188] That goes to show just how difficult the housing market became in certain cities when a person could be grateful that they had retained living quarters for nine months.

Mary wrote Fred that she would start looking for a place on a daily basis so as to not get into a bind and find herself homeless. The housing horror stories of the boomtowns of San Francisco, Detroit, and Washington DC motivated Mary to no end to solve this problem post-haste. Those cities experienced such an influx of war-related migrants that housing soon ran out. Even smaller cities and towns outgrew their housing and services. Mobile, Alabama's population grew by 65% while California gained two million new inhabitants. Four hundred and forty thousand of those new Californians moved to Los Angeles causing a housing crunch that resulted in families renting out basements and garages just to get a roof over their heads. The government tried hard to create more housing but simply could not do it fast enough. When the ultimate crisis was reached in mid-1942, as Mary desperately looked for a house, Roosevelt created an agency, yes another one, to tackle the problem. The National Housing Authority (NHA) built over eight hundred and thirty thousand new units of housing while private industry created an additional one million new living units. This massive effort only lessoned the problem as the boom towns continued to grow.[189]

Mary, along with Grace and Suzy, began their search realizing that it would be an uphill battle. Mary wanted a furnished house, which was a tall order considering the reluctance of landlords to rent furnished houses – or any houses for that matter – to families with children, of which Mary had four.

On one occasion Mary answered an advertisement to look at a house, which happened to be close to a cemetery. To avoid distractions while talking to the landlord Mary dropped Grace and Suzy off at the park-like cemetery where they could play while Mary conducted her business. Mary went to the house and was warmly greeted by the landlord. Mary's neat and attractive appearance immediately interested the landlord, after all if a person takes care of themselves, they probably will take good care of a house, even if it was rented. The landlord was very enthusiastic. He showed Mary the house and asked a few questions.

"Where do you live now?"

"Over on Calvert Street in Baltimore, roughly at 30th Street."

"Oh, I know that area, it is very nice. Where is your husband?"

"Oh, he is in the Navy."

The landlord suddenly did not like the way this interview was going.

"In active combat?" was his next question.

"Well, I don't exactly know since everything is so secret now and you know the mail is so erratic."

The landlord's skepticism grew.

"Do you have any young children?" he asked, zeroing in on another possible way to disqualify Mary from renting his house.

"Yes, but they are in the cemetery right now," came Mary's response.

A look of great sorrow came over the landlord's face. "I am so sorry to hear that. Life offers too many tragedies sometimes."

After hearing that Mary's children were in the cemetery the landlord decided to rent the house immediately to the poor bereaved woman right there on the spot. Just then Grace and Suzy ran up. The landlord was astonished at the incredible resurrection that rivaled Lazarus' own rise from the dead.

Mary clarified, "I meant they were at the cemetery down the street playing so you and I could better talk about renting the house." [190]

That was the end of that interview as the landlord sent Mary and the children on their way. Wartime America at times seemed rougher than peacetime America, as everybody "pitched in together" to win the war. But "pitching in together" could have a lot of different interpretations based on what a person's personal economic interests were at any one time. Mary was not angry about her problem. There were just too many people trying to cram into cities that had too few houses.[191]

In addition to that problem, the great house hunt caused Mary to cancel plans for a much-needed family vacation. She did, however, hold out hope of getting to Atlantic City for a few days with the children, if for no other reason than to beat the uncomfortable heat and humidity of Baltimore. In addition to the heat Baltimore became very dirty in the summer with a grey dusty film settling on most of the city. Some of that might have been caused by the lack of trash pickup. Most people at that time in Baltimore burned their garbage in backyard, which may have contributed to the sometimes bad atmosphere that Mary disliked. Fred Jr. concurred with Mary's assessment calling the city "stuffy." She enrolled him in a summer day camp, which he enjoyed very much. The fresh air, fishing, archery, and other outdoor activities kept him busy and happy, and away from Baltimore. The summer camp was a fitting reward after his hard work at his school Leonard Town, where his lowest mark for the year was a 95% in geography. All his other subjects were 98% to 100%. Mary Jr. also did very well attaining a "B" average, "Which is excellent considering the school changes," Mary thought.[192]

    The good family news buoyed Mary's spirits as the great house hunt continued. Baltimore was looking less and less likely to have available housing, so she began to consider more seriously Annapolis. Mary took a few day trips there to look around to see if that Navy city still appealed to her. While there Mary sat down to look through some real estate ads in the local newspaper called the *Evening Capital*. She found an ad for a nice little house for rent on German Street. However, Mary shied away from that house as a big controversy was brewing on that street. Some residents that lived on German Street wanted to change the name of the street to something that was, well less German. This controversy instantly became so much fodder for the wags living in Annapolis. One gentleman wrote a letter to the editor of the *Evening Capital* that the street in question should be changed to "Hitler Street" because German Street was a dead end, ("cul-de-sac" in our modern real estate language), and since Hitler was going down a dead end it would be an appropriate name for the street. Mary wondered if the residents of Germantown, Pennsylvania wanted to change the name of their city perhaps to "Americatown." The *Evening Capital* did report that Irving Berlin was not going to change his name to "Irving London," but a local restaurant changed Vichysoisse into De Gaulle Soisse, and Sauerkraut magically became Liberty Cabbage overnight. Presumably none of the ingredients changed with the name. Mary, not wanting to get involved in any large important controversies like that, looked for other renting opportunities.

    As Mary continued to peruse her newspaper another item caused her some incredible anxiety and near heartbreak. Authorities were considering canceling the Army-Navy football game in 1942. About two months before, Mary had sent Fred the form for him to fill out so she could get tickets for the game, writing,

And to a pleasanter subject, Football! I heard over the radio there is to be an Army Navy game in Philadelphia – November 28th. I'd like to go. Can you have the association send the order blanks to Sue – (In case I do move – and the mail would get mixed up). I will parcel out the tickets. This was successful last year. Perhaps you've already thought of it.[193]

Luckily Fred was between war patrols when the forms arrived in Australia. In all due haste the call to general quarters sounded, decks cleared for action, forms quickly filled out, airmail stamps purchased, couriers hired, and the forms sent. Mary then acquired the tickets in spite of the Japanese who were actively trying to sink Fred's ship, the erratic mail service to and from the United States, and those pesky V-Mail forms. She and Fred Jr. looked forward to attending the game with great excitement.

After reading the *Evening Capital's* story about the possibility of cancellation of the game Mary's excitement ground to a halt. After all the effort Mary and Fred had put in to get the tickets in the first place, Secretary of War Henry Stimson thought that transportation needs for the game would prove to be too much and cancellation loomed. The game is traditionally played in Philadelphia, roughly the mid-point between the Army and Navy academies. Wartime produced many shortages including sugar and rubber; and apparently Secretary of War Stimson thought that the country also suffered from a serious train shortage. When reporters from the *Evening Capital* asked Commander Perry, the Navy's athletic director, about the cancellation of the game, he claimed that he had heard nothing about it.[194] Suddenly it looked like the Army had egg on its face. Were the Army's football players too scared to travel? Of course not, objected West Point officials. Stimson, trying to avoid embarrassing himself further, stepped aside and the two academies worked out a solution. In 1942 The Army football team traveled down to Annapolis and played at Thompson Field. Attendance was limited to local football fans, newspaper reporters, and the Navy cadets; Army cadets stayed at West Point and listened to the game on the radio. Rear Admiral J.R. Beardall felt a little bad that the Army would not have any fans in the stadium, so he ordered half of his Navy midshipmen to root for the Army. The halfhearted cheering did no good however as the Navy beat the Army 14-0. Luckily Mary and Fred Jr. lived close to Annapolis and were able to attend the game enjoying the outcome immensely.

Hunting

The problems of whether Mary and Fred Jr. could attend the game palled in significance to the housing problem. Mary reported the current situation to Fred,

> I pause to write this in the midst of a house hunt that is a "wow." Baltimore like all other cities is jammed. Nobody wants to rent to a family of children for nobody has to. There are 15 people at least for every house or apartment to let. But I am not discouraged. If the worst comes to the worst I'll...buy. This I do not want to do. But I may have to in order to get a roof. I'm not losing any sleep over the situation I can assure you.[195]

Jammed was a complete understatement of the problem. Baltimore's housing problem got worse mostly because Washington DC's housing problem reached a point of complete impaction. "Government girls," those women that answered the patriotic call and came to Washington DC to become typists and clerks, slept four to a rented room and many times even "hot-bunked" where they could use the bed for an eight-hour shift. No hotel rooms could be found anymore for businessmen in Washington DC. The Mayflower Hotel offered a program where businessmen who had no room could use a lounge on the second floor, pay for access to showers and lockers, and use a desk. As things got worse many of Washington DC's "homeless" drifted to Baltimore, rented rooms and houses there, then took the train every morning to Washington DC. Later even Philadelphia became a city where people doing business in Washington DC might spend a night.[196]

Mary did keep a cool head as she methodically combed through the ads and went to look over several places. By mid-September she still had not located a house and she had to be out of the Calvert Street house by October. Out of desperation Mary contacted several rental agencies, but all those agencies had the same story; the kids were a problem and the fact that her husband was in a combat zone was a problem. Most rental agencies had policies that required proof that a husband was on his way back to the United States before they attempted locating a house for a client. In other words, Mary had two strikes against her. The people of wartime America could give a great show of patriotism while giving no leniency to the very people that were fighting for their freedom.[197]

Somehow in early October Mary managed to secure a house to rent on Deepdene Rd in Baltimore. The landlord, no doubt a patriot, was very nice to Mary and graciously put a Navy clause in the lease so that Mary could terminate the lease early in the event that she had to move suddenly on account of her husband. Located in the Roland Park area of Baltimore, about five miles north of her house on Calvert St., the new house had eight rooms and okay heating. Schools for the children were close by and shopping was within walking distance. Mary and the four children moved in on October 15, 1942. Sue and Carroll Pattison would have put the family up in an emergency, but Mary did not want to impose.

The new house pleased Mary very much. In fact, she liked it so much, and figuring that she would be there "for the duration," she sent for the family furnishings at York. When their small amount of furniture arrived, Mary inspected everything and reported to Fred that nothing was missing, a minor triumph. The movers helped Mary and the children unpack. It did not take long as they did not have too many things anyway. Among the few items that made the place seem like home was the "red carpet." As with many of the items that Mary furnished her house with, the red carpet had been acquired while following her husband around the world to his various assignments. The red carpet had been purchased from the beloved Boethe's in Tsing Tao. It was rather small, perhaps measuring only four feet by five feet, but meant a lot to Mary because it reminded her of the pleasant China days and the summer months spent in Tsing Tao before the war. As she unrolled the carpet Mary might have thought how much the world had changed since those days. Where were the Boethe's now? Were they safe? Had the Japanese destroyed their lives as they had so many millions of other lives? Mary could only wonder.

As the four kids began to explore the new neighborhood they could only be pleased. Just like at Calvert Street, the Deepdene house had lots of shade trees. A wide front lawn set the brown frame house well back from the street. Traffic noise almost did not exist as gas rationing cut down on car travel significantly. With such few cars and even less gas the convenience of the Baltimore trolley system could not be over emphasized. As luck might have it the trolley stopped only a few blocks from the new house. A short walk took the family to the trolley, where a short ride took the Warders' to shopping areas. Mary and the children enjoyed these forays into the local emporiums, one of which had a clown to entertain the children. The trolley also came in handy for Mary Jr. who used the trolley to get to school. Fred Jr., Grace, and Suzy all walked to school from their Deepdene home. In everyway the family was now settled, at least for the moment.

After getting the floors waxed and looking good the way she liked them, the curtains properly hung, and all the important family pictures up on the walls, only two items remained to complete Mary's picture of domestic paradise. First, the "hat picture" would have to be hung on a wall and then the blue star placard put into the front window. Mary's affection for blue hats knew no bounds. She bought one as often as she saw one. It became a sort of trademark with her. Early in her married life Mary bought a small oval print, about the size of an 8x10 photo, of a man and a woman in approximately 1890's garb. The woman in the picture wore a blue hat. When the "hat picture" went up on the wall that meant that they were truly at home.

Finally, to make everything absolutely official Mary put the small blue star flag in the front window. People with family members in the military put small flags, or in Mary's case a cardboard placard measuring about seven inches long and four inches wide, in the front window of their home's to let people know of there family's personal contribution to the war effort. Each blue star on the flag stood for a person in the household that was currently serving in the military. Mary's blue star flag had one star representing her husband Fred Warder. The War department greatly encouraged this patriotic display and it proved to be quite popular during World War II.

With those items taken care of the only missing piece to the puzzle was Fred Warder. Would he be coming home soon? As Mary, Sue and Carroll Pattison, and the four children sat down to Thanksgiving dinner they thought of all of the things they had to be thankful for. Later that night Mary wrote her husband, who at the time was on war patrol in the Pacific,

> There have been so many rumors of the possibility of your early return to the States that I haven't been able to take letter writing to you very seriously. I am optimistic enough to hope that you will come riding in with Santa on his sleigh – if not before.[198]

Chapter – 11
Bad Omens

Seawolf arrived at Fremantle harbor to a hero's welcome at the conclusion of the successful 4th war patrol. They moored next to the submarine tender U.S.S. Otus. After so many days at sea and under such stressful conditions the crew desperately wanted liberty. When informed the paymaster would not be aboard until 7:00 am on the following morning, the crew suddenly became anxious to remain on the ship. After receiving their pay the next day half the crew went to Perth for a little relaxation. The other half, as usual, stayed with the ship to help with repairs. In a few days the two groups swapped positions.

In addition to good fresh food, the Australians gave the men of the U.S. Armed Services great hospitality. The young Australian women seemed especially patriotic and philanthropic, dispensing much needed aid to the men on shore leave. There was a war on and people sensed that the next couple of days or weeks might be the final days on earth for many of those men; a little frivolity made everybody feel a little bit better and think less about the sad situation of war.

About a week after the Seawolf came to Fremantle the crew was summoned and ordered into "dress whites." Scuttlebutt became rampant as the crew came out onto the deck looking sharper than they had for several months. Rear Admiral Arthur Carpender came aboard with a small entourage. The officers and crew snapped to attention and the Admiral called Lieutenant Commander Warder forward.

Carpender began to read. "For heroism and especially meritorious conduct in combat with the enemy as Commanding Officer of the U.S.S. Seawolf in three separate engagements with heavy enemy Japanese Naval forces..." The Admiral concluded with the awarding of the Navy Cross to Frederick Warder as the crew looked on with pride. Afterward, Warder turned to the crew and told them they earned the cross as much as he did. To underscore that statement Warder awarded Capece the Silver Star for his quick action, using the 2x4 to trip the main circuit back on, and saving the lives of all the crewmembers at Lombok Strait a few weeks earlier.

Warder recognized other crewmembers with advancement in grade. Amongst them were Henry "Swede" Hanson. For his action during the battle Warder raised him to Petty Officer 3rd class, gunners mate. Predictably,

Bad Omens

Hansen went into town that night to celebrate. Also, predictably he got drunk. However, instead of coming back to the Seawolf and passing out on his bunk, which would have been predicable, he decided to end his night of revelries by firing off the .50 caliber machine gun. Luckily nobody was hurt. Unfortunately, Warder had to bust Hansen back down to seaman 1st class the next day. That might qualify for the shortest-lived promotion in the history of the U.S. Navy.

Repairs on the Seawolf's trim lines continued. The task fell to two Australian plumbers who worked meticulously, which made the work progress slowly. But the methodical pace resulted in high quality work and despite the lengthy repair period Warder appreciated the effort. Seawolf would soon be in battle again and the extra time spent now might help the crew survive later. It took about two weeks to finish that job and then Seawolf left Fremantle and headed for Albany, Australia. Technicians there installed a new secret weapon, the SD radar. In theory the new radar helped locate enemy airplanes just before surfacing and at night. In truth this early radar proved unreliable and Warder ordered Seawolf's SD disconnected only six days into their next war patrol.

After about a week in Albany the crew loaded onto the Seawolf and went back to Fremantle. Captain, soon to be Admiral, Lockwood hitched a ride. Lockwood's earlier passage on the Seawolf proved to be tense and turbulent. Some superstitious sailors might not have welcomed him aboard because of the past incident. The superstitions proved correct. During the short voyage from Albany to Fremantle produced more serious problems than Lockwood's previous trip on the Seawolf. One of the enlisted men on watch went to Warder's cabin, put his firearm to his own head, and threatened to kill himself if Warder did not let him off the Seawolf. Considering that they were at sea on a submarine the request could hardly be arranged immediately. But Warder, who had a certain sympathy about him that the men recognized and trusted, was able to calm the man and quietly defuse the situation. When they reached Fremantle Warder granted the sailor's request and transferred him, no harm done. After the incident Lockwood commented to Gervais and Thompson in the conning tower that, "It had been another rough passage."[199] Jinxes, bad omens, and old sailor superstitions aside, Lockwood's presence on the Seawolf surely inspired tension.

Finally on May 12, 1942, after more than a month on the sidelines Seawolf received orders to leave port and "conduct an offensive patrol against enemy combatant supply, and transport ships in the Philippine area." Those clear orders pleased both Warder and the crew. Their orders also directed them to gather intelligence around Manila and Subic Bay while finding traffic routes used by the Japanese to "strip the islands of their wealth."[200]

They pulled out of Fremantle harbor with hope and confidence. It took only three hours before the calm shattered though. Army troops illuminated the U.S.S. Seal and the U.S.S. Rottnest, roughly four miles ahead of Seawolf. Warder blew his stack yelling, "I complained about these people one month and five days ago."[201] Over half a year into the war and some of these flawed practices around friendly harbors still went uncorrected. Warder also commented on the bad weather, a persistent problem. During the first few days of the voyage the crew spent time on training drills to re-hone their skills after the long layoff. During a battle-surface drill the crew took one minute and three seconds to fire the first shot out of the 3-inch deck gun after broaching the surface. During another drill the crew needed just 49 seconds to crash dive.

On May 19th Seawolf arrived at Koepang. That city, located on the western most part of Timor, fell to the Japanese on February 23rd just after the savage air raid on Darwin, Australia. At 5:00am Warder ordered Seawolf to submerge for a reconnaissance into the harbor. The calm sea concerned Warder but just before diving he noted very discolored water that easily hid the submarine. After he looked over the harbor and town through the periscope Warder noted very little shipping and no fires in Koepang. He did see smoke in the hills about twelve miles away from the recent Japanese bombing. About the town itself Warder wrote, "The town presented an attractive appearance. Houses of Dutch architecture."[202] Warder's broad interests and detailed comments could, at times, sound more like a travel brochure rather than a naval report.

They left Koepang at about 5:00 pm, surfaced about an hour later and cruised to Dilli, the next stop on their way to the Philippines. On the way Warder spotted a troop transport ship of about 5,000 tons. Warder ordered a submerged attack. The men went to battle stations and fired two torpedoes at short range, about 700 yards. Both missed badly as Warder, watching in the periscope, saw they cruised right by the enemy ship. Very chagrined over the misses, Warder continued to follow the large transport. Unfortunately, just before nightfall, he lost contact with it. Missing a valuable target such as a 5,000-ton transport really hurt, but loosing it altogether was just too much for Warder.

Seawolf surfaced and the approach team got together in the control room. Making a few guesses from the enemy ship's last known location, they set a course to intercept it. Through some lucky miracle it took only about an hour before they spotted it again. Warder ordered a decrease in speed to about 13 knots after realizing he had actually outrun the enemy during the chase. The lower speed reduced Seawolf's phosphorescent wake, which helped to conceal her. Clouds blocked the low full moon as the crew prepared for a night surface attack against the Japanese ship. Warder calculated the enemy's range at this point at 6,000 yards, far too distant.

Suddenly the enemy ship zigged right towards the Seawolf. Warder, ever confidant, thanked his lucky stars saying, "I was expecting him to change course about this time to head for Dilli, so I attached no special significance to the zig except to thank him for helping me get up ahead."

As it turned out, Warder had gotten so far ahead that he changed his attack plan from surface to submerged. He gave the necessary orders and the crewmembers outside the ship began to move toward the hatch without any special hurry. Just as Warder started down the hatch the officer of the deck, Ensign Mercer, shouted that he saw a flash. An instant later Warder himself heard the report of single large caliber gun. It took less than a second for one of the lookouts, Gale Bennett, to shout that a shell had passed overhead. What began as a simple low-key submerging, turned into a mad scramble as the five men on top of the conning tower dove down the hatch and Seawolf disappeared from the surface of the ocean. Far from trying to run away from the Seawolf the merchant ship came after her, pursuing with relish. Warder, now not so grateful, took Seawolf to 90 feet. A depth charge exploded in the distance. He ordered 200 feet and the crew rigged for depth charge attack. Warder noticed the armed merchant did not drift off but rather, "milled around," for some time. Warder did not play much poker, but in battle he had a great poker face. This time though he could not hide from his face the astonishment at the night's events.

It had been a surprising night indeed. Being shot at by a transport ship was not necessarily a shock. Many transports and even merchant ships carried guns. But being hunted by a merchant ship, well that was almost too much.[203] It showed the incredible aggressiveness of the Japanese. Even their freighters had turned into submarine hunters. And being shot at by a freighter, well some of the crew found that to be insulting.[204]

Notwithstanding the ship overhead Warder needed to get on his way. The navy expected him to file an intelligence report regarding the port town of Dilli. They steamed for that port town and just before 8:00 am Seawolf entered the harbor at Dilli. He reported the "Buildings present a clean-cut appearance, no fires burning." He followed that with a gentle jab at the army, "According to press news, Army reported intensive bombing of Koepang and Dilli on May 18." Well maybe the Japanese rapidly put the fires out and fixed the buildings. Or maybe Warder was blowing off some steam caused by the army's bad habit of illuminating friendly ships near friendly ports.

Be that as it may Seawolf next headed for Ambon. On the way the crew reset their clocks one hour ahead as they entered time zone 9. Sometimes these little details go unnoticed, and their importance underappreciated. Ship's crew, and this is especially important in submarine warfare during WW II when sonar was fairly unreliable, must always be very aware of the proper time so that they can make the proper calculation as to tide conditions. "How much water is over me? How much water is under me?" These are recurring questions for a submarine skipper. To appreciate how the overlooked detail can cause huge problems one need look no further than the Marine invasion of Tarawa. A simple miscalculation of tides caused the Marines and their mechanized support to get stuck over five hundred yards from their landing beaches. That miscalculation caused a huge amount of killed and wounded for the U.S. In many books the problems at Tarawa are explained away as an important "training" period for the Marines in amphibious assaults. Realistically if planners can't figure out small details like tidal charts and time zones with any accuracy then the troops and sailors are going to be in some trouble.

With clocks set and tidal charts consulted the Seawolf continued on its way. Soon they found a freighter and fired three torpedoes at a range of only 750 yards. As the torpedo left Seawolf the crew felt the familiar popping in their ears as the residual air from the torpedo tube cycled into the ship. Warder watched through the periscope as one torpedo passed right under the ship but did not detonate properly. This freighter, like the last they encountered, also carried depth charges and guns. A mild counterattack began. After 20 minutes Warder came up to periscope depth. The freighter, to his utter surprise, now floated at a range of just 570 yards, bearing 31°. Warder needed no prompting and ordered another torpedo sent on its way. It too missed. The loathsome freighter's bow gun fired several rounds at Seawolf's periscope. Warder ordered 200 feet and reported hearing the explosions of three ineffective depth charges.

Twenty minutes later the Seawolf again came to periscope depth and, to no ones surprise this time, there floated the freighter bearing 243° on a course of 143° and at a range of 6,000 yards. Warder came to 55 feet in order to get his periscope higher for better observation. While being easier for the enemy to spot the Seawolf, the added elevation of the periscope gave Warder a better chance to observe the enemy. With the onset of dusk the chances of detection lessened until finally at 7:19 pm Seawolf surfaced and gave chase at full speed.

Warder wanted to pass the freighter at night for yet another stab at sinking her. At 11:20 pm he observed the freighter signaling with its blinker to some other unseen ships. Just after midnight Seawolf lost contact with the freighter. Warder however was not deterred and made a few guesses as to the course of the freighter and plotted a corresponding course to intercept the ship again. At dawn the Seawolf dove and believe it or not, only 20 minutes later found the same freighter! Oh so skillfully Warder had maneuvered ahead of the enemy during the night and now waited, at an initial range of 10,000 yards, for the enemy ship to close the range and steam into Seawolf's ambush.

Warder's crew calmly went through their paces; the men in the conning tower making the calculations, Deragon grinding away at the TDC, and the crew in the stern torpedo room finalizing the torpedo settings. In recent attack Warder thought the torpedoes might not have armed themselves properly, so he paid special attention to this, even personally inspecting them. The Japanese ship came in just as Warder had predicted. At a range of 1,600 yards Warder ordered the firing of the first of two torpedoes. Thompson repeated the order as Brengelman pushed the plunger to electronically fire the torpedo from the conning tower. Everybody waited. Nothing happened. The crew in the conning tower waited for the familiar popping of their ears signaling a torpedo had left the ship. It did not come. Thompson asked the men in the torpedo room to again fire, which they did with no results. Again, Brengelman hit the plunger and one more time the crew in the torpedo room tried to manually fire the thing. But it would not leave the Seawolf. The crew had tracked that freighter, been depth charged by it, been shot at by it, had gone through heaven and hell to get to it, and at the moment of truth, Seawolf's tube misfired.

Warder switched the attack to tube six and ordered, "Fire." Brengelman hit the plunger and the torpedo left Seawolf. Warder watched the whole scene through the periscope; a perfect shot that passed right under the bow of the enemy. He looked, the crew listened, and nothing happened.

"It should have hit!" was Warder's interesting comment, which is insightful to the consternation that these early submarine skippers were going through. More properly Warder might have commented that the torpedo "did not explode," but at the time the torpedoes were deemed reliable, therefore the only problem could be poor aim. Even though he saw the torpedo go right under the ship he still thought, "It should have hit." During the fifth patrol Warder constantly criticized himself for the misses, which were not misses at all, but rather malfunctioning torpedoes.

Despite his disappointment Warder continued to look at the enemy ship and seemed quite amused at the antics of the Japanese. "They did not see it [the torpedo] until it crossed their track," he reported. "The torpedo threw the Japs into great commotion and they ran fore and aft and up and down at a great rate; white uniforms predominating." He didn't sink them but at least he got a chuckle from the antics of the Japanese.

The Japanese mounted an insignificant counterattack. As Warder ordered "200 feet," they dropped the perfunctory three depth charges, all of which exploded far overhead. Early in the war the Japanese set the ignition of their depth charges at about 150 feet so American skippers simply went to 200 feet and avoided enemy depth charges. This explains why the Seawolf had a fairly easy time of these counterattacks near Timor as opposed to those experienced at Christmas Island, where shallow water kept them closer to the surface of the water. At 6:48 on the morning of the 24th Warder reported, somewhat pathetically, that the "target was fading out on 220° T." Then he remarked to the crew in the conning tower, "He must have been rubbing the Budda's belly a lot," accounting for the enemy's good luck and ending the great chase.[205]

The final exclamation point on the two-day travesty came from the crew in the after-torpedo room. They reported that the torpedo in tube number 5, the one that did not fire, could not be brought back into the ship. In fact it hung halfway out of the ship, which meant the torpedo door could not be shut. To make matters worse neither the depth nor the gyro setting spindles could not be withdrawn. All of this occurring only 12 days out of port where the Seawolf had supposedly been fixed. At least the trim lines worked, for now.

On the night of May 24th Seawolf was given orders to proceed north of Amboina, Seram because another U.S. ship was coming south by way of Djailolo. Warder felt he could not comply with the order, being so far out of position after pursuing that last freighter. He decided to disobey the letter of the order figuring the intent was to have Seawolf west of Buru to avoid friendly shipping coming south. Therefore, he set a course of 345° T and proceeded west. These are the decisions that can save lives, or cause disaster, and why the mantle of command is at times a heavy burden. In this case it was the correct thing to do.

While steaming north out of the Banda Sea into the Molucca Sea Warder received information about a large enemy convoy headed to Davao. If he put all four engines on propulsion and did a little daylight surface running through the Celebes Sea, Warder thought he might make an early interception point. The target rich environment might change Seawolf's luck,

Bad Omens

and a few enemy ships might go to the bottom of the ocean. After analyzing fuel consumption problems for the adventure, Warder decided that it could not be done. It is important to remember that Submarines operated behind enemy lines and could expect no help if they ran into difficulty, whether that be from mechanical failure or something simple like running out of diesel. Thinking back a week, it appeared that the Japanese freighter Seawolf chased in vain for two days, while taking her far out of position, was having a huge impact on this war patrol.

Given that Seawolf remained in the area that night, Warder decided to strike down torpedoes. In peacetime this was a risky operation and rarely performed on the open seas. In war time the danger multiplied exponentially. The Salmon class boats had a storage area in a watertight compartment outside the pressure hull for 4 torpedoes. If necessary, those torpedoes could be loaded into the ship proper. It required running on the surface with an open deck hatch at the loading ramp. If trouble came from the enemy during the operation, Seawolf could not dive to escape. With the deck hatch open a sudden rainsquall or heavy seas could spell disaster. The men worked rapidly but handling the huge torpedoes on the open deck required caution. The full moon greatly aided the crew, and all breathed a sigh of relief upon safe completion of the task 2 ½ hours later.

At dawn Seawolf dove and proceeded north to Kema where they spent a day, as per previous orders, and inspected the town. Due to heavy rainfall Warder gathered little information other than noting a road near the village. They proceeded toward their assigned station of Stroomen Kaap, crossing into the Celebes Sea via the Bunka Passage. During that part of the cruise crewmembers spotted many fishing boats. Which one had a radio? Which of the crew on those fishing boats bore allegiance to Japan? Should the crew of the Seawolf take action? Even in a war, or maybe especially in a war, you can't shoot everybody. Sometimes you have to proceed in a friendly fashion and hope for the best. Warder and crew took no action against any of those small fishing boats and suffered no perceived consequence for their restraint.

On the morning of May 31the crew of the Seawolf finally spotted another ship at a range of 14,000 yards. Casler plotted courses as the approach team in the conning tower worked out strategies to close on the enemy. If all went well a favorable firing position could be obtained within about 6 hours running at 6 knots submerged. After about five hours Seawolf closed to about 4,200 yards, but Warder decided to abort the attack. He rationalized that in the calm smooth waters the enemy could easily see incoming torpedoes and take evasive measures, especially considering the three-minute torpedo running time from the Seawolf to the enemy. Warder also hoped he might still run into that convoy headed for Davao but had to consider Adm. Lockwood's orders to conserve torpedoes as well. It is easy to understand Warder's clear reasoning and reluctance to attack in such an unpromising situation.

Unfortunately, Fred Warder was going to pay at least a small price for that decision. In the endorsement of the war patrol report Lockwood criticized Warder saying that, "A mere shortage of torpedoes should never be a deciding factor in withholding fire at a valuable target such as this ship was."[206] That written comment must have really steamed Warder since it was Lockwood himself that had cautioned submarine commanders against using too many torpedoes. In fact, at this stage of the war the Navy wanted its submarine skippers to attack capitol ships first and deemed merchant marine to be the lowest target priority. So in essence Lockwood criticized Warder for doing exactly what Lockwood had ordered Warder to do in the first place.

Seawolf hung around Stroomen Kaap for a few more days but the enemy convoy never materialized. Warder continued his itinerary of sights to explore including Tolong, Dalipe Point, and Looc Bay, sighting nothing of much interest. But then again it would have been hard to see anything because the attack periscope began fogging up making observations difficult and sometimes impossible. A couple of times Warder switched to the high-power lens hoping for a clearer view but it proved to be worse and therefore useless. A few days later the periscope fixed itself and Warder could almost see clearly. He didn't quite know what was worse, a piece of equipment breaking itself for no reason, or fixing itself for no reason. It was a good thing that Warder did not have all those superstitious leanings that certain sailors do have. Some of the problems during this patrol caused a few of the crew talking of a "jinx."

In the early morning of June 9th in the Tablas Strait, Lt. Deragon sighted what he thought was a minesweeper at just 1,500 yards. Deragon ordered a crash dive but was unable to locate the ship in the periscope; no kidding, it was fogged up. Sound picked up the ship but lost it. Warder now awakened and in the conning tower ordered the Seawolf to the surface. The men raced up the ladders and quickly looked for enemy ships. As it turned out the Japanese ship that nobody could see through the periscope was only 3,000 yards away and it was quite a bit bigger than Deragon initially thought. But Warder kept his cool and kept Seawolf on the surface hoping for a shot at dawn in about five hours.

Warder judged the enemy ship too close to Mindoro to overtake him on the shore side, so he planned to go around Maestro de Campo and intercept him at Bongabong. Due to great work in fixing the course of the enemy ship, three hours after rounding Maestro de Campo, there it was! Warder spent the next ten minutes getting the Seawolf into a perfect firing position. Then a violent electrical storm broke out foiling his completed setup. The huge bolts of lightning bisecting the skies made observations by Seawolf's crew nearly impossible. But the opposite was true of the enemy as the light perfectly silhouetted the Seawolf. To make matters worse for the submarine, the Japanese ship aimed a high intensity searchlight right at her. Warder ordered a crash dive, cursing the electrical storm that spoiled his perfect plan. He remained stubborn and held his course hoping for a break. Warder didn't get one though as the sound operator could not accurately track the enemy ship. Fifteen minutes later Warder looked through the periscope just in time to see a small black speck on the horizon – the escaping Japanese freighter.

The failures – bad luck to superstitious sailors – started to wear a little thin on some of the crew and very faint grumbling could be heard. Success in battle helps create the confidence that the mission is right and has an eventual end. This confidence in turn sustains morale. Soldiers and sailors cannot long endure failure before they start to lose confidence in their officers and their mission. The natural outcome of failure is low morale. Notwithstanding the failures on board Seawolf during this 5th war patrol, morale remained very high. This is a direct testament to Fred Warder's great ability to command and the enormous respect he received from his men. His prewar, and for that matter during the war, style of command, which emphasized strict discipline mixed with unusual amounts of compassion, helped to keep his crew together and focused during this, so far, disappointing war patrol.

Other commanders did not fair so well when the going got tough on their ships. One case in point was the Wahoo. Before the great skipper Dudley Morton took command of that ship on its third war patrol, Wahoo had a somewhat unpopular skipper, Lt. Commander Marvin Kennedy. It is true that Kennedy's soon to be famous Executive Officer, Richard "Dick" O'Kane, probably did not make commanding that ship very easy since the two men had such divergent ideas on how to engage in combat. Be that as it may the men on board Wahoo sensed bad decisions emanating from the bridge and knew of bungled attacks and un-aggressive pursuit of the enemy.[207] Additionally Kennedy did a few strange things such as changing all of the lights on the ship from white to red.[208] (Most submarines had red lights in the conning tower only, this to help the lookout's eyes adjust to night vision before going to the bridge). This sort of quirkiness does not hamper a successful commander, but as soon as the crew develops a feeling that things are not going well, those very quirks get them talking and wondering about the man in charge.

The Wahoo crew grew unhappy and discouraged during their first two war patrols. Lockwood reassigned Kennedy out of submarines. Kennedy later commanded the destroyer U.S.S. Guest with distinction. The irony is that Kennedy was not an unsuccessful submarine commander. In his two war patrols Lockwood gave him credit for sinking 3 enemy ships, including a destroyer, a fairly high score at the time.* Kennedy received a silver star for his second war patrol as commander of Wahoo. Later in the war he was decorated with a second silver star as the commander of Guest. In other words, Kennedy was a very successful naval officer, a hero even, both in submarines and surface ships but had some trouble none-the-less.

Some of the grumbling amongst the crew of Seawolf surrounded a Perspective Commanding Officer (PCO) on board named Lieutenant Commander Edward Stephan. PCO's came aboard a submarine for a patrol to observe only. For some odd reason, sailor superstition more than likely, a few of the crew decided he had jinxed the ship on this fifth war patrol. Other members of the crew took no note of the mild-mannered Lt. Commander and in fact Warder praised him specifically as successfully dreaming up a "fix-it" for one of the myriad mechanical problems on the ship. Such is the luck or lack of it, for officers in the Navy who are sometimes at the mercy of voodoo or other sailor superstitions picked up in the exotic places they visit.

Later, Stephan commanded the submarine Greyback on two war patrols. Lockwood found his results disappointing and relieved him. These dismissals were not exceptions. Fully 1/3 of the CO's that started the war had been relieved within the first year. Poor training and misguided strategy, the sphere of the high commanders doing the relieving, are partly to blame, which is somewhat ironic.

Intangibles however play a huge role in whether a submarine CO would be successful. In truth Warder was not much more successful than other CO's during his first five war patrols. But Lockwood liked Warder. Why? Who knows, maybe because Warder never took guff from him? Lockwood understood Warder's incredible courage and his ability to keep a cool head during even the longest periods of great stress. Warder's crew liked him too. That is because he took care of them in the face of the "brass hats." He recognized his crew as humans that were fallible but who could do great things if shown what to do and then were inspired to do them.

---

* After war credit was reduced to one ship sunk. This reduction was not unusual and has absolutely no negative connotation for any of the submarine commanders that received reductions in both number of ships and tonnage of ships.

Bad Omens

That is not to say he was soft on the crew because he certainly was not. As one crewmember said, "If you messed up on your job you needed to find a crack in the deck to crawl into."

Importantly Warder was able to lead by example. He had engineering and maritime law degrees. He put great time and effort into knowing about virtually every piece of machinery in his boat and he could also operate and trouble-shoot those machines on his own. He could even signal by semaphore, a detail not lost on the crew. In short Warder somehow magically understood command, which is probably the explanation for his success.

The next several days produced many ship sightings and several calls to battle stations but no attacks. The enemy thwarted most of those attacks simply by maneuvering, albeit by accident, away from the Seawolf. One approach looked especially promising but came apart when Seawolf hit a rip tide and then a cold-water pocket. The crew lost depth control over the ship as it bucked like a mad bronco. Hanging on, they kept Seawolf under the water, safe from the enemy, but they had to abandon the attack.

At 6:00 pm on June 10th the battle stations alarm sounded, and the crew ran hopefully to battle stations. Over the next 30 minutes they closed in on the enemy target. As they got closer the target turned out to be a rock. That might have been funny a couple of patrols ago but during the current situation the officers and crew were not amused at tracking a rock for 30 minutes.

Two hours later Seawolf surfaced and commenced charging batteries. Over the previous month they had investigated just about every cove and bay from Fremantle up through the Celebes on their way to their ultimate destination, Manila Bay. Seawolf had not been in these waters since the fall of Bataan and Corregidor. As the crew made their way through the Verde Island Pass one might think they had a special excitement, returning to the Philippine Islands, their own home just 5 months before, now in enemy hands. But the truth is the captain and crew simply considered this to be another war patrol. Survival topped their "to-do" list followed closely by sinking enemy ships. The crew did not spend too much time waxing nostalgia.[209]

As the Seawolf closed in on Subic and Manila bays, Warder's periscope observations, fog and all, provided no initial results. On June 11th Seawolf took up position at Fortune and Lubang to intercept shipping headed towards the conquered Hong Kong or the home islands of Japan. Although eager to change his luck in the heart of the areas conquered by the Empire of Japan, bad weather intervened making Warder's periscope observations uncertain and blurred. Rain and wind reduced visibility down to about 500 yards. As they searched, sound reported screws to the starboard of the ship. Warder saw nothing. During this patrol Warder was completely flummoxed by sound giving him inaccurate information. A little later a lookout spotted a ship to the port side. Then a searchlight from land illuminated the Seawolf. Warder sounded the alarm and Seawolf dove. Two hours later they were back on the surface searching in vain for ships to sink. Rain continued and heavy seas hampered the men on the bridge, making life miserable for the crew as the submarine pitched and rolled through the ocean.

Several hours after submerging Warder finally found a ship to attack. Unluckily the ship turned out to be a Japanese destroyer that was in truth hunting Seawolf. The enemy destroyer dropped a few well-placed depth charges causing Seawolf to spring a leak in the compensating water line in the forward engine room. Then an airplane flew overhead. In the extremely high seas, the Japanese airplane caught the Seawolf in a trough that clearly exposed the periscope. For some reason Warder and the crew simply could not establish a good consistent rhythm of problem solving during this war patrol. Down they went again to avoid being depth charged by the airplane. It was just as well anyway. The rough seas were nearly intolerable on the surface, and even at a depth of 150 feet the crew felt the violent ocean overhead.

In the morning Warder decided to head into Manila Bay. They went around Corregidor Island, now inhabited by the Japanese. Warder plainly saw the dock where Seawolf rested only a few months before. Japanese sentries now walked on that same dock, not knowing they were being watched.

After their "inspection" tour Seawolf headed about 10 miles west of Corregidor to surface and charge batteries. A couple of times they saw some smoke only to find it came from small "station vessels." A little later Warder found a large merchant ship, "Hull down," and waited for an ambush shot, but the ship did not come his way. He reported that the "Entering Maru altered course to starboard to head for Station Vessel, which is about midway between old points *"A" and "B"."* That must have hurt; reporting an enemy ship's location by the names of old navigation points, now changed by the enemy, much like the people in East Berlin waking up and finding some of their streets named "Lenin Street" or "Trotsky Street" after the communist takeover.

In the early hours of June 13th Seawolf headed up towards Subic Bay where Warder spotted some ships. They headed toward them, the alarm sounded, *"Bong, bong, bong..."* and the men headed for general quarters. Within 30 minutes Warder found a line of 4 merchant ships being protected by one destroyer. This looked like a very promising development. The leading merchant ship zigged radically while the other ships held fairly steady courses. A station vessel joined them and pointed a searchlight at the escorting destroyer. That was nice of him. It appeared that both sides had a penchant for illuminating their own ships in their own waters making it easier for their enemies to find them. The irony was not lost on Warder as he ordered a course of 276°, "To watch the development of the problem."[210]

A few minutes later the enemy destroyer came to within 1,500 yards and his estimated track would bring him to 390 yards, far too close for an attack. Warder turned the Seawolf away to lengthen the range, bringing the stern tubes to bear. This attack developed rapidly but the continuing rough seas hampered periscope observations (not to mention the continuing problem of the fogging periscope). If Warder could get good information from the sound operator, he might still press home a successful attack. But Eckberg was having trouble locating the enemy ships. After about eight minutes an exasperated Warder noted, "Sound finally picked up target bearing 170° relative." The constantly changing situation and poor conditions caused Warder to switch his attack to the second target, which now offered a more favorable track.

"This was a mistake," Warder later conceded.

Eckberg failed to locate the next ship on the sound apparatus,* yet he managed to report a contact about five minutes later. Warder thought the contact to be, "doubtful," although the approach party continued to work through their problems. The ships did not come into any favorable range of attack for about an hour. Then one of the merchant ships zigged into range at about 1,500 yards. Warder decided against attacking the rather small ship. He also thought Seawolf's overall position so favorable that he did not want to give it away without at least waiting for a much bigger ship, so they waited.

About 3 hours later Warder's patients paid off. A Japanese destroyer and merchant ship appeared at 5:10 pm. Seawolf's attack against them developed quickly as the approach team worked away in the conning tower. At 5:21 pm, just 11 minutes after first sighting the enemy, Seawolf opened fire with a spread of four torpedoes against the two ships. All four torpedoes had a depth setting of just 6 feet. By now Warder had an inkling about poor torpedo performance including deep running torpedoes. His last attack missed with a torpedo depth setting of 8 feet. It is an indication of his frustration that he ordered the depth lessened by another 2 feet. Sound

---

* In his defense the sound sensing equipment did not work very good, especially by modern standards.

reported the torpedoes running, "Straight, hot, and normal." Be that as it may Warder thought he had missed both ships. However, Lt. Syverson in the after-torpedo room, (and the torpedo crew for that matter), thought he heard one large explosion. At the periscope Warder reported,

> I also saw one torpedo explode on far side of the destroyer throwing a column of water up between his stacks to a height well above them. There is no indication on the destroyer that they were aware of our presence until this explosion took place, when activity became tremendous.[211]

Later that afternoon Warder saw, an unusually large cloud of smoke, probably a burning ship. It seems peculiar that he did not claim sinking the enemy ship. Other COs had done so on much flimsier evidence. Maybe his, by now, total lack of confidence in the torpedoes caused him to think it was hopeless so he should not claim a sinking. To Warder's thinking the torpedo probably passed under the destroyer and blew up a safe distance away on the far side.

Here is another insight to Warder's success as a commander. He possessed unbending character and integrity. If the CO fudges a bit certain members of the crew will begin to fudge a bit. If a CO allows himself to be influenced against his own intuition and character, then deep down the crew will begin distrusting and second-guessing him. In this case all Warder had to do is give himself the benefit of the doubt. His officers and crew would have supported a claim of a ship sunk or at least damaged, after all at least one officer, Lt. Syverson, insisted that he, and many of the crew, heard a loud explosion. However, if Warder thought he missed, that was the end of it.

A few minutes after Seawolf's failed attack the Japanese commenced a counterattack. During the next hour and a half twelve depth charges exploded nearby. When the counterattack ended the crew felt relieved at the mild Japanese response compared to the battering they took just two months before at Christmas Island. Seawolf surfaced that evening about 21 miles from Corregidor and spent an incident free night recharging the batteries. The next morning Seawolf submerged and continued her patrol in front of Manila. They quickly found two ships despite increasingly bad weather that included the usual electrical storm. Warder identified one of the ships as a sub-chaser but decided it was only a small threat and continued patrolling just outside of Manila Bay.

The increasingly rough sea forced Seawolf to 120 feet. At 3:20 pm the sound operator picked up some screws. Warder ordered a depth of 63 feet to make a periscope observation. He saw a destroyer cruising around at about 20 knots. In a sad sort of way Warder wrote that, "He evidently came out North Channel but turned west as soon as he passed point "S" (as our destroyers used to do)." Warder also saw two additional ships – one an oil barge and the other a small merchant ship about 250 feet in length. He considered both ships too small to attack. He waited and waited and...

Then it appeared – a cruiser! Warder could not believe it! In their previous war patrol the Seawolf sank a couple of cruisers.* If they could turn that trick again the officers and crew would become legends. Warder noticed an empty airplane catapult on the cruiser, which might present a problem in the near future.

After his initial sighting Warder did not waste a second and he, "immediately went to collision course at high speed."[212] The range was 11,000 yards as Seawolf took twelve minutes to chug up to 13 knots. It took ten more minutes before Seawolf was going 17 knots. By that time the Japanese Cruiser had put a total of 13,000 yards between her and the Seawolf. One minute later Warder sighted a seaplane at an elevation of 1,500 feet. That plane probably belonged to the cruiser, but Warder continued the chase theorizing that the rainy weather ruffled the water surface enough to hide his submarine. But within the next 14 minutes the cruiser extended the range to 16,000 yards and Warder abandoned the approach.

Later that afternoon a destroyer and a sub-chaser came out and started to hunt for the Seawolf in earnest. "They pinged the hell out of the area," is how Warder described the enemy's search. In the morning of June 15th they sighted a destroyer and Warder called the crew to battle stations. Only 600 yards separated Seawolf from the enemy, much too close for a shot. Then the destroyer turned and came within 300 yards of the Seawolf. The men braced themselves, but the ship continued on harmlessly overhead.

With the destroyer safely away a merchant ship came into view. Warder attempted an echo range with no luck.* He therefore used the old-fashioned method and estimated the range 1,700 yards. The attack team carried out their duties perfectly and sent a spread of three torpedoes on their way.

Unfortunately, the diving officer improperly trimmed the submarine to compensate for the weight loss of the three torpedoes. Seawolf tilted upwards and headed for the surface, and when the mast broached, the enemy saw the

---

* Post war assessment reduced that to one cruiser heavily damaged.
* This was the second time he ordered an echo range both being unsuccessful. The device worked sometimes and at other times didn't. It was best when used under 2,000 yards.

submarine in broad daylight. In the emergency Warder quickly ordered, "Flood negative."   Seawolf tilted the other way. The diving officer lost control. Unbeknownst to him the trim pump broke the day before. The ship plunged down as the men fell and rolled around the inside of the ship. After a brief struggle they regained depth control and brought the ship back to 120 feet.

While careening out of control the crew of the Seawolf heard a huge explosion. The screws of the enemy ship stopped. Suddenly the entire Seawolf crew heard sounds of a ship breaking up and sinking; they listened intently to the dramatic crackling of small explosions and crunching sounds, as the enemy ship broke apart. Seawolf had her first sinking of this 5th War Patrol. Writing in his report Warder triumphantly, if modestly, proclaimed, "At 0701 and 20 seconds, Commenced successful attack."

Things had turned around for the captain and crew and it felt good to them. Now all they had to do is survive the counterattack that began 4 minutes later. The initial depth charges exploded far in the distance. Then a string of 6 depth bombs from a plane crashed into the sea near Seawolf. The Japanese seemed to be especially annoyed about the ship they just lost. They redoubled their efforts to get the Seawolf. Another plane came in. Enemy ships pinged all around as the Japanese put in a major effort. About eight more badly placed depth charges gave the Seawolf crew more confidence in their survival. A little latter they comfortably slipped away and waited for nightfall to surface and recharge their batteries.

During the war Adm. Lockwood did not give credit to the Seawolf for sinking that Japanese ship. Unusually, postwar analysis did credit Warder with a sinking. It is one of the few times that a CO was actually given an *increase* in his ships and tonnage sunk after the war. Most postwar analysis reduced the number of ships sunk as well as the tonnage.

As the sun rose on the 16th Seawolf resumed her patrol outside of Manila Bay with little luck. Rough seas and the now highly motivated Japanese required Seawolf to patrol at 120 feet, only coming to observation depth of 63 feet every 15 minutes for a look around. Other than that, little happened that day except for about 20 depth charges exploding a little too close for the crew's comfort.

As per orders the Seawolf left the Manila area that day and entered the Sulu Sea around the island of Panay. At dawn Seawolf dove. For the next 10 hours nothing much happened. The weather was so bad that even at nightfall Seawolf did not surface. Then at 6:05 pm Warder spotted some smoke on the horizon. They headed toward it hoping to find a target to sink. As it turned out they found two ships moving rather slowly. With some coaching from

Bad Omens

Warder the man in the sound shack, Paul Maley, accurately fixed a bearing on the lead ship. A little later Warder came to 63 feet for an observation but when he sighted the ship the bearings from sound seemed all out of whack. The level of frustration was growing rapidly.

"Could I now be looking at the trailing ship?" he asked rhetorically. Warder had not seen the second ship for some time so he reasoned that is what happened. Visibility dropped. The expected full moon had not yet materialized. It started raining. What to do? Warder decided to take two shots at the ships using only the sound instruments for aiming. That was a bit desperate. In his writings Warder did not demonstrate too much faith in ability of the sound sensing equipment to get a really accurate fix on the target. He also decided to take the shots from a depth of 120 ft, the only time he did from such a depth. Was he getting tired? Was the crew drained of energy? They had been out to sea for over forty days. During that time most of the crew never saw the sun and never breathed fresh air.

Even considering the bad weather and the decision to fire from such a depth, the attack seemed somewhat lackadaisical. The outcome can be guessed, "No hits," reads the laconic entry in the report. They pursued the ships for a short time then stopped. Warder cited bad weather, "questionable value of ships," and, "paucity of torpedoes," as reasons for breaking off the pursuit. One almost wonders why they took two shots at the ships in the first place.

Two hours after the attack Warder was going over his notes and found some serious discrepancies. He had called the all-important angle on the bow at 345°. But the TDC operator, probably Deragon (although not mentioned by name in the report), did not lock that angle into the TDC at the time of firing. Rather the torpedoes went out at the default angle of zero gyro, a perpendicular shot to the target. What a mess. Because of the bad weather Warder could not see the target and so decided on aiming by sound. Since Warder did not do the aiming through the periscope, Deragon did the actual firing from the TDC, where the sound bearings were being entered. Deragon pressed the plunger but forgot to lock in the gyro setters. If the firing had been done from the conning tower, then either the Assistant Approach Officer or the Firing Key Operator would have asked for a check on the gyro setter. Warder, for whatever reason, always went easy on his X/O Deragon, and this case proved no exception. Warder wrote of the incident, "[TDC] operator was devoting all his attention to watching sound bearing input and white light and matching the generated and observed bearing dials…I didn't give the officer operating the computer [Deragon] much of a chance to get "squared away."" That was very generous of Warder to say the least.

Between June 19th and July 2nd Seawolf made her way back to Fremantle without finding any enemy ships and without any incident. The only thing that Seawolf stalked during that period were the mountain tops in the Kangean group. They tracked those mountains for a good 30 minutes before Warder realized the mistake. After 51 days at sea – half of that underwater – the crew seemed to be tired. A foggy periscope, broken trim pump (that was usual), a drain pump that didn't pump or drain, sparking exhaust (Warder couldn't count the times he had asked for mufflers), and a missing negative tank flood valve could not have helped moral. In spite of all these problems and the fatigue the crew remained upbeat; after all they had survived another war patrol. That was a pretty big reward in itself.

* * *

Upon docking in Fremantle, the men cleaned themselves up and readied themselves for a little R&R. They enjoyed another warm Australian reception. The Japanese had attacked the mainland of that island continent during Seawolf's absence, and the Australian civilians understood better than many what was at stake. When the crew got into town the few hotels and nightclubs offered great hospitality. The unattached women in Fremantle and Perth continued to be friendly and easy-going according to one crewmember, while the older married folks extended warm heartfelt greetings. With a war on nobody could really be sure about tomorrow. All the people on Bali for instance, now lived under the severe authority of the Japanese.

While the crew reveled in fresh food, sunlight, exercise, and some Australian companionship, Warder was busy taking it on the chin. Adm. Lockwood wrote a severe endorsement to the 5th War Patrol Report. Lockwood criticized Warder for patrolling too close to Corregidor. That must have sent Warder through the roof. Imagine being criticized for being too aggressive while returning to port with no casualties! Lockwood noted that Seawolf underwent several depth charge attacks that hindered her ability to attack the enemy. He certainly had a firm grasp of the obvious there. He then went on to all but blame Warder for the Japanese trying to keep him out of Manila!

Lockwood continued, "This patrol might have been more successful had the patrol been maintained at a slightly greater distance from the entrance [to Manila Bay]."

If Warder had done that Lockwood would have hammered him for not being aggressive enough. Luck played such a huge role in submarine warfare during WW II that these sorts of criticisms are laughable. Never mind the torpedoes that did not work, which begs the question, "Just how many ships would Warder have sunk (or any submarine, torpedo plane, PT boat, or destroyer using torpedoes) if the ordinance had been good in the first place?"

Lockwood gave Warder one final jab for not attacking that small merchant ship on June 18th noting, "[A] mere shortage of torpedoes should never be a deciding factor in withholding fire at a valuable target such as this ship was." Was that a joke? Lockwood himself had cautioned against using too many torpedoes. The PCO, Lt. Commander Stephen who was on this war patrol as an observer, would later be sacked from his command of the submarine Greyback, for expending too many torpedoes! Furthermore, to consider a tramp steamer that seemed to have a top speed of about 10 knots a "valuable target," is not really serious. This is especially true when one considers that Seawolf, as of June 18, was on its way *out* on patrol, to Manila no less. Any thinking CO, which Warder certainly was, could comfortably speculate on a large amount of good targets emerging in the future. Lockwood's endorsement was the worst kind of "Monday morning quarterbacking." To add to the injury, as previously stated, he did not credit Seawolf with a sinking. Warder and his crew had to wait until after the war to get their credit for the sinking of the enemy ship in front of Manila.

One last note of irony on the situation: Warder received a letter of commendation and a Bronze Star for the fifth war patrol. In part the citation reads

> During this tedious patrol the Commanding Officer displayed skill, courage, and determination. He patrolled within a radius of twenty miles from Corregidor for four days and was subjected to frequent and severe depth charge attacks...

That seems to be the last word in a world turned upside down. At least the board of awards tried to make things right for Warder and his crew, recognizing their incredible determination under the most severe conditions.

*   *   *

The rest in Fremantle lasted 22 days. But the Seawolf crew did not rest that whole time. They rotated in and out of town while working on the Seawolf. In reality the crew had not been off duty since the beginning of the war, and it started to show in the general declining health of the crew. Be that as it may they boarded Seawolf on July 25th and left for their 6th war patrol.

While still in friendly waters they went through several drills including battle surface. At the outbreak of the war U.S. Fleet submarines carried a three-inch deck gun and had two posts for mounting .50 caliber machine guns. When the captain ordered, "battle surface," the gun crew would assemble in the conning tower. Just as the hatch broke the surface of the water, the quartermaster undid the hatch. The air pressure inside the sub then blew out sending a spray of water upwards and slightly lifting the quartermaster as he scrambled out of the hatch. The rest of the team then scrambled up the ladder in a shower of water.

Once out of the ship one crewman unlimbered the gun from its braces. While he did that the loader put a round in the breech and the trainer and aimer took their positions. Next, they took aim and fired. While this was going on crewmembers formed a line, a sort of bucket brigade, passing the 3-inch shells up and out of the ship to the gun. The .50 caliber machine guns would already be set up ready to fire, protecting the men at the 3-inch gun.

During this drill the gun misfired, a bad omen – but only if you're a superstitious sailor. In fact, somebody had packed too much grease into the firing mechanism jamming the firing pin, a perfectly logical explanation. Unfortunately, logic is trumped by superstition. "It could have been serious," was Warder's laconic assessment of the situation. The next day they repeated the drill and successfully fired 3 rounds.

Despite this training Warder never ordered a battle surface engagement with the 3-inch gun. They did come close one time when they happened on to a large Sampan in Lombok strait during their 6th war patrol. Warder was on the bridge at the time. He sighted a large sampan and figured it might have a radio or possibly carry machine gun mounts. Warder ordered the diesel engines cut and the electric motors engaged. Gunners mate Bennet opened the gun locker and distributed small arms amongst the crew. They mounted the .50 caliber machine guns and silently crept up to the sampan. Seawolf got to within about thirty yards of the vessel as Warder carefully looked the ship over. Suddenly there was a movement on the sampan. The men felt the triggers of their weapons waiting for the order to fire. Everything rested on Warder with only a few seconds to decide if the sampan was a friend or enemy. Suddenly he noticed a child on the ship and then a woman. He ordered his men to stand down their weapons. It appeared that a fisherman and his family were out plying their trade. But was it a trick? Warder did not see any antennas or gun mounts, so he ordered Seawolf away without any incident. It is those cool-headed decisions that save lives but rarely show up in the newspaper reports or are cited as points of heroism for commanders and crew.*

After drilling and getting their "sea-legs" under them, the crew headed for their old hunting grounds of Lombok Strait arriving on July 30th. The terrible rip currents and tides in the strait held the ship up. "We spent the day on practically a stationary patrol in the southern approaches," a frustrated Warder commented.[213] Since the ship was burning 350 gallons of fuel per day it was somewhat important to make some progress and have something to show for all that burnt fuel. Warder thought in hindsight that he should have gone through Badung Strait. Later that night lookouts spotted a ship. After being called to the bridge Warder decided it was a fellow U.S. submarine, possibly the Sailfish. These chance encounters could prove dangerous, so Seawolf quickly turned away.

Unlike the last time Seawolf patrolled these waters, the captain and crew sighted many small native fishing vessels. Then on August 2nd the officer of the deck, Lt. Whitman, sighted a large Japanese tanker, estimated at 7,000 tons. One of the statistics evaluating submarine crew performance was total tonnage sunk. A large tanker could statistically equal several merchant ships; therefore, this tanker presented an exceptional opportunity.

Whitman excitedly called for Warder who immediately bounded up the ladder into the conning tower. He confirmed the sighting and called for general quarters. The quartermaster slammed the alarm, "*bong, bong, bong...*" as the men raced to their battle stations. The approach party squeezed into the conning tower; Gervais at the helm, Brengelman at the torpedo-firing panel, Warder at the periscope with Mercer to his right, Casler at the plotting table, and Thompson wedged in between Mercer and Casler. Below them in the control room Deragon worked the TDC.

Warder looked through the periscope, which unfortunately began to fog up again. However, he did see well enough to put the wire on the ship, and in his elevated combat voice gave the order, "Mark."

Gervais called out the heading, "084°".

Mercer immediately checked the rings on the outside of the periscope, "096°."

---

* The next CO of Seawolf, Royce Gross (hugely successful), often ordered battle surface using the .50 caliber machine guns to suppress fire from small enemy sampans in Imperial waters.

It took Casler a few seconds to work the math and call out the true bearing, "180°T."

Then it was Warder's turn. Using the statometer on the periscope he called out the range, "12,000 yards."

At that range he might as well have said 12,000 miles. Casler and Warder bent over the charts and planned and guessed. The temperature in the conning tower climbed to over 90° as the men sweated, dressed only in shorts and sandals. After 37 minutes of steady maneuvering, calculating, and sweating, they actually closed the range to about 5,000 yards, still an almost impossible shot. Despite poor lighting, the foggy periscope lens (Warder conceded that his last reliable observation came fifteen minutes earlier), and the great range, he decided on firing a spread of 4 torpedoes. As usual Warder looked through the scope and coaxed the helmsman while taking aim at the inside of the stern, the outside of the stern, inside of the bow, and the outside of the bow. Each time those points crossed the "wire" Warder ordered, "fire," and Brengelman dutifully hit the plunger, Thompson repeated the order to the torpedo room, and the torpedoes left the ship.

Then catastrophe. The quick loss of weight somehow confused the diving officer, just as it had at Manila Bay on the 5th patrol. The ship heaved upwards. Warder screamed to lower the periscope, which Lt. Holden quickly did. Despite their fast action the periscope and shears broached. He ordered 200 feet to evade a probable counterattack from some sub-chasers that Seadragon reported seeing in the vicinity a day earlier. By now the diving officer got a hold of himself and ordered the planes-man to dive at 7° down bubble. In such an emergency too steep a dive exposes the stern of the ship to the enemy. Worse, if the stern comes out of the water, the propellers spin wildly possibly damaging the engines. Additionally, and maybe more importantly, the submarine descends, not by taking on more ballast (water) as many think, but rather by positioning the planes at an angle that forces the nose of the ship down when water passes over the planes. If the propellers are out of the water, they can no longer push the ship forward so the planes cannot force the ship down. In this case the diving officer calculated correctly, the screws stayed submerged, and the Seawolf descended, hopefully to safety.

As the Seawolf descended past 70 feet, a huge blast rocked the ship. Paint in the conning tower peeled from the walls and showered the men. The diving station barometer cracked and broke. The crew anticipated a severe counterattack. But nothing else came. Warder later reasoned that a "Most satisfactory hit," had taken place and not a depth charge explosion. He sighted no cavitation sounds that accompany a depth charge attack. Warder also thought the target could have been about 2,000 yards closer to Seawolf than originally thought during the attack, (that would account for the explosion being heard about a minute before they had originally calculated). His third reason, "The detonator [of the depth charge] was not heard to fire, as it usually is heard to do, when charge is at all close." It gives one a cold chill to think that the detonator of a depth charge actually signals to the submarine crew that a potential life-ending explosion is about to erupt.[214] Eight minutes after the explosion, Seawolf came back to periscope depth. Warder looked around and found nothing, "But the dark land background of the Celebes."

Seawolf surfaced. The approach party worked furiously, making calculations and guesses on the position of the Japanese tanker. Even though Warder claimed a solid hit on the tanker, he knew it probably didn't sink. Tankers are designed to carry liquids so creating a hole in one with a single torpedo wouldn't affect it much. The trick was to catch a tanker fully loaded with oil, diesel, or even better – gasoline. In that case a huge explosion and spectacular fire usually followed a successful torpedo attack. As they searched for the enemy tanker, Warder sent a dispatch reporting the last known location of the tanker. He knew that the submarine Swordfish, commanded by Albert Burrows, followed Seawolf by a few days and might be able to intercept the huge prize if it escaped.

As luck would have it, and luck does play a huge role in military action, Warder found the tanker at 11:11 pm. He decided against a night surface attack, reasoning he could not get close enough to the enemy undetected (the mufflers were sparking again). The periscope continued to fog up so a night submerged attack remained out of the question. Warder had to improvise. He decided to head westward and go up ahead of the target, keeping the tanker in sight, submerge at dawn, and attack with the periscope. At about 4:00 am on August 3rd Seawolf found herself about 7-8 miles ahead of the tanker and slowed to 9.7 knots. The crew shifted to battery power and dove at 4:50 am.

About nine minutes later Warder picked up the tanker in the periscope but then lost him about 15 minutes later. "Now how can a tanker disappear so fast?" the approach team wondered. Using intuition Warder ordered a course change of 090° to close on the Kapoposang entrance to Makassar. Twenty-eight minutes later the tanker magically reappeared bearing 023° T, at a range of 5,000 yards and an estimated speed of only 7.9 knots. Things began to look rosy again until, to the consternation of the crew, Warder reported at 5:36 am in his elevated voice, "Destroyer bearing 054°."

That certainly was unwelcome news. The destroyer did not get any closer than 6,000 yards to Seawolf, but the enemy captain took its escort duties serious enough for Warder to comment with some exasperation, "In combination with flat glassy surface [of the water] he constituted a serious nuisance." In addition to the destroyer Warder also spotted a small merchant ship of about 1,200 tons at a range of only 1,500 yards. With all the pieces in place on board and the players all at their stations, this most serious of games began again.

Over the next fifteen minutes Warder maneuvered into perfect position for a three-torpedo attack against the tanker. Twelve seconds elapsed between each torpedo fired, with a gyro angle of 101.5° S, 101° S, and 196° S and a calculated range of 2,800, 2,800, and 2,750 respectively. Sound reported all torpedoes running, "Hot, straight, and normal." In the smooth glassy water Warder could easily see the torpedoes going toward the enemy tanker (notwithstanding the foggy periscope).

One of the torpedoes began to smoke badly. That wasn't good. Then another torpedo hooked wildly left and appeared to be making a circular run. Warder almost ordered Seawolf to 200 feet to avoid his own torpedo but at the last second the "fish" straightened out and continued toward the tanker.

"I watched this smoke make a perfect mating with the tanker at about the stacks and one to the right of it intercepted the tanker at the bow," Warder wrote. Continuing he reported, "Sound and the torpedo Officer [Syverson] tracked one torpedo down to a perfect interception with the target's screws." What could be more perfect? That made three hits on the tanker not counting the hit on the previous night. Warder watched through the periscope but not one of the torpedoes exploded. There was absolutely no mistake about two of the torpedoes hitting the ship because he visually witnessed them run into the tanker.

What should they do now? Warder did the only thing you can do in such a situation, try again and hope for the best. Maybe if he fired all of his torpedoes at it one time they might tip the ship over, not likely. Two more torpedoes went into the ship with no effect. The Japanese destroyer, now thoroughly engrossed, turned towards Seawolf at full speed. Warder ordered left full rudder and aimed the stern tubes at the incoming destroyer. He couldn't get a shot in. Would it have mattered? Warder ordered Seawolf to 200 feet and the crew rigged for depth charge attack. The Japanese destroyer threw only about five depth charges as it churned the water above Seawolf. About ten hours later Seawolf surfaced and headed for a new station in the Makassar Straits.

Bad Omens

The next few days proved uneventful, but things got exciting again on August 9th when Lt. Syverson spotted a couple of ships, one being a tanker and the other a small anti-submarine vessel. Hopefully this new tanker would cooperate and sink if Seawolf got a torpedo into it. The Japanese by now must have felt invincible. Seawolf attacked the tanker with a 3-torpedo spread set to a depth of only two feet. Apparently, Warder had finally had it with deep running torpedoes and was going to take a chance on the "fish" porpoising on their way to the target. None of the torpedoes broke the surface, due either to a minor miracle or, being so fouled up that even a two-foot depth setting sent them ridiculously deep. Sound recorded hearing a "flop," presumably a dud torpedo hitting the side of the tanker, but nothing else. Armed with a three-inch gun the tanker fired a few obligatory rounds at the Seawolf, missing wildly. Both parties then left the area none the worse for the encounter.

The next day Seawolf traveled to Tarakan where a small torpedo boat hassled her for about 9 hours. At one point the enemy ship came within about 4,000 yards of Seawolf, pinging madly. Warder took Seawolf to 200 feet noting a "dense layer" at about 120 feet. Temperature differences in the ocean created "layers" in the water, which the unsophisticated Japanese listening devices bounced off, thus concealing any submarine below.

After a few days off Tarakan they left for Sibutu. Favorable currents caused their fuel use to decline to only about 700 gallons per day contrasted with about 3,000 gallons earlier in the voyage. On August 14 the OOD, Lt. Mercer, sighted enemy ships, ordered a change of course to intercept them, and called the captain. Warder took one look and called for battle stations. The mad scramble began and it took less than a minute for the approach party to assemble in the conning tower. The war gods smiled on Seawolf as the enemy crossed her bow and allowed Warder to set up a perfect stern shot. Warder made his last observation, the echo ranger confirmed the range (about 950 yards), Deragon worked the TDC, and a two-torpedo spread left Seawolf.

Warder could not see the torpedoes as they went toward the Japanese freighter due to the "smoke screen" put out by the torpedoes.* They waited for one minute and four seconds. Then a huge explosion sent debris and flying objects everywhere. Warder reported that the decisive hit, "Blew hell out of the shaft alleys, No. 3 hold, steering engine room, after steering station, mainmast rigging, and after gun platform." Warder was not sure if a gun had been mounted on the platform but commented, "If there was one, it went overboard."

---

* No doubt Warder's attempt at some dark humor.

The devastating explosion caused the quartermaster, Henry Thompson, to spontaneously utter, "I think we killed some of my friends."

Everyone in the conning tower, now in silence, raised their eyebrows. Henry glanced down wishing that had not slipped out. After a moment everybody turned back to what they had been doing.

As Warder watched through the periscope, he noted that the enemy crew took about thirty minutes to abandon ship. He then watched them row away in two rowboats. The surface sailor in him came through when he noted that; "They rowed poorly but signaled smartly with semaphore." He also observed two wounded men in the boats as their crew raised a mast, unfurled a sail, mounted davits and oars, and headed for land.

Always thinking, Warder took this opportunity to do a torpedo test of his own. Using the now abandoned and "dead in the water" enemy ship as his test target, he lined up a shot of 1,500 yards. Warder and Casler double-checked the data. Lt. Deragon triple checked the settings on the TDC. The normal depth setting for a MK XIV torpedo was about fifteen feet and Warder had taken shots with a depth setting as shallow as two feet. In this case he put the depth setting at six feet, as the sinking ship sat low in the water.

They fired the torpedo. Warder searched in the periscope but found nothing. Fully 40 seconds after firing, and halfway to the target, he finally found the wake. The torpedo had taken its sweet time getting to proper attack depth. Sound reported the shot ran, "straight, hot, and normal." The torpedo approached the ship, and then Warder clearly saw it pass right underneath, about one foot aft of the aiming point. He absolutely proved that the torpedoes ran too deep. The enemy tanker finally sank amidst the unmistakable and dramatic sounds of it breaking up beneath the ocean.

After everything settled down the approach team left the conning tower. As the men left Warder hesitated and asked that Thompson remain behind obviously interested in his unusual remark. When asked, Thompson related that as a child living for a few years in Torrance, California, he had a few friends that were Japanese. They played together, their favorite game being marbles. Just before their teen years the Japanese boys left for Japan to learn the language and culture of their ancestral home. As the Japanese ship blew up there must have been a flash in the back of his mind, to his childhood, that caused him to (in his words), "pop off."

Warder was satisfied with the explanation. It showed the difficulty of making war in America. No matter where the United States' military reluctantly fights, in this case the Pacific in an unprovoked war against Japan, there is always some group of citizens who must fight against their home country or that of their friends.

Seawolf passed the next several days near Sibutu. Boredom set in amongst the crew. That is the nature of military life in general, long expanses of incredible boredom broken up by short instances of shear terror. After several days Lt. Holden sighted the bright barrel of a periscope. Everyone agreed that it was probably U.S.S. Grampus commanded by Edward Hutchinson. Seven days later Lt. Mercer sighted a ship and the Seawolf gave chase getting into attack range, albeit at "excessive range," within an hour and a half.

Warder and the rest of the approach team worked away under the usual poor conditions. Dressed in their usual shorts and sandals they dripped sweat and breathed in the foul air, putrefied with the constant stench of body odor mixed liberally with diesel fumes. The enemy ship, another 5,000-ton tanker, smoked heavily making it hard to see. At first Warder thought the range too small to fire, then too big. The swirling smoke gave him the impression that the ship had zigged, so he canceled a bow attack in favor of a stern attack. After "fumbling" about, (Warder's description), he opted for a long shot. After firing a lone torpedo and watching the tanker for the next 4½ minutes with no result, he gave up the attack, very disappointed.

If Warder came down on his fellow officers and crewmen when they came up short in performing their duties in battle, he doubled the scorn on himself. He devoted half a page of his report to what he perceived to be his mistakes during this approach and concluded, "Such type of attack shall not be attempted again."[215]

Just past midnight Seawolf surfaced. Warder still wanted to try for that tanker, being an especially big prize. After looking over the last course headings taken on the enemy tanker, Warder guessed it might be headed for Tarakan. With a little luck and skilled sailing, he thought he could arrive there first. After completing the battery charge, he ordered all four diesel engines put into the screws and they sped forward. Unluckily it started to rain heavily, and visibility dropped to less than 500 yards. No matter though, they simply followed their already fixed course.

When they arrived at Tarakan, at just before 4:00 am, the tanker was nowhere to be found. Warder, Deragon, and Casler continued to look over the charts. During the night run Warder thought he might arrive first, so he decided to backtrack. They changed course to 60°. If that tanker did not materialize Warder might be in some trouble with his superiors back in Fremantle. First, for his unsuccessful approach of the previous day resulting in a dubious and failed attack scheme, and second, for not being able to track down a tanker steaming unescorted in his patrol station.

At 6:35 on the morning of August 25th, Lt. Holden the OOD put any concerns of Warder's to rest when he sighted the enemy tanker hiding in a rainsquall. Quickly the approach team worked the math as the helmsman Rudy Gervais guided the ship as per Warder's commands. They crossed the enemy's bow and set up for a stern shot. Warder called the out the numbers on the statometer and Lt. Mercer, reading the scale on the side of the periscope, called out the range, "1,300 yards," a perfect shot.

Hank Thompson repeated the range into his phones and Deragon worked the TDC below the conning tower. When the wire crossed the inside of the stern Warder ordered, "Fire!"

Bringelman hit the plunger just as Thompson repeated the order to the aft torpedo room. Warder decided against a spread opting to completely re-aim for the second shot. Everybody made new calculations and Deragon fed the numbers into the TDC. A few seconds later the green solution light lit up on the TDC, signaling that the gyro angle had been solved. Deragon reported, "Okay."

The wire crossed the same exact spot on the enemy ship 19 seconds later and Warder ordered, "Fire two."

Now the only thing to do was wait and wonder. Did they aim right? Would the torpedo work? Then 59 seconds after firing of the first torpedo a titanic explosion erupted into a burst of light that caused Warder to blink at the brightness flowing into the periscope. The tanker had a full load of fuel, and the ensuing conflagration was a "Marvelous spectacle," in the words of Warder. He continued to watch as the forward third of the ship burst into flames and plunged downwards. The tanker's propellers almost immediately came out of the water as the great ship tipped forward and sank in just over two minutes.

About twenty minutes later Seawolf surfaced to inspect the debris floating in the water. Warder noticed six survivors clinging to boards with one of them in a life preserver. The wreckage included much wood including empty boxes floating around and canvas tarpaulins. Warder ordered crewmembers of the Seawolf to throw the enemy survivors six life jackets. A Japanese life jacket (unused) floated by and a crewmember of the Seawolf retrieved it for a souvenir.

"After they have recovered from the shock, they will be able to make a raft out of the wreckage," Warder commented satisfied with the materials he saw. The canvas tarpaulins could be used as a sail and to catch rainwater if the enemy crew happened to be on the sea for more than a day, which Warder doubted since he saw a small fishing boat not too distant away.

Seawolf spent the next seven days in the area without sighting any ship other than another U.S. Submarine. On September 1st they received orders directing them to a new station. Once they arrived at the new station Warder opted to change his position slightly because of the terrible reefs in the area. He felt it would be unsafe to engage in combat (as if that wasn't unsafe) when all the crew's attention could not be focused on an attack. Considering Seawolf's close call on February 19th during the fourth war patrol when she grounded hard, one can see why Warder erred on the side of caution at this moment. Additionally, the number four engine broke down requiring a new piston pin bearing and connecting rod. Engine room personnel needed a safer place to make the necessary patrols.

Seawolf patrolled for about a week longer near Makassar in very bad weather with poor visibility. That last week proved uneventful and on September 9th they turned for their temporary home in Fremantle. At 3:45 am on September 15th an escort vessel sighted them, they exchanged signals, and came into harbor safely from another war patrol.

After tying up and getting a few hours of sleep Warder went to submit his report. After 51 days at sea, he said that "In fact, it was the easiest patrol conducted to date." He did have to report on a few varying illnesses none more severe than Rheumatic fever. Despite these troubles morale remained high with only one man, a chief electrician's mate, needing to be transferred out on account of a nervous condition (who can blame him?).

As for the torpedo situation Warder was well armed and "loaded for bear" as the saying goes. Of the 17 torpedoes fired during the war patrol 11 had actually exploded. Regrettably of the 11 torpedoes that detonated properly, only 6 exploded under the target. That means that out of the 17 torpedoes fired during the 6th war patrol 11 malfunctioned. Warder wrote in the war patrol report:

> The submarine torpedo situation is considered most unsatisfactory on the following counts: 1) Erratic warhead behavior; a) non-firers, b) prematures 2) poor exploder design; a) Too great a distance required for arming. This tends to make Approach Officers take greater firing range than they should. 3) Smokey exhaust. 4) Uncertain depth performance. 5) Uncertain tactical characteristics makes use of small gyro angles mandatory and thus robs attack of flexibility. It is my opinion that as many targets have

escaped being hit during this war patrol by reason of the foregoing deficiencies as there have been target hits.

At least Warder had his say in print. His direct superior, Adm. James Fife, did give him some compliments including calling the attack at Sibutu (August 14), "Well Executed." He also liked Warder's initiative of sending the third torpedo into that ship writing,

> The experience of firing third torpedo at ship dead in water and abandoned and having it pass under without exploding emphasizes need of modern testing equipment for Mark 6-1 exploders in all submarine tenders. Holland and Otus have been handicapped by absence of such equipment since beginning of war.

Fife seemed to think the exploder's design was still viable and it appears from his comment that manufacturing quality might be the problem. Fife backed up Warder's decision to break off the attack against the tanker on August 2nd saying that the excessive silhouette of the U.S. submarines handicapped night surface approaches.[216]

Fife managed to wipe out all the good feeling though when he wrote, "Two hits out of seventeen torpedoes fired is far below the expected standard of performance." It was as if Warder and the other COs were talking to a wall.

While Warder's pre-emptive attack in his war patrol did make a small impression on Fife, it was not the case with Adm. Lockwood. Lockwood shafted Warder saying point blank, "The failure of Seawolf to inflict greater damage on the enemy can be attributed principally to improper solution of the fire control problem." He also lambasted Warder for not attacking the Japanese destroyer on August 9th. Lockwood was unimpressed with Fife's defense of Warder's decision to break off the August 2nd attack stating, "A submarine coming up astern of a slower target at night even under adverse light conditions presents its smallest silhouette and if sighted will have the advantage if torpedoes are fired at this time because any movement of the enemy increases the length of the target." No matter that the enemy would probably be shooting at the approaching submarine.

Lockwood did credit Warder with the sinking of 2 ships for 8,100 tons and one ship damaged, which by the standard of the day was a very successful patrol. To add to the irony Frederick Warder received the Silver Star for this sixth war patrol that Lockwood and Fife criticized so heavily.

Warder put the last stamp on the ridiculous situation using his typically unambiguous language, "The goddamned torpedoes were no damned good."[217]

Chapter – 12
On All Fronts

While the Seawolf was in Fremantle getting the obligatory patch job, Mary continued to fight the battle of Baltimore. The latest catastrophe to strike occurred in the form of tonsillitis. For some reason, coincidence more than likely, some family disease hit the Warder's at each of the homes that Mary and the four children occupied since 1940. In Pomona the mumps struck everybody down and on Calvert Street it was the chicken pox. Deepdene Road became the staging area for the removal of the children's tonsils, all within the space of a few weeks. Except for some discomfort in the hospital, the sum total of the suffering amounted to a few weeks of the children sitting around the house in pajamas eating ice cream, a standard prescription at the time. Aside from the unfortunate health problems life continued very smoothly for the family. All the children did very well in school, despite the many upheavals and school changes of the last two years.

As everybody settled comfortably into the new house the children thought it lacked a certain spark or charm – or something, they could not quite put their finger on it. Mary figured out what was missing with only a little thought; along with her other talents Mary played piano very well. Now that she felt very secure on Deepdene Road Mary splurged and bought an upright piano. Aside from entertaining herself and friends and family, she could teach her children how to play, plus singing songs around a piano always brightens a house.

When not doing homework or playing the piano the Warder's loved to play board games. Two games dominated their competitions, as they did most of the American households: Parcheesi and Monopoly. Parcheesi, an ancient game from India was brought to America in the 1860's. By the turn of the century, it was by far the most popular board game in America. Fred Jr., Mary Jr., Grace, and Suzy loved to play Parcheesi. Nearly every night they would have a game going. Sometimes there would be an argument during the game and a few cross words. No matter who won or lost or cried, a new game was sure to start within a day.

When not playing outdoors or board games indoors the Warders loved to listen to the radio. During the day or in the evening when their favorite shows came on the family crowded around the huge vacuum tube driven device. The well-known shows of the time included Dick Tracy, Ellery Queen, and The Shadow (the favorite catch lines included "Who knows what evil lurks in the hearts of men," or "The weed of crime bears bitter fruit"). While crime shows were a big staple of 1940's radio silly family comedy was also very popular with the most popular being "Fibber McGee and Molly." Fibber McGee lived at 79 Wistful Vista, which was probably the best-known address in America at the time. The show featured funny skits with lots of funny sound gags that always got laughs. For instance, Molly was always telling Fibber, "Don't open the hall closet," at which time he always opened the hall closet and all the contents spilled out with a loud crash. Edgar Bergen and his trusty wooden sidekick Charley McCarthy were the main attraction in the Chase and Sanborn Program. At the height of that show's popularity about one third of the listening audience in America tuned in to hear the wise cracking dummy that set everybody straight. As in our modern times, the stars of the 1940's teamed up to make films. Fibber, Molly, Edgar, and Charlie got together and made, "Look who is laughing," where they try to entice a manufacturer of military airplanes to build a factory in their town, a typical story line of the early war period.

The Warders had their own favorites and listened to Our Gal Sunday, Jack Benny, Amos & Andy, and of course – Stella Dallas, the soap opera story of an orphan girl's ups and downs in the big bad world. Commercial breaks came during the shows and advertisers vied with each other to create the best jingles hope-full that the listeners would sing along, which they did. Orchestras like "Les Brown and his Band of Renown" had regular music shows, but one of the most popular songs during the era was a silly number by Milton Drake called "Mairzy Doats (Mares eat oats)." When that song came on the radio Grace especially liked to sing along.

Even though there was a war on Mary and other people in the country still managed to live their lives in a way that resembled prewar days, however after about six months the war began to make more serious intrusions into the civilian lifestyle. The war affected the amount of material available for civilian use, the growth of cities, and civil rights. President Roosevelt wanted people to attend to those problems and issues by voluntarily "pitching-in" in small ways back home that would in large ways help the soldiers fighting at the battle fronts. Traffic in some cities became so congested because of the "boom-town" atmosphere that people literally could not get around anymore. The Roosevelt administration decided to solve the problem through a voluntary "ride-sharing program. This would also help cut down on gas consumption and rubber use. The Automobile Club of America tried to promote this government plan across the nation, but after about six months reported that in the Baltimore-Washington DC area most cars arrived in government parking lots with only one passenger, if that. What were the reasons?

> There are only two conclusions to be drawn from this; 1) The national Capital's car owners are uncooperative; 2) This is one of the country's most unfriendly cities. Washington is no longer a friendly town...Only New York can tie wartime Washington in its reluctance to accept newcomers.[218]

Because few people cooperated with ride sharing, gas consumption did not go down and soon a shortage hit the eastern states. Mary did not have a car, but other people in the country did and were hit hard by the gasoline shortage, which encompassed many issues including the sinking of American tanker ships on the east coast.

Germany's entry into the war against the United States brought aggressive German submarine tactics right up to the shores of America. The German submarine onslaught in the early stages of the war nearly paralyzed east coast water borne shipping. The rising star German submariners such as Ulrich Folkers of U125, Reinhard Hardegen in U123, and Peter Cremer of U333 tabulated huge scores against American tanker shipping, sinking them almost at will, off the east coast of the United States in 1942.

Hardegen was the first to strike when he slipped into New York Harbor by way of Long Island on January 14, 1942. It was something of a nostalgic trip for him as he had been to New York some years before as a young sea cadet in the German Navy. At that time, he enjoyed walking around Manhattan and took pleasure in the sights of the great city as he marveled at the huge skyscrapers and the lights at Times Square. On his 1942 trip to New York, he also saw lights through his periscope, the lights of Rockaway beach, neighborhoods of Brooklyn, and of course one of his favorite spots, Coney Island. Finally, after waiting awhile near Sandy Hook, he spotted the tanker Coimbra and fired a couple of torpedoes into her. The fully loaded tanker blew up in a spectacular fireball. Of the thirty-six-man crew only six survived. Hardegen then proceeded to New Jersey where he blew up a small steamer, the San Jose. He then went to Cape Hatteras where he sank five more ships, all in one night.

It was amazing what those audacious German sea dogs were pulling off, but they had a lot of help from the Americans. In order to counter the German submarine threat, the U.S. Coast Guard directed that American coastal shipping travel with dimmed lights at night so as to not attract the attention of the enemy. But nobody thought to dim the lights on the American east coast; those lights remained brightly lit, perfectly silhouetting the huge tankers that the Germans found to be such great targets. A latter cruise by Hardegen into the Chesapeake Bay would net him ten more ships, for the Germans it was almost too good to be true.[219] While Mary read about those German sea raiders so close to her home in Baltimore, she might have had an eerie feeling thinking of her husband busily observing Japanese strongholds in the Pacific.

By sinking so many tankers the Germans caused a serious gasoline shortage on the east coast of the United States and the administration took the unpopular step of rationing gasoline on the east coast. The task of administering the rationing went to Leon Henderson and the Office of Price Administration (OPA). The Americans were first introduced to rationing when sugar supplies ran short. That rationing program was also introduced by the OPA, which produced ugly scenes as plenty of people resented not being able to buy exactly what they wanted to buy, including the amount of sugar they wanted to buy. When it came to issuing ration booklets some not very smart person thought public school teachers ought to distribute them. Teachers traditionally go the extra mile for their students, so why not go the extra mile for the country as a whole? Teachers in general thought that it would be a benign and harmless even patriotic thing to do. They would have to man the ramparts of the distribution tables for only three days, a small price to pay for living in the land of the free. Little did those naive teachers realize the amount of bravery and heroism that would be required to fend off the frustrated and angry Americans who considered it their birthright to buy anything they could afford to buy.

As only a few people predicted, when the distribution of ration books began, all hell broke loose. The teachers did not mind so much the volunteer hours they had to put in to distribute the ration books, rather it was the abuse they received in so doing, that really frustrated them. One teacher complained that the public showed little consideration for the teacher-volunteers, while another thought people in Washington DC should distribute the ration books because, "They don't have to work for a living." One outraged "customer" spilled ink all over a table filled with ration books.[220] One man wanted a ration book for his mule because it would not pull a plow unless it had a bag of sugar in front of him.[221] On it went for three solid days...

Since the teachers had been so easily manhandled and manipulated by the OPA for sugar rationing, the U.S. Government decided to overburden them with the gasoline rationing. Unlike sugar rationing, the OPA created a "class" system for gas rationing. Rationing cards were issued that permitted the holder a certain amount of gasoline per week. An A card allowed the purchase of three gallons of gasoline, a B card about five gallons, but a person holding an X card could purchase an unlimited amount of gasoline. The United States Constitution says in Article I section 9, "No title of nobility shall be granted by the United States." While the X card definitely was not a "knighthood" and those people who received them did not have to be addressed as "your lordship," The X cards definitely set a person apart from the rabble. The X cards were really only supposed to be for people engaged in vital war work, but when the cards were issued it turned out that a lot of people thought that they were engaged in vital war work. The members of the Senate and House of Representatives were the worst offenders. Of the 531 total members of Congress in 1942, over two hundred applied for and received an X card. Why the members of Congress could not ride a streetcar or even walk to work is another of the great mysteries of the war. The reaction of the people against those special privileges should not have been a mystery to the politicians who constantly claim to have their fingers on the pulse of the Americans. The violent and great protest caused the OPC to revamp the program with only A, B, and C cards available, no more unlimited gasoline.[222] Teachers distributed the new cards in the middle of July during their summer break.

After the books were rationed came the enforcement. It took only a few weeks before the arrests began. Mary's copy of the *Evening Capital* reported 14 people busted for "pleasure driving." One guy was driving home from a friend's house and given a thirty-day ration suspension. Another man was busted for driving to the countryside to fish, while another got caught driving to his weekend house. All were punished with ration suspensions or being fined a certain amount of gas ration coupons. The east coast became a hotbed of pleasure driving criminals – soon though real criminals would get in on the act.[223]

Gas rationing started on the east coast, due to shipping problems and the German submarine offensive, but soon spread across the country. Just as in the east, gas rationing had nothing to do with the amount of gasoline itself, as there was plenty of it. The latest round of rationing occurred due to a rubber shortage, which happened because the Japanese had taken over all the places in Southeast Asia that produced natural rubber. The Roosevelt administration believed that rationing gas would conserve rubber tires on cars since less gas per car meant less miles driven; the idea made sense. A few members of the administration thought that more rationing would be just too much for the Americans, and the indefatigable Secretary of the Interior, Harold Ickes, convinced Roosevelt to hold off on west coast rationing for a while. Ickes thought that he could scrounge up enough scrape rubber throughout the country to get everybody through the war without more gas rationing. Ickes calculated that he could get the Americans to collectively bring in one million tons of scrape rubber. Events were held with movie stars and singers asking people to bring in their scrape rubber. Public service announcements heard on the radios throughout America explained the need for everybody to help out and bring in their scrape rubber. Even the President's dog Fala, donated her rubber bone.

Early on things looked pretty good for the rubber drive. Maybe Ickes was correct and painful political decisions could be avoided. Maryland State Senator Louis Phipps optimistically declared that the rubber drive was bringing in more scrap rubber than predicted.[224] Just two days later though, the Roosevelt administration announced that the rubber drive would be extended, "because collection through Saturday had brought in a disappointing total of 219,000 tons."[225] The double speak could not undue the latest failure of the "volunteer system" system of fighting the war. Less than half of the one million tons Ickes predicted he could bring in, materialized. Roosevelt now had to make another unpleasant decision and the new gas rationing books with their neatly perforated coupons went out to the entire nation.

As might be predicted all the rationing produced a new industry: ration book counterfeiting. A couple of members of the infamous "Purple Gang" of Detroit resurfaced after ten years of inactivity and became so expert at ration book counterfeiting that the Secret Service had to develop an infrared detection system to ferret out the genuine coupons from the counterfeits.[226] It was estimated that by 1944 black market gasoline sales using counterfeit coupons reached nearly 2.5 million gallons per day. The OPA turned up three million counterfeit coupons between November and December 1944. When people could not get their hands on counterfeits, stolen coupons were available as bags of the gas rationing coupons routinely disappeared from post offices.[227]

Far from all of the "lets stick together and win" nostalgia that we hear about World War II, people for the most part were only willing to sacrifice what they actually absolutely had to. After a while the OPA realized this and committed about thirty percent of its personnel to enforcing the rationing laws. Patriotism runs deep when it comes to singing songs or watching a buddy's back in a foxhole, but when it came to gasoline, Americans showed the standard level of self-interest.

Living in Baltimore in the spring of 1942, Mary Warder came into close contact with two more war-produced issues: race and labor. Dot, the young and beloved housekeeper that meant so much to Mary and the children, left to pursue other better paying manufacturing jobs produced by the war. The manufacturing labor shortage that produced higher wages for some people as well as pushing women like Dot into jobs traditionally held by men, in turn created higher wages and opportunities for others. Many of those "others" were black Americans who had existed at the lower end of the economic sphere since before the founding of the Republic in 1776.

President Roosevelt addressed the issue of race even before the war began. As war production began with some urgency after the final defeat of France on June 25th, 1940, white unemployment came virtually to an end, but Black unemployment continued. Initially the United States government did not insert anti-discrimination clauses into its war material contracts, and without any pressure from the government, industry was not going to move too swiftly to change its hiring practices. This fact certainly did not go over the head of A. Philip Randolph, the director of the Brotherhood of Sleeping Car Porters, which happened to be an all-black trade union. Randolph desired that Roosevelt hasten social change at home by awarding military contracts only to companies that did not discriminate against blacks. He wanted to drive this point home by having a large demonstration/march in Washington DC. Randolph already had a great slogan for the march, "We loyal Negro American Citizens demand the right to work and fight for our country."[228] One could hardly argue that point.

However, as of early 1941 President Roosevelt did find a way to do just that. Roosevelt liked to gloss over problems with his charm, a tactic that almost always worked. He tried his very best to gloss over race/civil rights problem, but Randolph was not a man easily charmed as he and Roosevelt set a collision course over civil rights. The two men had a meeting a month before the scheduled march in Washington. Roosevelt was determined to stop the march guessing it would be good propaganda for our potential enemies.

"Hello Phil," was the Presidents opening gambit when Randolph came to visit the White House on June 18th. The President was famous for "first naming" people he had never met in an attempt to psychologically establish a familiarity that really did not exist.

Then the President, supposing Randolph was in his crosshairs, pored on the charm with his next line, "Which class were you in at Harvard?"[229]

"I never went to Harvard, Mr. President," was Randolph's respectful reply.

"I was sure you did," Replied Roosevelt, almost as if he meant it and believed it. Thinking that his usual charm routine was working, Roosevelt leaned back in his chair, took a few drags on his cigarette, which was held by the usual cigarette holder, and began to talk about this and that, the nostalgic stuff that he thought interested people. The President used this device to stall a person, use up their appointed time in the oval office, and then shoo the unsuspecting citizen on his way. Roosevelt one time dealt with a delegation he did not want to talk to by showing them tricks performed by his dog Fala. After several tricks – sit, stay, role over, speak, the whole routine – the President looked at his watch and declared that he had gone way over their scheduled time, as if he had done them a favor, and excused them. However, Randolph was different. As Roosevelt waxed nostalgia, Randolph cut him off by stating that time was running out and they needed to talk about U.S. Government policy and Black Americans.

Roosevelt did not want the march in Washington DC, Randolph wanted an executive order saying that discrimination in defense plant work would disqualify that plant from defense contracts. Roosevelt told him to call off the march and they could talk later about an executive order. Randolph told him to issue an executive order stopping discrimination in factories that received government contracts, and then he would call off the march. Roosevelt did not like that. Randolph went on saying that the executive order should not be for defense contractors alone but should apply to the federal government as well. Roosevelt allowed how the U.S. Government was making strides towards equality and inclusion.

"The Government is the worst offender!" rejoined Randolph.

Well, that tore it. FDR nearly lost his temper informing Randolph that he was not used to being told what to do with a gun to his head. Luckily the governor of New York Fiorello La Guardia, who was a friend and supporter of both Randolph's and Roosevelt's, was at the meeting and intervened saying that it was obvious the march was going to happen in the absence of an executive order and the President should accept that. On the other hand, La Guardia asked all parties to come up with a formula so that the march could be avoided. He suggested that a committee should be appointed to draw up an executive order. That is exactly what happened, and the President signed it on June 25th, victory to Randolph. Roosevelt even gave a speech on the subject a few months later saying,

> In some community's employers dislike to hire women, in others they are reluctant to hire Negroes. In still others older men are not wanted. We can no longer afford to indulge such prejudice.[230]

At the time that Roosevelt gave that speech the United States' military had very few blacks and was completely segregated, except for the Navy. In point of fact though, most of the non-whites in the United States Navy at the beginning of the war were stewards. Roosevelt was a most pragmatic man and knew that the overseas armed forces and society at home had to change rapidly to give America its best chance to win the war. To that end black combat units were created that would have the same level of combat responsibility as white combat units. For instance, the 99th fighter squadron, or the Tuskegee airmen as they are now better known, were an all-black air unit that fought mainly in Italy escorting American bombers to and from their targets in Germany. They never lost a bomber they escorted to enemy fighter plane fire; however, they did lose three bombers due to enemy planes ramming American bombers. Otis Cowly, or Big "O" as his fellow fliers knew him, was one of those men who flew the p-51's with the big red tails that became so notorious to the German fighter pilots. The 761st Tank Battalion, also all black, entered combat operations in November of 1944 while fighting in Patton's 3rd Army. Two other all black tank battalions also fought in Europe, the 758th and the 784th. There were also numerous all black infantry units that would fight in Italy and France.

Despite Roosevelt's various speeches on the subject and his executive order, racial inequality in the workplace continued unabated until the real serious labor crisis came in late 1942. At that time a mass migration of black workers came north to work in the factories that were beginning to churn out war related material. Those cities became overcrowded causing tension as people vied for a place to live in the northern boomtowns, and the worst of those cities was Detroit. The influx of black workers and the hiring and promoting of black workers, or the lack of it, led to a serious race riot in Detroit in 1943. The riot was put down when the army was called in to keep the peace. People went back to work, but it was not comfortable for a long time. Regardless of racial tensions the war needed to be won, blacks would have to be hired into factory jobs, and Mary would have to hire black domestic help.

In the spring of 1942, after Dot left the Warders for a better paying factory job, Mary looked in the want ads, made a phone call and a few days later "Black-Bessie" showed up. Mary never had a black housekeeper before, but she was not a bigot. The opportunity simply never came up, after all the America that Mary grew up in was strictly segregated in most areas of the South. In the North there were no segregation laws, but there did exist strong social lines and mores that few people crossed, therefore Mary's minimal contact with black Americans was not unusual. Most of Mary's racial attitudes were formed while living in the Orient. While staying at the various bases and ports-of-call where Fred was stationed in Asia, Mary generally had household help and nannies that were always indigenous to the area in which she lived. Mary had a deep respect for all humans and treated her domestic help with great kindness and consideration. For instance, when in China Mary and the kids walked a great deal as Mary had an aversion to taking rickshaw rides. She did not like the implication that one human should act as a draft animal for another human. Even so the new housekeeper Bessie was to be a new experience for Mary and the whole family.

One question that might have been on Mary's mind as Bessie began to work with the Warder's; how would Fred feel about this? He would be coming home on leave someday and it might be best to test the water or at least give a fair warning about the new domestic situation. Mary informed Fred by letter that she had hired a "darky" to help around the house and do some cooking. A few letters later Mary was praising Bessie's efforts and referred to her as "Black Bessie." A few weeks later Bessie became simply, "Bessie." Mary reported to Fred that, "She is the best." In the past Mary must have had some household help that was less than hard working and possibly dishonest. According to Mary, Bessie worked without supervision and needed no "Watching." Bessie also babysat Grace and Suzy from time to time while Mary ran errands. When Mary took her occasional short two- or three-day trips to visit friends in Philadelphia, Bessie was able to stay with the children back in Baltimore. Just as with Dot, Mary helped in the kitchen and continued to clean along with Bessie. When not cleaning or cooking Bessie and Mary sat on the porch and had long talks while smoking a cigarette or sipping some iced tea. The four children loved Bessie even though she only worked part time, Bessie became an important part of the Warder's everyday life.

In addition to the good friendship that developed between Mary and Bessie, Mary considered Bessie a vital part of her permanent recovery, writing to Fred,

> Bessie is a real help, though expensive. I'm keeping her in spite of the cost – for the excellent reason that though I might try to do everything and succeed for a time – I might set the stage for a future "flop" in so doing.

Bessie's labor was expensive to purchase. In addition to every other kind of shortage, the amount of domestic help that was available declined rapidly. In 1940 nearly 60% of the black women in the work force labored in domestic service. By 1944 that numbered declined to 45%. Black women engaged in industrial jobs before the war amounted to about 6% of the black female work force. By 1944 that number rose to about 18%.[231]

However, it took almost a force of nature for black women to break into the better war industry jobs. One woman named Maya Angelou answered an ad for a position as a streetcar conductor. When she got to the office and asked for an application the people working there literally laughed in her face. But she went back every day for about a month and finally got an application and got the job as a streetcar conductor. The level of tenacity demonstrated by black women in America to break into the wartime job market is almost without comparison and was a tough business to say the least. Be that as it may those that got war industry jobs created a ripple effect that benefited people like Bessie who could now charge significantly more for their domestic labor. Mary felt the pinch of the new labor circumstances. After going over her finances and finding it increasingly difficult to pay for Bessie's services Mary chided Fred, who had a personal steward assigned to him to take care of all of his personal needs including clothes washing and meals, wrote, "I wish you could bring one of your mess attendants [to me]."

* * *

While Mary and the rest of the Americans adjusted to rationing, housing shortages, and social change, Fred Warder continued his battle with newfound, and unwanted, fame. The nation needed heroes and President Roosevelt set out to give them the heroes that they craved to know. Fred wrote to Mary a typical letter explaining his exploits,

> Naturally we have been lucky as hell and all this hero stuff is very over done. I liked the way you [Mary] handled the Sun Reporter. The credit for our performance belongs first of all to superior authority for having the ship in the right place at the right time and the rest of it belongs to these grand officers and men who are an inspiration to me. They can "take it" – and they like to "dish it out."[232]

Fred was a very sincere and modest man, so he must have been taken aback when Mary wrote him in a lighthearted way about what was becoming a very embarrassing situation for both of them,

It seems – my sweet – you have made the "funnies." As Dr. Carol puts it – that is a real achievement. It gives you a fair idea of the general excitement over your exploits.[233]

Yes, a real achievement indeed thought Fred. In addition to fighting "the battle of the books" Fred was confronted with the battle of the comics; and the Hearst papers, notorious since the Spanish War days, jumped wholeheartedly into wartime comics with their "Heroes of Democracy" comic strip series. Being a Hearst owned enterprise one could safely assume that truth would be an early casualty in the comic campaign. One of the comic strips that appeared in the Hearst papers was authored by Stookie Allen and shows the Seawolf in a daytime "battle surface" action apparently sinking an enemy ship with a .50 caliber machine gun. That would have been quite a trick, sinking a 5,000-ton ship with a few bullets. Further, if it were true that subs could safely operate on the surface during daytime hours as depicted by Hearst, a lot of money was being wasted in giving submarines the ability to dive under the sea. The last frame of that comic is very typical of Hearst's favorite type of text reading, "Rumor has it that the daring raider [Warder] had a large part in the Coral Sea Battle where the Nips lost too, too many ships!"[234] That was some crack reporting job done by Hearst's men since Seawolf happened to be in an Australian port at the time of the battle of Coral Sea. Reporting on Rumors, or purposely making up rumors was the basis of Hearst's fine reporting techniques. Seeing how Hearst never let the truth get in the way of a good story one can easily see why a man of such outstanding character as Fred Warder would be a bit disgusted by all the silly publicity aimed at him.

But there was more to come. Look magazine ran Warder's story in its August 25, 1942, edition with a small amount of copy accompanied by very large and stylized illustrations. This is an article that Fred would have laughed out loud at since it pictured him at the periscope of the Seawolf wearing a dress shirt and his Lt. Commanders epaulets. As noted, because of the extreme heat and discomfort while submerged, most of the crew including Warder, wore only shorts and sandals during submerged operations.

Dell comic books had its own series called, "War Heroes," in which Fred appeared in the January 1943 issue. The Dell version of what happened at Christmas Island had almost no relation to the truth whatsoever. However, the Dell version included some schematics of U.S. submarines, an explanation of torpedoes, and a map of Indonesia where Christmas Island is located making it somewhat educational.

The privately owned press did their best to exploit men like Fred Warder. At the same time, the Roosevelt administration did their very best to control information about the war. President Roosevelt's first efforts at trying to shape public opinion, aside from his own speeches, consisted of the formation of the Office of Government Reports (OGR) in September of 1939. That agency, headed by Lowell Mellett, was a sort of clearinghouse agency that was supposed to collect information from various government agencies and then produce literature to assure the public that the United States Government was busy protecting their freedom and their improving prosperity. The OGR got their letterhead, started slowly, then petered out to nothing as hostile Republicans accused it of being nothing but a advertising agency for the administration.

The OGR's lack of success caused the President to try again. The Division of Information of the Office of Emergency Management (DOI) was created in March of 1941. In the true Roosveltian style the OGR was not disbanded with the arrival of the new agency; Roosevelt simply plastered the DOI over it, which caused problems for everyone except Roosevelt. Robert Horton led the new agency, which in turn was an agency of the Office of Emergency Management (OEM). It could get confusing from time to time, but Roosevelt was certain that he was not getting his version of the facts out and he wanted this new information agency to work. Horton, a former editor with the Scripps-Howard news service, knew a little about facts and propaganda and Roosevelt looked on with the keenest of optimism. The attempt was doomed to failure from the beginning as Horton lacked any kind of authority to enforce a coordinated effort at getting the government's story out in the first place. Often a story released from the DOI conflicted with one or more news releases of the several agencies that Horton was supposed to be coordinating.[235]

It appears Roosevelt had hit a dead end, but because of his deep distrust of the private press including Hearst, and his unwillingness for the comic strips to be the main providers of war information, Roosevelt pressed on. His trusted Secretary of the Treasury, Henry Morgenthau Jr. attempted to span the information gap with a spring 1941 campaign to "use bonds to sell the war." Morgenthau's advertising efforts in selling the bonds included information about government policy and the war in general, however the focus of Morgenthau's campaign was really finance. Roosevelt liked Morgenthau, but he thought his ad campaign lacked punch.

After three defeats Roosevelt tried an entirely different approach based on several of the local Civil Defense Committees, which resembled a sort of well-intentioned yet amateurish vaudeville act. But Roosevelt believed that along with their other activities the CDC's could get some information out on how best to cope with attacks against the United States and of course show that the government was busy staying ready to repel our enemies. This attempt also lacked success. In desperation Roosevelt asked his Friend Mayor Fiorello La Guardia to come in and make sense of the information problem.

La Guardia and Eleanor Roosevelt proceeded to supercede the Civil Defense Committee with the Office of Civil Defense (OCD). This organization was to have a practical defense aspect to it while also having a morale boosting function. Unfortunately, like the other organizations, the people running it could not focus on the central problem of informing the public about the government's strategies and activities relating to the war effort. For instance, Mayris Chaney was hired by the OCD to be the "National Sports Coordinator" for the employees of the OCD. Her duties consisted of leading some of the women in dancing and other exercises on the roof of the agency's headquarters in Washington DC. For her efforts Miss Chaney received $4,600 per year, quite lavish considering the pay of an army enlisted man amounted to $21 per month.[236] The American press had a field day with that tidbit of information even going so far as to accuse Miss Chaney of being a former fan-dancer. Far from distributing positive information about the administration's efforts on defense the OCD quickly became a laughingstock.

Not to be overcome by failure Roosevelt started yet another agency that hopefully would fix everything. The new agency was called the Office of Facts and Figures (OFF) and on name alone it never had a chance. The New York Herald Tribune ran an editorial saying, "This is where we get OFF."[237]

> OFF is just going to superimpose its own well-organized facts upon the splendid confusion, interpret the interpreters, re-digest those who now digest the digesters, explain what those who explain what the explainers of the explanations mean, and coordinate the coordinators of those appointed to coordinate the co-ordinations of the coordinated."[238]

That about summoned up OFF. In addition to ridicule, all of the aforementioned agencies still continued to operate as they saw fit and OFF did not have any clear authority over any of them. Soon the press referred to OFF as the Office of Fun and Frolic. That is a real blow considering what the drivel and half truths that the various newspapers around the country continuously passed off as facts and figures.

These failures spurred Roosevelt into creating more agencies, which was his usual remedy for curing the ailments of the previous failed agency. William Donovan's Office of Coordination of information (OCI) soon followed the Coordinator of Inter-American Affairs (CIAA), with Nelson Rockefeller at its head. When that proved inadequate the Foreign Information Service (FIS) directed by Robert Sherwood became the OCI's unwanted stepchild. And lastly amidst the chaos a new agency under the direction of Elmer Davis emerged called the Office of War Information. His principal assistants were Archibald MacLeish and Robert Sherwood, both holdovers from other agencies. The date was June 13, 1942, about the time that Fred Warder had, "Made the funnies." Help indeed had arrived.

The Office of War Information didn't engage in unseemly farfetched propaganda. The OWI rather tried to convey to the American public propaganda based on solid facts demonstrating that progress was being made in the war effort. That agency had the difficult task of explaining why gas rationing was needed even though we had a surplus of gas. The OWI was more successful than earlier attempts at propaganda and survived to the end of the war. They did have problems though with two major departments of the United States Government, namely the Army and the Navy, neither of which wanted anything to do with OWI. The irony is that most of the information Americans desired had to do with the Army and Navy, but because those two agencies were completely uncooperative as far as information went, Americans were forced to receive most of their war news in over-the-top made-up newspaper headlines or from comic books or even from Dr. Seuss.

The stories came and went; Fred Warder being the star of some them while other heroes were displayed or created in such a fashion as the free press or the OWI thought would be useful to the war effort as well as newspaper sales. In January of 1944, after the public had become at least little acclimated to heroism due to its constant display on the battlefronts, the West Virginia Review ran a very nice story about the U.S.S. Seawolf, Fred Warder, and the crew. Gone were the intense bigger than life hero hysteria that earlier publications presented. What emerged out of those pages is something Fred Warder and his crew preferred, an honest rendition of a well-trained crew at work, doing their duty, and especially, surviving a close fought battle.

As with all extraordinary times intense emotions are often coupled with the silliest of occurrences. War to defend our freedom against the heinous Empire of Japan and Nazi Germany was coupled with the ridiculous proposition that eating sauerkraut was somehow unpatriotic. A serious showdown over civil rights and race relations at the White House, is balanced by two women, Bessie and Mary, sitting on a porch in Baltimore, exchanging a story as they sipped iced tea, then pausing to say hello to a neighbor who happened by to swap a few coupons from their ration book

Chapter – 13
Success

While the Seawolf crew rested at Fremantle, repairmen worked hard getting her back to combat readiness. After that all-out effort it was decided that the ship was too worn out for extended operations anymore. Seawolf needed an entire overhaul, so the next war patrol would end at Pearl Harbor with the crew never returning to Fremantle again. Leaving that wonderful little town in Australia was a blow to some. It had been home for the crew after finishing several war patrols, and the Australians had been very hospitable. Families made the crews welcome in their homes and many young women enjoyed the attention they received from the Americans. As for Fred, he had made the acquaintance of Mary Lewis, a young English mother with two kids. Her husband was in the British army but had been reported missing in Burma. Fred had written Mary, his wife, on a few occasions about Mrs. Lewis. Now that his stay in Fremantle was coming to an end Fred related to his wife Mary the events of their last meeting,

> My division commander and the skipper of the tender and I took out three families for a Sunday picnic – two of the families don't know where their daddies are (defense of Singapore). Two children each and a bunch of young mothers. Also Mary Lewis and her two youngsters of whom I have told you [was also there]. They were all grand kids and it was a wonderful day – but there are no kids who can appeal to me like our own; nor is there any companionship I can enjoy like I can yours (sic).[239]

Being with the Lewis family from time to time and understanding their pain and hardship caused Fred to seriously count his blessings and take stock of some of the simple things that now eluded him.

> I would like to have made the Fourth of July picnic with you – I never thought I would go for "such thing's" and used to regard mother and dad's predilection for them with great sympathy. But – I have changed.[240]

Success

On October 7th with the exchange of hugs and handshakes between the Americans and Australians, U.S.S. Seawolf, 8 officers and 66 crewmembers, left on their 7th war patrol. Seawolf's trip to Pearl Harbor included scheduled patrol stops at the usual hunting grounds of; Lombok Strait, Makassar City, Balikpapan, Tarakan, and Davao Gulf. The tour guide also placed a few new destinations into their travels, Palau, and Yap.

As the Seawolf left, her armaments included 12 Mark XIV torpedoes and surprisingly, 8 Mark IX torpedoes left over from WW I. This brings into stark view the latest torpedo problem, a shortage. The Japanese helped create the shortage by their well-placed bombs at Cavite on the third day of the war, which destroyed about half of the U.S. supply of torpedoes in the Pacific. Also, America's great manufacturing companies had not yet organized their war armaments production, so the Mark IX's, relics and museum pieces from World War I, were dusted off and brought back into service. The sailors aboard the Seawolf could only look at those old torpedoes, scratch their heads and wonder, could they be any worse than the Mark XIV's.

Over the next three days Seawolf's crew went through the usual drills to shake off any rust their short shore leave might have produced. Warder remarked that the SD radar seemed to work, a pleasant surprise. However, on October 10th, just three days into the patrol and not even out of the air-restricted area,* Seawolf's fuel oil started leaking into the compensating water system when using the drain pump on the bilges. Seawolf surfaced at 11:00am at Exmouth Gulf, near the Northwest Cape in Western Australia, in order to make an appointment with an oil barge where they took on 8,000 additional gallons of fuel oil. After that they headed for the familiar hunting grounds of Lombok, Indonesia. During the first few hours of the voyage, they spotted many U.S. PBY's, a testament to the increasing vigilance of the United States armed forces. They did a few battle surface drills with their usual quick time to the first shot, about 1 minute and ten seconds.

On October 12th the Seawolf arrived at Lombok Strait and the crew reset their clocks to time zone 8. That night, while cruising on the surface, they spotted a ship only 600 yards away and went to battle stations. Warder, on the bridge and looking through his binoculars, identified the ship as either U.S.S. Sargo or U.S.S. Seadragon, both United States submarines. He ordered emergency speed and right full rudder. Warder wanted to get away from that U.S. submarine as fast as possible to avoid accidents. Apparently, the CO on the other ship had the same idea because it rapidly disappeared.

---

* Certain corridors were designated as areas where friendly planes could not bomb any targets for fear of sinking friendly submarines.

By October 14 they had come as far as Surabaya, on the island of Java, and by the 16th were in front of Makassar City, in the southern area of Sulawesi. All the while they spotted small boats called "vintas,"[241] but no enemy ships of any substance. Then on the 17th the OOD, Lt. Mercer, spotted a big ship, pressed the alarm, and the men ran to general quarters. Warder came up to the conning tower and the approach team got to work. The target, a 4,000-ton transport, offered the Seawolf a pretty good setup. It took an hour for the approach team to work the Seawolf into a good firing position. Warder received continuous reports from the echo ranger, which seemed accurate to him until the last ten minutes of the approach, the most critical period. Despite that recurring problem Warder felt sure of his estimated range of 1,500 yards. Seawolf fired two Mark XIV torpedoes at the enemy ship, but they passed harmlessly by, exploding about 5 minutes later at the end of their run.

Warder felt he caused the miss by incorrectly estimating the enemy's speed by about half a knot. He could have blamed the echo rang finder, which didn't work on this occasion. Also, the "plot ready light" on the TDC burned out causing a critical time lapse in accurate firing, but he didn't blame that problem either. About the inaccurate speed calculation though, Warder did say in the future he would employ the Voge speed spread and chastised himself for not using it in this instance.[242] Sometimes Warder disparaged his own abilities much more than even his friendly critics.

Seawolf followed the enemy transport ship toward the northern approaches of Makassar City near Kapoposang hoping for a second chance at sinking it. The glassy surface and clear water made this chase especially dangerous for Seawolf. Eckberg, operating the sound equipment, could easily hear waves breaking on the shore and against the coral reefs as strong currents whipped around and slowed the Seawolf's progress. Because of the danger of grounding Warder opted to stay toward the southern approaches of Langkai, a less used entrance and exit.

As Seawolf headed south, the Japanese, warned by the ship Seawolf attacked earlier, sent up an airplane to see if they could find Seawolf and put her out of the war. Just as Seawolf arrived at Langkai a Japanese plane spotted her. Warder ordered a depth of 100 feet to avoid the expected enemy attack. The Japanese plane circled back took aim, then dropped a string of depth bombs. The crew in the Seawolf heard them splash into the water. They didn't sound close. Soon after the depth bombs sank to the preset depth, the detonator exploded the bombs. The concussion from the explosion did not even slightly rock Seawolf.

Success

After the evening's excitement Seawolf headed through the Makassar Strait to Balikpapan located halfway up the western side of Borneo. While cruising on the surface that night, Seawolf again came upon a small vinta that unfortunately spotted them. Warder quickly ordered the .50 caliber machines guns mounted and manned by the crew in case of trouble. Seawolf drew up along side the small vinta. Suddenly they saw a flash from the ship, which turned out to be reflected light. All the same nervous fingers tightened on their triggers. Someone shouted for the people on the vinta to come out. Two men appeared. The Seawolf crew gave them a close look then noticed a woman and child cowering on the deck. Warder scrutinized the vinta and its family crew. He again used his tour guide expressions describing the family as clothed, "In colorful native dress." He judged the vinta and the family aboard to be harmless. The Seawolf crew stowed their weapons and moved on into the night.

On October 20th Seawolf arrived in front of Balikpapan. The importance of this area to the Japanese cannot be exaggerated. They wanted oil. Indonesia, especially Balikpapan, possessed an abundance of that resource. In fact, the whole of the attack against the United Stated revolved around that commodity and the Indonesian/Borneo area. For quite some time before the war against the United States began, the Japanese wanted to take oil from Indonesia to support their war in China. The Philippine Islands sat directly on the sea-lanes between those two countries. That made the Japanese very nervous because the United States had a large commitment to the Philippines. And those islands were still nominally a territory of the U.S. and would be until July 4, 1946.* The Japanese thought they needed to eliminate the U.S. as a power in the Pacific in order to steal the Indonesian oil. They were probably wrong about that considering the very high isolationist feeling in the U.S. before the war began. One idea that apparently never occurred to the Japanese; why not just buy the oil from Balikpapan? That would have been much more cost effective, and millions of people would not have suffered at the hands of the Japanese. In the end, the war that the Japanese started caused the destruction of their home islands, and the killing of hundreds of thousands of their own people. Clearly the Japanese did not think things through very well in the 1930's and 40's.

When the Japanese took over Balikpapan in mid-December 1941 the Dutch, thinking they might slow down the Japanese, broke up all of the oil field machinery. The enterprising Japanese, with full knowledge of their intentions, came prepared. Their oil refinery engineers landed almost

---

* As per the Hawes-Cutting Act of 1932.

simultaneously with their invasion forces. In only a few weeks fuel oil streamed from that area to the Japanese home islands and areas of their conquest. When Seawolf showed up in late October the crew had every reason to believe that huge amounts of shipping, especially oil tankers, would be moving in and out of the area.

Enemy merchant shipping also meant a large amount of enemy anti-submarine activity. At about noon on October 21st Lt. Holden, the OOD, observed a lightship and proceeded toward it for further inspection. He changed direction one time in order to avoid the swarming vintas. This unfortunately, and no fault of his own, brought the Seawolf face to face with a sub-chaser. The crew went to their battle stations and Warder toyed with the idea of a quick shot but decided against it as per guidelines of CSSWP Adm. Fife.* Also the sub-chaser presented only a small problem and did not interfere with Seawolf's activities. On the afternoon of the next day the same sub-chaser, or one that looked just like it, came into view escorting a tanker. Warder estimated the rage at 9,000 yards. After about an hour the approach team managed to get within 3,200 yards of the tanker but no closer, so they abandoned the approach. After a few disappointing days, Seawolf left Balikpapan for Mangkalihat and then Tarakan, both north of Balikpapan by a couple of hundred miles.

Tarakan should have contained about the same amount of shipping as Balikpapan, but upon their arrival the crew found no shipping at all. Seawolf even stayed on the surface well into mid morning, "In broad daylight, with no shipping in sight."[243] It looked as if the deeper the Seawolf roamed into enemy territory; the less they saw of the enemy. It was another frustrating and perplexing situation.

Then on October 27th, finding the enemy became the least of the crew's problems; the Seawolf attempted to sink herself again. That night Warder surfaced the submarine as usual to charge batteries. The lookouts took their positions on the deck. For the five men, three on the deck and two perched on the shears, it was a very pleasant evening with calm flat seas, but no shipping in sight. Then one of the lookouts noticed that the stern seemed a little low in the water. It continued to sink so the lookout shouted a warning to Lt. Mercer, the OOD who was scanning the horizon in front of the Seawolf. When Mercer heard the warning he headed for the back of the conning tower, passing under the two lookouts on the shears, to the cigarette deck. There he could plainly see the stern quickly sinking. Then, for some

---

* Commander Submarines South West Pacific.

reason Mercer ordered, "Sound collision," and the sharp ascending whistle of the collision alarm split everybody's ears.

A few seconds later, Lt. Mercer realized he gave the wrong order and belayed it since they were not in danger of a collision, but in fact were sinking. He next ordered a dive. That made some sense, after all the Seawolf, in a sort of quirky way, was currently in a dive, a stern first dive to be exact. At least with a dive order all the hatches would be closed. But a few seconds later Mercer, now grasping the situation in all its horror, realized that course of action was also incorrect. The ship was obviously sinking, and the problem had nothing to do with the hatches. To close the hatches and "dive" would only cause the Seawolf sink faster and dive permanently.

Time ticked away as the ship continued to slip beneath the ocean. Mercer, attempting to get control of the desperate situation, ordered the main ballast tanks blown. That made a lot of sense as it addressed the immediate problem and stopped the Seawolf from sinking, at least temporarily. Unbeknownst to Mercer though, water continued to rush into the pressure hull. In a matter of minutes Seawolf would begin sinking again and this time without the luxury of blowing the main ballast tanks to keep afloat.

By this time Warder had come into the control room to take command. In addition to his other training and coursework, including maritime law (capturing prizes and piracy of all things), he was a skilled engineer. He knew how every bit of machinery worked on his ship and on many occasions demonstrated his knowledge when bandaging poor Seawolf.[244] Warder rushed to the rear of the ship and found the auxiliary generator room completely flooded for some reason. He waded through ankle deep water tracing the problem back to the engine room. Only the #1 engine was running at the time, but all the outboard exhaust valves were open and on the "power" setting, as they should have been for surface running. But the exhaust valve on the #4 engine malfunctioned and wasn't tightly closed. Water rushed into the after-engine room. From there the flooding poured into the auxiliary generator room, filled it with water and ruined a generator. Despite the chaos created by the flooding and spraying water, the men were able to tightly close the faulty valve and stop the flooding. They turned on the ships pumps and pumped the water out of the Seawolf. Gradually Seawolf began to rise out of the ocean. It had been a close call and Warder himself thought Seawolf, "Almost went under."[245]

After patrolling a few more days off Tarakan Seawolf headed for Davao Gulf. Warder wanted to go there by way of Sibutu where on August 25th, during a previous patrol, they sank a tanker. Additionally, Warder and the crew were familiar with Sibutu because it is in the Sulu Archipelago where the island of Tawi Tawi is; a place they spent time doing maneuvers in the months leading up to the war. Who knows, familiarity might lead to good fortune as it had before.

As they steamed in that direction they received and decoded a message from Adm. Fife. A large amount of Japanese shipping had been spotted by another U.S. submarine at the Cape San Augustin entrance to Davao Gulf, on the Philippine Island of Mindanao. Warder immediately put all of the engines to the screws and Seawolf actually got up to 17.9 knots in the rush to get into combat. As they got to Balut Island just off of Mindanao, Seawolf hit a stiff current of almost 3 knots. After they churned around for an hour or so Warder commented, "I realized I was just throwing away precious fuel for no good reason." They dove and ran on the batteries for the next seven hours surfacing at about 5:30 that night, still fighting the current, much to the consternation of Warder.

By 5:00 am the next day, November 2nd, the currents had reversed, and Warder made another effort at getting to the San Agustin entrance to Davao gulf. At 11:45 am they arrived and Lt. Mercer, the OOD, immediately sighted some smoke bearing 348° T. He raised 12 feet of the periscope out of the water for a quick elevated look. This could be dangerous as it made it easier for the Japanese to spot a submarine with so much periscope exposed. The advantage of being able to see a significantly longer distance with an elevated periscope overrode such concerns, especially for an aggressive crew like that on the Seawolf. About two hours later the next OOD, Lt. Syverson also exposed the periscope 12 feet and spotted a couple of topmasts at 350° T. In that situation he didn't need to think. He gave the order, and the battle stations alarm rang, "*bong, bong, bong...*" throughout the ship. Warder quickly came up to the conning tower with the rest of the approach party. The big game began again.

Warder looked over the situation and gave the first order, "Full speed, collision course." Examining the enemy ship through the periscope he saw one gun at the stern of the 350 foot ship and two passenger decks. To him it looked a lot like the ex-British SS Wenchow, which the Seawolf sank back in August.

Dripping in sweat the approach party worked doggedly over the next couple of hours. To add to their discomfort all the men in the conning tower had to stand. Then, after hours of effort, as often happened, the merchant ship suddenly zigged toward Seawolf, ruining the setup developed so painstakingly by the approach party over the last hour.

Warder ordered the speed cut to 2.5 knots. Dutifully Thompson repeated the order to the men in the maneuvering room and Seawolf immediately slowed down, but not fast enough. This presented Warder with a huge problem, or so he thought at the time. The initial setup had been for a bowshot. The modern Mark XIV torpedoes were in the forward torpedo room. When the enemy changed course, Warder found himself too far in front of the enemy. He now figured that only a stern shot was possible. But the aft torpedo room was loaded with the old WW I era Mark IX torpedoes. In the few seconds available, Warder quickly decided on a stern attack with the old Mark IX's.

The museum curators in the aft torpedo room loaded in the WW I relics. Despite the gloomy situation everybody performed their duties with the usual precision. The new Mark XIV torpedoes had not performed well, and the crew could not expect the old Mark IX's to do any better. But in the words of one crewmember, "We were submariners, we were going in and going to fire whatever torpedoes we had."

At the beginning of the chase the crew enjoyed clear skies with flat seas, but as time progressed the weather steadily turned sour. The approach team, sweating in their shorts and sandals, worked the new set of problems in the conning tower. After wrestling with the 2,300-pound torpedoes the crew in the aft torpedo room reported tubes 5, 6, and 7 loaded and ready to fire. The Seawolf continued to move at 2.5 knots while the enemy traveled at about 7 knots. Warder lined up the periscope and called out the final setup including the all-important angle on the bow. Deragon, just below in the control room feed the data into the TDC. The green solution light, now replaced and working, came on and Deragon gave his usual, "Okay!"

Warder noted a periscope bearing of 195° for all three torpedoes, while the TDC automatically figured the gyro angle at 180°, a fairly "straight-in" shot at a range of about 1,100 yards. Unlike the Mark XIV's, the Mark IX's gyro had to be set by hand by the men in the torpedo room. The crew worked methodically to ensure a correct setup despite the 98% humidity. Warder aimed the torpedoes one-quarter length ahead of the ship, the middle of the ship, and one-quarter length behind the ship (the Voge Speed Spread). He then "eye-balled" it through the periscope and when his imaginary point ahead crossed the wire of the periscope he called out, "Fire one."

As usual Brengelman hit the plunger, always a satisfying feeling, and Thompson repeated the order to the aft torpedo room. The ancient weapon, built to battle the Kaiser's *Kriegsmarine* in World War I, left the Seawolf bound for a new enemy in an entirely different ocean, war, and era. As Warder looked through the periscope two more torpedoes were fired. Eckberg, in the radio shack, listened with his sound equipment and reported all three torpedoes running, "hot, straight, and normal." They waited and they waited. Just as they were about to lose hope, they heard a sharp "crack" that rocked the submarine.* Seawolf's old World War I vintage Mark IX torpedoes hit the enemy ship decisively and blew a huge hole in it. The concussion was so fantastic that when the smoke from the blast began to clear, Warder saw that the ship was already sinking rapidly. Maybe they should have been using the Mark IX relics during all of their patrols.

Lt. Mercer had contrived a way to take photographs through the periscope and Warder was anxious to get a good picture of their collective success. Warder told Mercer to get his camera fast. Mercer retrieved it from his room as the enemy ship took on water. Mercer put the camera onto the periscope and snapped a picture, but no more than the bow of the ship remained above water. The enemy ship sank in less than 10 minutes.

After Mercer took his pictures, Warder looked again through the periscope. Warder counted 41 survivors in the water with no lifeboats. The starboard boat of the stricken ship had not been manned due to the ship's heavy list. As the crew on the Japanese ship attempted to get that lifeboat into the water, the sinking ship pulled it under. The port lifeboat went down with the front part of the ship. As for the crew, most of them abandoned the ship on a rigged-up cargo net. With no lifeboats they clung to various pieces of wreckage.

The ship sank at about 2:00 pm. Warder stayed in the area thinking a destroyer might come out and rescue the crew giving him an excellent chance at sinking another ship. No ship came out and when darkness came, about four hours later, Warder ordered Seawolf to the surface. They cruised into the debris field. A few survivors still bobbed up and down in the gentle swell of the ocean. A couple of the Japanese drifted close to the Seawolf. They seemed very young. Warder ordered a line thrown to them, but the Japanese refused to grab it. After attempting to rescue them and being refused for about ten minutes the crew of the Seawolf gave up. Maybe the young Japanese, in their inexperience, thought they could swim to shore despite the swift and treacherous currents. These young Japanese might have known how brutally the Japanese treated Chinese, Filipino, Korean, and American POW's and thought they would receive the same from the Americans. If they had known how hospitable the Americans were toward enemy POW's they would have gladly grabbed the line and saved their own lives.

---

* The Mark XIV's made a very large "boom" sound whereas the smaller warhead of the Mark IX made more of a "crack."

Success

As it was Warder ordered life vests thrown to the young Japanese. He also ordered that a bottle of Australian Whiskey be passed to them. The gesture was magnanimous but with a grim edge. Warder opined,

> It is believed [that the] sinking was not observed on [the] beach. With prevailing weather and strong southwesterly current [in] this locality it is believed that there will be few, if any, survivors.

Perhaps the whiskey would tranquilize them before the sea swallowed them up in a few hours, making their final descent into the ocean less uncomfortable. It is hard to know what to do in such a situation fraught with the extreme ambivalence war creates.

The rain started to fall in earnest. Visibility dropped so low that Warder did not think he needed to exit Davao Gulf, which ranges from about thirty miles to fifty miles across and is about 60 miles deep with the large island of Samal at the northern end of it. At 5:25 am Seawolf dove about 12 miles from Davao Harbor, at the north end and well inside the gulf. Wary of mines Warder remained outside of the 300-fathom line trying to establish the existence of a swept channel, (no mines), before going into shallower water. The lack of any perceptible currents inside the gulf made controlling the submarine easy while the choppy water above kept the Seawolf safe from enemy patrol planes. After about three hours Warder still could not definitely confirm a safe swept channel despite seeing a few anti-submarine ships milling around.

During one of his periscope observations Warder noticed a very large 9,300-ton freighter anchored at Talomo Bay, just south of Davao Harbor. He immediately ordered a course change to attack the new larger Japanese ship. It took about 45 minutes to get into a reasonable position and at 9:21 am Warder ordered battle stations. Sizing up the situation he thought it could not be any better. The big ship lay at anchor and the enemy posted no lookouts. Perhaps the Japanese remained somewhat overconfident despite their recent setbacks at Coral Sea, Midway Island, and Guadalcanal.

The stationary ship produced an easy setup for the approach team; target speed 0, gyro angle 0°, periscope bearing 0°, and the target bearing 11°. After feeding the final data into the TDC a spread of four Mark XIV torpedoes sped towards the Japanese ship. Warder watched the torpedoes with great confidence through the periscope. He watched as the first torpedo went right under the ship and exploded on the beach. Warder had ordered the second shot set for a contact detonation and that torpedo hit the ship resulting in a small explosion with no effect. Probably the detonator fired but did not trigger the explosives in the torpedo, a typical problem producing a "dud.". The third and fourth torpedo followed the example of the first. They went right under the ship, continued to the beach, and dutifully exploded. At least the crew of the Seawolf could be assured that no enemy sand crabs remained in the area. Warder had ordered a depth setting of just 4 feet on those last two torpedoes. Considering the enemy ship's draft at 24 feet one can see just how out of whack the torpedoes continued to be.

As Seawolf withdrew to reload and try again the Japanese began to fire at her with their two mounted guns. But they didn't seem to be particularly good shots (thankfully), missing 500 yards to port and 500 yards to starboard consistently. Warder did note that the explosions from the shells were quite a bit louder than anything encountered before.

At 11:31am Seawolf commenced a second attack against the ship firing one Mark XIV torpedo with a depth setting of 8 feet. This time the torpedo hit the ship but again with negligible damage. That really frustrated Warder. Most of the Mark XIV torpedoes malfunctioned and could not even get to the target. The few that did actually find their targets misfired consistently.

Warder turned the Seawolf to line up a stern shot with one of the old Mark IX torpedoes. After a quick setup Brengelman hit the plunger. About forty seconds later the crew heard a perfect hit, punctuated by a loud "crack," the signature sound of the old Mark IX's. A fire immediately spread rapidly throughout the enemy ship as it began to sink. Warder wrote again,

> The failures of the first attack are typical and merely add weight to the previous complaints of other CO's and myself as to the erratic performance of the Mark XIV torpedo and its warhead attachment. All six of these fish smoked.[246]

Warder looked upon the scene through the periscope. Only two men remained on the enemy ship. The rest bobbed up and down in five whaleboats and rowed toward the dock where a number of men witnessed the events. Lt. Mercer snapped a few pictures as the crew basked in their success. It felt especially good watching the enemy ship sink as the crew of Seawolf had been through a period of undeserved criticism. Mercer's photos guaranteed to stop those controversies.

As Seawolf slipped away from the burning wreckage Warder spotted another ship with a tripod mast moving at high speed; very likely a sub-chaser, he thought. A few minutes later Warder spotted three Japanese planes. Two flew away but one came right at the Seawolf. This was truly a desperate situation. The plane dropped five depth bombs as Warder ordered

Success

Seawolf to 200 feet in order to evade the enemy. Two Japanese ships lackadaisically made runs over Seawolf's position but after a few hours they moved on.

By now the wind had picked up creating a good chop on the surface of the ocean better concealing the Seawolf. Because of that change, Warder thought the Seawolf could safely remain deep inside the gulf a while longer. (Although by now he and the crew had become so confident and aggressive they probably would have stayed whatever the weather conditions.) At 3:15 pm Warder sighted some smoke and ordered a course change to investigate it. Despite being confined in the small space of a gulf, and the enemy knowing Seawolf was in the area, Warder exposed 12 feet of periscope for a greater view. He could not see anything in the harbor but rationalized the excessive range, about 9 miles, could be the reason. He proceeded with a mixture of caution and aggressiveness; he wanted to sink the merchant ship earlier sighted in Davao Harbor but did not want to tangle with any additional depth charges. The good submarine COs judged the proper balance between these two disparate goals.

About thirty minutes later Seawolf reacquired the original target and closed the range enough to discern a 5,000-ton freighter. The alarm was pressed, and the men rushed to their battle stations. Warder planned a two-shot spread from the bow torpedo tubes. It took only twelve minutes for the approach team to arrive at an acceptable firing position. However, unlike the last attack, this freighter traveled at about 8 knots. As the approach team worked through the problems, Warder decided Seawolf was too close to the anticipated track of the enemy freighter. He immediately swung the ship around in order to lengthen the range. This maneuver also had the happy effect of creating a stern tube shot with the old, but proven, Mark IX torpedoes.

Warder began to line up for the final shot as he coaxed the helmsman Gervais, "A little port, a little more..."

The surface water began to flatten, and Warder became very concerned about detection taking only the briefest time to make his periscope observations. Using the Voge speed spread chart in his calculations, Warder now planned three shots, one-quarter length ahead of the enemy, in the middle of the ship, and one-quarter length behind the ship. At 4:11 pm the Seawolf fired the first of three shots. The second being fired 18 seconds later, and the third, 19 seconds after the second. Each time a torpedo was fired the residual compressed air came into the submarine and the crew felt the familiar popping in their ears.

Sound reported the first and third torpedoes running, "straight, hot, and normal," but the second torpedo sounded funny. In fact, it had turned to the right and circled back towards the Seawolf. That was a new twist. Instead of the Seawolf trying to mechanically sink herself, her torpedoes were now attempting the suicidal feat. Warder ordered a fast dive to 150 feet to avoid being blown up by his own torpedo. As the Seawolf descended the crew heard a large explosion followed by the sounds of a ship breaking up. Two minutes later the Japanese threw off their lethargy and a concerted hour-long counterattack began. Warder counted twenty depth charges or depth bombs. Two ships made close runs above them but none of the attacks inflicted any serious damage on the Seawolf.

About two hours later the counterattack ended. Warder ordered the diving officer to bring Seawolf up to 63 feet for a periscope observation. The sub-chasers were gone but Warder spotted smoke coming from another freighter. It was evening and he decided it was dark enough to make a surface approach undetected by the enemy. He ordered Seawolf to the surface. The crew remained at battle stations; that meant that Thompson, the quartermaster who usually handled the duties of opening the hatch, was predisposed with the phone apparatus. Lt. Casler, Jughead as he was nicknamed and sometimes known, was assigned to open the hatch. Because of the great pressure that builds up in a World War II era submarine, opening the hatch is a little trickier then simply popping it open. The best way to open the hatch is to open the tightening dog wheel a little bit first in order to equalize the pressure. Unfortunately, Casler swung the wheel violently and the hatch literally blew open. Normally the sudden change of pressure would only hurt the crew's ears. But Fred Warder was especially susceptible to headaches from sudden pressure changes.[1] The pain inflicted on him caused by the sudden pressure change made him bellow at the top of his lungs. Warder's sinuses hurt and he experienced a continuous headache for the next several days. Needless to say, Casler was a bit shaken by the incident. Nobody wanted to be on the wrong end of Warder's temper.

After the brief excitement the men on lookout duty climbed onto the bridge. Immediately visibility dropped due to rain and wind. The weather in the South Pacific could literally change in a matter of minutes from sunny, hot and calm, to violent rainsqualls and heavy seas. The weather notwithstanding, Chief Machinist Mate Lober, on the deck as the port

---

[1] Even latter in life Fred Warder preferred to drive instead of taking an airplane even for long trips such as his home in Florida to his in-laws' vacation home in upstate New York.

Success

lookout, spotted a ship smoking heavily and moving as fast as its one funnel could take her. Alerted, Warder saw the ship about one minute later, but soon after he and the lookouts lost the ship in the bad weather. Then suddenly out of the mist and violence of the storm an enemy ship appeared within 1,500 yards. Warder whacked the klaxon for a crash dive. The lookouts scrambled down the hatch and the Seawolf went to a depth of 100 feet narrowly missing the enemy over her own stern. The Japanese did not drop any depth charges. Either they did not see the Seawolf in the bad weather or they had no depth charges aboard.

The lack of aggressive Japanese counter measures during the seventh war patrol indicates just how far the Japanese had sunk after their first five months of nearly unbroken success beginning in December of 1941. Mindanao and certainly Davao Gulf, were important areas, yet the Japanese mounted the lamest counter submarine effort sending only small, slow, coal burning, ships, and the occasional airplane, to attempt rooting out the Seawolf. Compare that to the long and sustained counter attacks against the Seawolf just eight months past at Christmas Island.

The brave, lengthy, and largely unsupported stand of the Americans and Filipinos at Bataan and then Corregidor, helped deteriorate the Japanese military's capabilities in the Philippines and allowed the Americans time to get some organization to their military effort. Emperor Hirohito himself intervened and pressed his generals to finish off the Americans at Bataan quickly. The extra Japanese effort, while successful, helped wear down the Japanese and increased their casualties.[247] That stand by American and Filipino forces led directly to the battle at Coral Sea where in May Adm. Frank Fletcher's Task Force Seventeen, which included the carriers Lexington and Yorktown, turned back the Japanese sea invasion of Port Moresby. The defeat of the Japanese at Midway in June irreversibly crippled the Japanese fleet. The battle in the Solomon Islands, including the ferocious fighting on Guadalcanal, thoroughly sapped the strength of all of the Japanese services. While the fighting did not get easier, at least there were a myriad of signs, such as the Japanese not being able to put a maximum effort against the Seawolf in Davao Gulf, to indicate that the tide of war had turned. The forlorn defense of Bataan made those later successes possible.

After all of the excitement and success of the day Warder ordered a withdrawal to the southern approaches of Davao Gulf. He admitted that he needed a rest. After nearly 24 hours of continuous battle and two enemy ships sunk, the crew needed a rest as well. But for some in the crew there would be no rest. The bow plane-tilting panel needed repairs. The other usual areas also needed attention; the trim and drain pumps needed service, the drainpipe leaked and needed plugging, the main motor air cooler leaked, and one air conditioner was broken. Moreover, nearly everybody on the ship still had a headache.

When Seawolf arrived at a safe position just outside the gulf it was time to surface. Warder thought the headache epidemic had been caused by the too fast release of pressure upon surfacing earlier that evening. When Seawolf surfaced that night, the quartermaster Thompson (the usual man) opened the hatch at Warder's personal order. Thompson had a knack for equalizing the pressure just right. However, Warder's pain and understandable bad attitude toward the hatch situation caused him to kibitz the operation. He ordered the boat vented, the main engines on, and the low-pressure blower turned on, which is what usually occurred when the ship was on the surface and the hatch already open. Warder was taking no chances with his ears and was determined that the pressure hull would have no pressure in it when the hatch was finally opened.

Whether or not the quartermaster rolled his eyes at this series of instructions we don't really know. What we do know is that the hatch would not open; it didn't even budge. Warder had completely overdone it and far from pressure building up inside the submarine, all of the air was being sucked out creating a vacuum in the pressure hull. Under those conditions there was no way the quartermaster could open the hatch. Discretely the quartermaster ordered the engines and the low-pressure blower turned off. He also requested that the men in the control room give the interior of the ship a short blast of high-pressure air. The air pressure quickly equalized, and Thomson opened the hatch, ordered the engines back on, and the high-pressure blower turned on. Later Warder, possibly a little embarrassed, only cautioned against opening the hatch too fast. He never again hovered over this operation giving his unneeded advice. However, Warder made sure that anytime the hatch was to be opened, Hank Thompson would be the first man up the ladder to open it, exiling Jughead Casler to a distant part of the ship during that singular operation.

After repairs Seawolf headed towards Tarakan. Warder gave two reasons for this. First, he needed to send some radio transmissions back to headquarters reporting on his activities and intelligence gathering since October 7th. He wanted to make sure he had enough time on the surface to get the message off. Secondly, he knew that due to his planned lengthy radio transmission, the Japanese had a good chance of getting his position and even his direction. Warder wanted to take the Seawolf back into Davao Gulf in the morning and deceiving the Japanese into thinking he was headed away from the Gulf was a smart move.

Success

After completing those two tasks on November 4th and early 5th they submerged and headed again towards the Cape San Augustin on the eastern side of the Davao Gulf. As they went, the crew tuned into Tokyo Rose's radio program. After playing the usual selection of sentimental records, Glenn Miller, Bing Crosby, and Doris Day, Tokyo Rose reported an American submarine had been sunk around Davao Gulf. Peaking Warder's interest he commented, "I hope they meant us." Warder already knew his course and he wanted every advantage. If the Japanese reported sinking the Seawolf, maybe they believed it giving Warder an edge in the combat that would take place in just a few hours.

On the morning of the 7th Seawolf was back deep inside Davao Gulf just south of Samal Island. Warder liked this position. From there he could control both traffic routes inside the gulf. After six hours of patrolling on a north-south axis Warder found no shipping, but no enemy anti-submarine activity either. His Tarakan ruse seemed to have paid off. As he searched for the enemy Warder's balancing act between caution and boldness continued. He commented often about the dangerous glassy surface of the ocean, which made it too easy for the enemy to spot Seawolf from airplanes. At the same time he exposed twelve feet of periscope to better search for the enemy.

As the sun began to set Warder decided to clear Samal Island and proceed south. The island was described in intelligence reports and the pilot book as being, "sparsely inhabited." According to Warder the island, "is now well cleared, under cultivation and several houses appear on the bluffs." All good reasons to not be around when it was time to surface and recharge the batteries.[248]

As the nighttime of the 7th turned into the small hours of the 8th, the OOD Ensign Casler spotted a minesweeper coming at them at a range of about 3,000 yards. He ordered a crash dive and a depth of 100 feet. Due to the atrocious weather Warder was not sure the enemy saw them. He decided to play safe and patrol just outside of the gulf. An easier escape could be achieved from that position if it became necessary. As it so happened Warder noticed a small powerboat that started and stopped at regular intervals in the area. He suspected some kind of listening device being used against Seawolf.

Despite the elevated danger embodied by the Japanese boat actively hunting the Seawolf, Warder's attention was drawn to a nice 5,000-ton passenger freighter leaving Davao. He thought it might be the same one he spotted on November 3rd and called for battle stations. After a few days of low activity, it seemed a good way to start off the day. A small mine sweeper escorted the freighter out. The Japanese freighter zigged wildly with a minimum course change of 10° and a maximum of 60° never holding course for more than four minutes. The Japanese apparently did not believe their own false reports on the sinking of a submarine in the area.

As usual the men in the approach party sweated away in the conning tower as they worked through the difficult approach problems hour after hour. As with many protracted approaches the men ate at their posts, and either Gus Wright, the ship's cook, or one of the ship's stewards made the rounds with trays of sandwiches and steaming cups of coffee. In the conning tower the men tended to not eat, but coffee flowed liberally. One might wonder whether drinking hot coffee in an environment typically over 95° F with about 96% humidity, could be pleasant. It might be proof that people can get used to, or at least put up with just about anything, just to have a cup of joe.

After quite some time the approach team finally worked Seawolf into a, "fair position if he'd zig a little," in Warder's words.[249]

The freighter's course proved to be too erratic though. Just two minutes later the ship closed from 1,550 yards to 0 yards. In such a situation one must be flexible. First Warder needed to protect the Seawolf, so he ordered 120 feet to let the ship pass overhead. Seawolf continued at standard speed to open up the range for a stern tube shot.

"But then the target turned left and came up my port side and crossed our bow very close abroad. He was a tough ship to lose," Warder's calm tone belying some of his frustration.

After an additional hour of what amounted to blind man's bluff, the crew of the Seawolf finally mounted an attack. A spread of two Mark XIV torpedoes left Seawolf's bow torpedo tubes with a shallow depth setting of just four feet. With a little luck just maybe they wouldn't pass under the targeted ship. After a running time of just about 30 seconds, the range being a very close 800 yards, the first torpedo detonated next to the boiler room of the ship. A few seconds later the second torpedo hit the bow and detonated perfectly. Warder could see steam billowing out of the smokestack and the uptakes at the base of the stack. The ship looked bent in the middle and the forward gun had been blown right off the ship. In spite of the obvious damage, the enemy ship did not sink.

Then the Japanese "Went to work on us," in Warder's words. They fired their remaining gun, located at the stern of their ship, at Seawolf. From all the small splashes around Warder supposed the shells to be shrapnel. That was a good piece of intelligence. Were the Japanese already running low on high explosive and armor piercing shells? Less than a minute later the Japanese crew brought a .20mm machine gun into action, probably an anti-aircraft weapon.

Success

As the tenor of the battle increased Warder noted that the Japanese moved calmly around their ship with no panic. Their white clothes indicated they were probably in the regular navy and not just merchant marine. While some members of the enemy crew continued to fire at Seawolf, others began to clear the lifeboats from the ship and throw floating material overboard. Other than that, the Japanese showed little inclination to abandon their ship. Their damage control appeared to be quite successful.

Because the enemy ship refused to sink, Warder ordered the helmsman Gervais, to swing Seawolf around for a stern tube attack where they had one last Mark IX torpedo. Seventeen minutes had elapsed since Seawolf launched her first attack against the freighter. The approach party worked the new set of problems. A few minutes later when everything was set Warder gave the command to fire. As usual Brengelman hit the plunger just as Thompson repeated the order to the torpedo room. A second later the last Mark IX torpedo left the Seawolf and headed for the stationary enemy ship. Casler had calculated a running time of about 50 seconds, another short-range shot. Warder watched the torpedo head for the ship. The Japanese sailors on the freighter also saw the torpedo. Most of them headed for the upper works of the superstructure.

While Warder watched the torpedo, Eckberg, in the radio shack, heard the sound of a ship heading their way. Warder swung the periscope to take a look. A minesweeper, possibly loaded with depth charges, chugged towards Seawolf. Tension mounted, as everybody knew, the attacker would soon be attacked.

Warder switched the periscope back to the freighter. About 55 seconds after firing, the lone torpedo detonated with extreme violence. Water, smoke and spray, flew up in a huge geyser over twice the size of the Japanese ship. A flash of fire fantastically illuminated the daytime scene. When the smoke and mist cleared, the ship was gone. All that remained in the area was an empty troop landing barge and a small whaleboat with about 12 men in it. The few Japanese in the whaleboat must have launched it from the port side and manned it shortly after the initial torpedo attack. Warder looked for the minesweeper. It was still over four miles away so Warder lingered another minute to further inspect the debris. Then, just as he was about to leave, a titanic and sustained explosion moved throughout the ocean. Warder theorized that the ship must have been carrying munitions of some kind, which finally exploded under water.

A distracted Warder, fascinated by the incredible destruction, had to refocus and affect an escape. He ordered Seawolf to a depth of 120 feet as he anticipated trouble from the air as well as from the minesweeper bearing down on Seawolf. The Sweeper made it's first run against the Seawolf about 19 minutes after the freighter sank. Two depth charges missed badly. Then another dropped but it too missed. The crew of the Seawolf, now at depth charge stations, sweated while they waited for the next one. It dropped off far astern. Eckberg, at the sound equipment, reported just one ship making runs. Then another charge exploded in the distance. The screws of the enemy faded away along with the cavitation sounds they made.

Seawolf surfaced that night. The hatches opened and the stale, carbon dioxide poisoned air inside the submarine rushed out, to be replaced by fresh oxygenated air. As the lookouts went to their positions on top of the conning tower, they soon spotted Cape San Augustine about 14 miles in the distance. The Seawolf crew looked back on two exhausting but extremely good days worth of work, depriving the enemy of bullets and guns destined to be used against their fellow Americans. They had survived to surface again and to breath the fresh night air. How much longer would their skill and luck hold? Nobody knew, but they went forward with confidence of more days like these to come.

From Davao the Seawolf turned to the east and headed for Palau. To make better time Seawolf traveled on the surface until just a little after the noon time hour. Lt. Holden (OOD) standing on the bridge spotted a floatplane. He slammed the klaxon, and a crash dive began, not stopping until Seawolf reached the fairly safe depth of 120 feet. Warder was fit to be tied. Not at Lt. Holden, who did his job as lookout and OOD perfectly, but rather at the lousy radar, which did not detect the plane. Five and a half hours later Seawolf surfaced. As the lookouts, including Warder, climbed onto the bridge a reminder went out, do not depend on the radar or any other equipment on the Seawolf.

As it turned out the malfunctioning radar was the least of their worries. The real problem for the crew continued to be the Seawolf in general. The ship was simply worn out and a new serious problem came up. Edward Mocarsky, one of the excellent electricians on the Seawolf who everybody new as "Pop," (apparently the nickname "Pop" applied to anyone over the age of thirty-five in a submarine), found the main generator cables had deteriorated and were heating up to an unsafe level. Warder immediately shifted propulsion to the batteries and cut out the No. 2 generator. After stripping back, the insulation around the cables it was plain that they were very moist with much verdigris between the copper and the adjacent insulating layer. After cleaning the cables, they attempted fixing them using 3 layers of phenolic tape, 2 layers of varnished cambric, a layer of linen, and then they covered the whole area with glyptal. Despite this effort the cable remained a problem for the rest of the patrol.

Notwithstanding the cable problems, Seawolf arrived safely at Palau on November 11, at about 6:00 am. That is the anniversary of the armistice ending the last Great War. There were no celebrations, after all that was the war to end all wars. The crew could only hope that this would be the last Great War.

Seawolf continued her voyage and headed for the Toagel Mlungui pass. After that Warder intended to turn north and head for Yap. He sighted some smoke but even after exposing 12 feet of periscope he found no ship. As Warder continued to look through the periscope, he noticed a nice lighthouse off of Palau and attempted to snap a picture, but every time they set up the picture it started raining, ruining the shot. If not for his choosing to be a professional sailor, Fred Warder probably would have made a great photographer.

While the men in the conning tower fiddled with the camera, Eckberg, down in the radio shack with the sound equipment, heard a ship coming at them. Warder looked through the periscope and found a small patrol vessel headed for them. He saw this unimpressive boat a few hours earlier and decided to do nothing about it at the time. As it zeroed in for an attack against Seawolf Warder continued to be unimpressed. He did not call the Seawolf crew to depth charge quarters and did not order any depth lower than periscope depth, about 63 feet. The enemy patrol vessel dropped one depth charge that hardly registered a yawn from the Seawolf crew.

About a minute later Warder ordered, "Up periscope," to take another look. The little thing was about 4,000 yards away. Two minutes after that he took another look around and found two enemy destroyers. He ordered battle stations, the alarm sounded (bong, bong, bong…), and the men scurried to their positions. Who had been watching whom?

Or maybe the Japanese were oblivious to the Seawolf's position. Warder started to think that the probability of the Japanese having two destroyers randomly in the area quite remote. There must be a reason. Then appearing out of the grey weather, almost as if scripted in a movie, Warder sighted an enemy aircraft carrier at a range of just 3,600 yards. His hunch had been right; those two destroyers were escorting the carrier. He ordered full speed attempting to close to a respectable range. Running submerged the Seawolf could not keep up with the great ship. This best illustrates the ambush nature of the World War II era submarine. If a Submarine happened to find a fast military ship steaming on the open ocean, the submarine had to necessarily be in a good firing position from the beginning since the submarine had no chance of staying with a fast surface ship.

It took just seven minutes for the Japanese aircraft carrier to stretch the range to 6,000 yards. Another five minutes put it at 9,000 yards distant with Warder, "trying to hang on," in his sad description of the one-sided race. The engineers in the motor room were also trying to hang on because all that chasing caused main generator cables heat up making the crew very nervous.

Fourteen minutes later Warder reported the carrier, "About out of sight."

He ordered Seawolf to the surface in a last desperate attempt to get at the ship. All four of Seawolf's huge diesel engines were put to the task and her speed increased to 17.5 knots. They sighted one of the escorting destroyers. However, it was the worn-out cables that raised most of Warder's anxiety, not to mention the reef that, "Juts out to south and west," in his words.

The truth is that the bad weather caused the men on the bridge to lose sight of land, let alone the stars or any other navigational help, which caused a dangerous situation around the reef. Warder took two engines off propulsion to do a "quick charge." While he did that, he ordered a communication to headquarters' relaying the position of the enemy carrier. Maybe one of his fellow skippers, most likely Kenneth Hurd of *Seal*, who Warder knew followed behind by about a day, would be in a better position to ambush it. That was a good idea except that they could not raise NPM with their radio and get the message through. What else could go wrong?

Warder had the cables checked again remembering that a few months early the Searaven, under the command of Hiram Cassidy, had caught fire in a similar situation. After considering his previous cable failures in August, Warder, "decided to call the whole thing off and head for Pearl." That was a good idea and he transmitted as much over VIXO. It was about that time that he heard the repeat of his NPM message to Seal concerning the Japanese carrier, *only 7 hours and 35 minutes after he sent it.* He should have gotten that message back within minutes. That really fried Warder. His ship was falling apart while a prime target in the aircraft carrier got away from him, and the rest of the fleet, because of a communication snafu.

While Seawolf steamed toward Pearl Harbor, Warder ordered a small portable cooling fan aimed at the ruined main generator cables hoping to reduce their temperature. During the passage from Palau to Yap Warder checked the cables several times and determined that the cable performance improved enough to warrant a three-day patrol at Yap. This once again demonstrated Warder's "never-say-die" attitude and his complete

Success

determination to keep Seawolf in the war, which happened by his will alone at times. Warder's success at rigging up yet another repair on the Seawolf caused another problem; he had been scheduled to be at Yap on the 15th, and 16th, but because of his early abandonment of Palau Seawolf would be arriving at Yap a day early on the 14th. To further complicate the schedule Warder had already radioed that he was going straight to Pearl Harbor because of all his mechanical problems. With all the malfunctions, he could not even be sure that any of his radio messages had gotten through.

In the end Warder put all these cares aside and Seawolf arrived in front of Yap's main harbor, Tomil, on the morning of the 14th and began to patrol. While there the crew snapped a few pictures and saw a small schooner in the harbor. The next day it was gone. Warder did note a large radio antenna and some structural concrete reinforcement on top of one of the hills. That was the sum total of that.

Seawolf left Yap and headed for Pearl Harbor, but just two days into the final voyage home Warder spotted a large freighter and gave chase. Looking around at the choppy white capped seas adorned by many rainsqualls, Warder thought the concealing weather allowed Seawolf to stay surfaced, enhancing his chances of tracking down the freighter. The approach team was called to the conning tower and started some preliminary work. In addition to the usual routine, the quartermaster, Hank Thomson, kept in close touch with the men in the motor room. Warder wanted constant information on the main generator cables.

Warder's plan began to work a little too well. After about twenty minutes it appeared he had closed too fast on the enemy, so he changed course to 260° to put his stern on the target and open the range a little. Nine minutes later the lookouts on the shears could only see the tops of the enemy masts. Due to the bad weather Warder had miscalculated the direction. He ordered Seawolf back to a course of 160°. But soon after changing course it looked like Seawolf again closed on the enemy too fast. Apparently, the Japanese ship moved so slowly the approach team incorrectly gauged its exact speed and direction. Warder ordered a course change to 175° T, now guessing the enemy moving at just 11 knots with a base course of 162°T.

The men in the conning tower could feel the tension rising as they went through their final calculations. Their coffee cups lay around on various surfaces neglected. Warder's usually soft voice increased slightly in volume, a tip-off that they were getting close. Then from nowhere a plane appeared. Warder shouted, "Dive." The klaxon was hit (Ahoooga, ahooga), the two lookouts standing on the shears jumped to the deck and down the hatch, followed closely by Warder and the two other lookouts. The last man down grabbed the lanyard, and the quartermaster spun the locking wheel.

They escaped detection by the plane and Warder quickly switched his immediate area of concern to the generators: No. 1 read 250,000 ohms, and No. 2 read 200,000 ohms. No cause for concern just yet. While submerged Warder kept a close eye on that plane, checking it about every two minutes. He must have really wanted to bag another freighter on this last voyage home because he exposed 7 feet of his periscope on his next observation and 12 feet after that, all with a plane flying within ten miles of Seawolf. He did finally see the topmasts of the freighter and noticed the enemy plane, circling overhead protecting it. At this point Warder realized that unless the freighter radically zigged, he had no chance of catching it. He ordered 90 feet and set, "A normal approach coarse," in the general direction of the enemy. Having lost sight of the plane and the ship Seawolf surfaced at about 5:18 just as the gloam set in.

When the sun rose on the 19th of November, instead of diving as usual during daylight operations, Warder kept Seawolf on the surface. At about 7:00 am he spotted the mast of a ship and pursued it, "bending on all 4 main engines at 80% power, just keeping the tops in sight."[250]

It would take some luck to overcome that ship. Then a tanker suddenly came into view about fifteen miles away. Warder switched his attention to it being a more valuable target. It took the approach team about an hour and a half to establish an estimated course for the tanker. As Seawolf continued the chase the voltmeter readings on the ground detector at the main generator cables climbed steadily. What a completely imperfect time for the daily breakdown to occur.

"Tanker now bearing 047°T and situation obviously hopeless so decided to drop back and take second ship," was Warder's sanguine backup plan.

After only two hours of operation the No. 1 generator had dropped from 1.5 mega ohms to 100,000 ohms and No.2 from 0.7 mega ohms to just 40,000. The mechanical situation was getting out of hand.

Still, something in Warder just could not let go. Two hours later he again sighted some smoke and changed course to investigate. At 11:30 am Seawolf closed in on what appeared to be the original target in the chase. Warder ordered Seawolf submerged. The diving officer ordered the ballast tanks filled, the diving planes depressed to about 1°, and the submarine again glided down beneath the surface of the ocean.

Steady progress over the next two hours brought Seawolf to within 2,000 yards of the not spectacular 3,500-ton Japanese coal-burning freighter. After he closed the range Warder discovered eight Sampan fishing boats in a

Success

small group with the freighter shifting from side to side "patrolling." This was really one for the books. As Rudy Gervais guided the Seawolf through the water Warder commented, "It's a miracle we didn't get tangled up in the trolling lines or nets. We were in a spectacular school of fish. Sea was rough and swells were deep. Observations were difficult. We finally threaded through the sampans."

With the range down to a nearly perfect 1,700 yards Warder ordered a two-torpedo spread fired from the bow torpedo room. Both missed. Warder surmised the cause; he thought he miscalculated the length of the enemy ship by 40 feet, and after the torpedoes were fired the enemy ship slowed considerably causing the torpedoes to run by in front of the ship. Dodging around those Sampans didn't help either.

If nothing else the Japanese showed some pluck in this case. That old broken-down coal burning ship (moving at about 7 knots), turned, came after the Seawolf, and dropped four depth charges. They also had two guns on the deck of the ship both were dutifully, if not quickly, manned. They did not fire a shot.

Warder decided he "Did not want to play with this outfit of not much worth, either on the surface or submerged in the moonlight." The cables continued to be a problem and fuel on the Seawolf was getting low. Warder ordered that a course for Pearl Harbor be held. Their action on the seventh war patrol had ended.

Chapter – 14
Last Patrol

After the action at Davao Gulf, Seawolf needed to be completely overhauled. The long time at sea, repeated depth charging, initial faulty equipment installations, and the corrosive effects of the saltwater environment all conspired to ruin the ship. The men had been at sea a long time surviving seven war patrols one of which lasted nearly two months; they were all worn out physically and emotionally. When the ship docked, the crewmen unloaded their seabags and exchanged their berths with the relief crew who would begin the process of overhauling the ship. The officers and men went to the Royal Hawaiian Hotel where they relaxed, ate fresh food, exercised, swam, and soaked up the sun on Waikiki Beach. Combat proved so exhausting for some of those sailors that their first two or three days in port might be entirely spent in sleep.

When Fred Warder got off the Seawolf he went and spoke with Admiral Lockwood. After filing his reports, he received his orders for leave, acquired the necessary transportation, and left for Baltimore. Fred arrived in late November 1942 to a tearful and happy reunion with Mary and their four children. The homecoming was tremendous. It is those first moments of reuniting that make such great and enduring pictures. The hugs, kisses, and tears were all fueled by the desperately long periods of separation causing an emotional outpouring impossible to contain. Soon after the initial embraces though, most returning servicemen, their wives, and their children entered into a period of confusion. In the case of Fred Warder, he came home to a home he had never seen before. Fred liked to garden, but there was no shovel to turn dirt with because there was no garden. How he would have liked to come home and sit in his favorite chair, but he did not even have one. His home consisted only of his wife and four children, but even they had changed dramatically in the last two years since Fred last saw them. And what was the family's impression of Fred? Being away for so long required that they also had to adjust to an entirely new person when he returned. The pressures of leadership had made Fred more serious. Combat had etched grimness into his face, which was reinforced by a personality sterner in character. Time changes people; war changes them more.

Last Patrol

After a weekend at the Deepdene house, Fred and Mary arranged for Bessie to stay with the children for a few days while they went away to visit friends and relatives. The two also wanted to have some time to be alone together. The four children did not understand that very well. They had waited all that time, written all those letters, struggled with jarring changes for two years only to be left alone again at the drop of a hat without any explanation. After several days the two fugitives reappeared. Fred's leave continued with all of the trappings of happy family life: home cooked meals, a few nights at the movie theater, tossing a football with Fred Jr., and listening to the radio together in the evenings. It was autumn and in the eastern United States that means leaves on the ground. Although Fred had no garden, he could rake leaves. He raked and he raked, putting the leaves into piles and then burned them such as was the custom at the time. Maybe he thought it would help him relax or give him some semblance of home doing a few traditional chores around "the house." For married military men and their family's, leave was often this way; they came from places where they were performing deeds of great valor amongst incredible danger and living a life of great and immediate purpose, then went to "home" where they were to drop everything and be civilians for a short period of time.

Fred and his family were not the only people that felt some discomfort during leave periods. Fred's good friend Wreford "Moon" Chapple wrote to Fred about a leave period where everything went wrong from transportation, to mixed up orders, and even an unexplained illness that landed both Chapple and his wife Grace, whom he had not seen for two years, in the hospital. Chapple poured out his frustration to Fred who understood perfectly how reunions of people who are desperately in love with each other sometimes do not work out as planned. Fred tried to console his friend,

> I appreciate exactly how you and Grace feel. All my leaves have been exactly the same way, involved with too much travel and family difficulties, and I found the leave periods more or less of a strain. Tell Grace to keep her chin up – Mary has been though more or less of the same thing from time to time, but everything always comes out all right.[251]

One additional problem arose during leave periods and readjustment from combat to civilian life; men like Warder and Chappel gave orders that that other men followed without argument. Families rarely operate that way, and women almost never do. Going from a situation where an order was followed quickly with a "Yes sir," to giving suggestions or bargaining with a seven year old or an adult with thoughts of her own, or trying to give an order and have it not followed, was quite a shock to many officers on leave. Everybody had to try and blend into the new social order; some could do this with just a little strain others could not accomplish it at all.

For all of that, Mary and the children – and Fred – enjoyed his leave period and were extremely sad to see him go, for how long nobody knew. Fred had desired to get a shore command near Baltimore, but the more he thought about it the more he realized his place was out in the Pacific fighting the Japanese. Mary understood perfectly and agreed. She had always been Fred's biggest supporter and confidant when it came to his career. Mary was the one that facilitated the moves, and kept things together in the Philippines, China, Panama, and now Baltimore. Mary was the kind of woman who married a man to be with the man, not to change him. Her commitment to Fred was as great as Fred's commitment to the Navy and the country, but their relationship was not one sided. He did "forsake all others" and put every once of his mind and muscle into the Navy career that meant so much to both he and Mary.[252]

*   *   *

After Fred left Baltimore, things quickly settled into the routine established before Fred's leave. After school the children in the neighborhood would gather for a game of baseball or kickball played in their front yards. Many times, as the children played, the adults also gathered to talk while enjoying a cigarette. Often the women brought their rationing books and cards and gave to each other what they did not need, while receiving extra coupons that they were short of.

While the country coped with the rationing and blackouts, Fred received orders directing him to his next assignment as a perspective division commander at Pearl Harbor. Just as he was leaving for Oahu Adm. Lockwood ordered him up to Portsmouth, New Hampshire where some important torpedo research was being conducted. Lockwood needed somebody he trusted who had a lot of experience with torpedoes to report to him personally about progress on the problem. Fred fulfilled both prerequisites and spent a few weeks helping the other engineers at the navy yard there solve some problems with torpedoes. That was Fred's first return to that city since helping build the Seawolf four years before. Four years did not seem so long ago in one sense, however so many experiences had been compressed into that short period that it could have been several lifetimes ago that Fred last walked upon those docks. In 1938 the Navy counted itself lucky if they received five new submarines a year whereas in 1943 twelve submarines were being completed each month at Portsmouth alone.

His work in the east completed, Fred reported to Pearl Harbor where he joined Lockwood's staff as a Prospective Division Commander preparing to take over as a Division Commander. Warder's time as a Prospective Division Commander came to a sudden halt when the commander of division 122 suddenly left Pearl Harbor due to a death in the family. Warder immediately assumed command and flew his flag from the U.S.S. Jack. Among the ships in his division were: Hake, Flasher, Snook, Jack, and Harder. These would all become successful and even famous ships, each making the top 25 list in terms of enemy ships sunk, while under the overall command of Fred Warder.

Fred worked and trained his crews and ships constantly. When a ship went out on war patrol, usually about 1/3 of its crewmembers were completely inexperienced in submarines and combat, magnifying the pressure and importance of creating meaningful training. Fred preferred a hands-on approach to training and went out to sea many times during training periods giving personal guidance to commanders and enlisted men alike. Warder was so energetic that Adm. Lockwood's Chief of Training and Commander of Squadron four, John "Babe" Brown, sent a personal note to Warder's direct superior reporting on what a wonderful job he was doing.

It did not take much coaxing to get Warder out to sea on a submarine. He wrote Mary,

> I have been kept fairly busy of late – riding the ships a great deal – Our old ship [Seawolf], my first love, is still doing a great job. I am going to arrange it for him [Royce Gross the current CO] to take some leave here soon and let me borrow her back for a trip.[253]

Most former COs wanted to get back into a submarine and reenter the fight, but "barrowing" a submarine was just wishful thinking on Warder's part. But as luck might have it, Lockwood was becoming dissatisfied with combat results in late 1943, which gave Warder a chance to get back into combat.

Adm. Lockwood could see that the tactics of the Japanese were changing as far as defending their merchant shipping due to large losses inflicted by American submarines. The Japanese started to convoy their merchant ships, which proved to be effective in lowering their losses to submarines. To counter those tactics Lockwood decided to experiment with groupings of submarines called "attack groups" to overcome the Japanese convoys. Three submarines would go out together under the command of the division commander who would coordinate attacks against enemy convoys. The first such "attack group" consisted of Shad (CO – MacGregor), Cero (CO – White), and Greyback (CO – Moore) with Swede Momsen in overall command. This first attack group sank three ships. Lockwood labeled the effort a compete success while the three COs on the spot thought the effort was completely unsuccessful.

Despite that opinion Lockwood forged ahead and tapped Warder to lead a second attack group. Warder jumped at the chance and thanked his good fortune for getting him back into combat. Harder (CO – Dealey), Snook (CO – Triebel), and Pargo (CO – Eddy) made up the group with Warder commanding from Pargo.[254]

They sailed out of Pearl Harbor on October 30 and got to Midway Island about four days later, topping up on fuel and provisions. The final patrol area was to be west of the Gilbert Islands hoping to intercept any Japanese shipping going to Tarawa where the U.S. Marines were planning an invasion in late November. On the way out to the Gilberts the supercharger hood broke on Pargo's #2 engine and put it out of commission. The equipment jinx continued when the teeth on Harder's blower drive gear ground off putting its #4 engine out of commission. Warder must have thought about all the bandages he had put on the Seawolf while on war patrol in that ship. Despite the problems the three ships pressed on.[255]

The patrol started calmly with no enemy contacts until November 12th. At about 2:20 pm on that day Sam Dealey on Harder sighted an enemy ship he thought to be a freighter. He sent out a contact report over the radio. Five seconds later he received a contact report from Ian Eddy on Pargo indicating that the two men spotted the enemy ship almost simultaneously. Pargo moved in to attack what turned out to be a small freighter and an escort. Just as Pargo closed to set up an attack against the Japanese ships, he heard four violent explosions. "Sounds as if the Harder beat us to it," was Eddy's disappointed comment in his war patrol report. Dealey described the attack this way,

> Fired 3 torpedoes from the bow tubes with 2 degree divergent spread and 8 foot depth setting. Range 750 yards, track angle 80, gyros near zero. Twenty-seven seconds after the first shot #1 torpedo struck the target just aft of the stack and a few seconds later #2 was seen to hit just forward of the stack. The destructive effect of those 2 hits was the most instantaneous and complete yet witnessed on three war patrols. The target broke in the middle, the stern port went down, tail high, in less than 10 seconds, and the remainder of the

ship seemed to disintegrate – large and small parts of it were hurled high into the air.

That was quite a show. When Pargo put up its periscope Eddy saw absolutely nothing, as if the ships had vaporized. Eddy was happy that Dealey defeated the enemy, but the COs of the U.S. Submarines competed with each other keeping track of damage done to the enemy and to a certain extent glorying in the success of their own ships. The competitive spirit probably helped morale to a certain extent and kept the COs aggressive, but because of the quasi-competition one can understand Eddy's mixed emotions after setting up a perfect shot and then seeing his target blow up before he could get a shot in. For these reasons the submarine COs did not necessarily like to operate in attack groups and definitely did not like having senior officers aboard their ships, as was demonstrated by Warder when he had to take Lockwood to Australia during the early months of the war. Now Warder was the senior officer on board somebody else's ship. Did he mind his manners? All indications say that he did. As for Snook, during that action on the 12th, an enemy plane had forced it down. This was definite evidence that the attack group idea worked because while poor Snook drew off the Japanese counter-submarine measures, Harder moved in for the kill increasing Dealey's score, something he cherished.[256]

After the attack Harder dove deep to evade the inevitable depth charge counterattack from the Japanese. As Harder passed a depth of 100 feet the crew heard two depth charges explode very close. When Harder got to a depth of 250 feet they heard another very loud explosion, then nothing. About 30 minutes later Harder came to periscope depth and saw the escort vessel that had been trying to sink her. Dealey reported that the escort was dead in the water with its starboard section completely blown off and the crowsnest on the ship dangled by a single cable like a damaged appendage. Evidently one of the depth charges on the Japanese ship exploded while still on the ship, ripping it apart. What perfect luck for Harder's crew! An hour later after the sun went down Harder alerted his men for battle surface against the disabled escort ship. As Harder broke the surface of the ocean the crew raced to their weapons and sprayed 20 mm shells at the topsides of what remained of the enemy to subdue any fire that might come from that vessel. While that happened the 3-inch gun crew put 21 rounds into the badly damaged ship. Finally, the target burst into flames and sank.

After the initial attack the frustrated Eddy on Pargo surfaced and found another potential target on its radar. After pursuing the target for about an hour Eddy finally figured out that it was Harder that he was tracking. Eddy must have been a little red faced having to give Warder that tidbit of information. However, Fred Warder was nothing if not reassuring to the men he commanded and probably soothed him with a few stories of how Seawolf once tracked seagull for a few hours and on another occasion a sunken yacht, not to mention a few clouds and several islands from time to time. With the submarines operating in a group though, the danger of misidentifying objects at sea became much more significant.

After that action the group moved to the Marianas Island chain. Warder ordered that each ship set independent courses because the route would take them within easy flying range of enemy planes. He did not want one plane to be able to keep all three submarines down in the event that they were spotted. While on the way, Pargo detected a target with its radar. As they positioned for an attack Warder noticed that the target was emitting radar itself and the signal looked strangely like the old SJ radar signal used on older U.S. Submarines. Warder checked the schedules and theorized that the ship they encountered was not an enemy ship but rather the U.S.S. Scorpion, which was supposed to be in that area at that time. Warder noted that this would have been a good time to have an IFF (Identification Friend of Foe) radio system in place on all U.S. submarines and airplanes.

Once the attack group reached the Marianas the three ships formed a patrol line spaced at 20 miles apart. It took nearly another week before the group made any meaningful contact with enemy shipping, but on November 19 Snook and Pargo found a five-ship convoy. Once again poor communications caused Harder to miss Pargo's contact report. Strangely Harder was able to transmit a contact report at the same time about the same convoy to Snook. Things got more tangled as 30 minutes later Harder sent to Snook the true bearing of the enemy convoy, which Triebel on board Snook characterized as, "Worthless as we did not know Harder's movement during the last three hours."[257] That was not Harder's fault though. The Japanese were busy jamming the frequency to prevent communications by anything in the area.

Then the soundman on Pargo detected three explosions that were interpreted as depth charges but were in fact three torpedo hits from Harder on the convoy that they both were tracking. Why the soundman misinterpreted the explosions is hard to explain since a depth charge gives off a distinctive "click" just before it explodes. In the melee Harder achieved seven more hits on two more freighters. Triebel on Snook was completely flummoxed thinking that Pargo was taking the shots when in fact it was Harder. Triebel was very angry writing,

Heard depth charges or torpedo explosions all morning. This was the most frustrated I have ever felt. On the surface at full speed, hearing explosions, and we couldn't make contact.[258]

Triebel sent an annoyed message to Warder on Pargo asking that contact reports be accompanied with a position report of the ship making the contact as he, Triebel, had been "chasing the moon" because of Harder's report.[259] Warder tried to calmly clear the air,

> No possibility of ambiguity [concerning the position of the convoy] was apparent to me at the time as Pargo was on assigned station at the time of originating two letter contact. We learned afterwards that Harder had sent a contact at about 0200 on Empire [Japanese home islands] bound convoy which had been received by Snook but not by Pargo and that Snook had first chased this Harder contact and was properly non-pulsed by Pargo's "two letter" bearing and distance signal and "two letter" target and course signal at 0507 and 0530. Decided in the future to use aircraft code.[260]

This, frankly, is what is termed the "fog of war." Even after sixty years the events are confusing to follow. In the heat of battle the CO's had to make decisions based on assumptions, not good solid facts. Those men wanted to make a meaningful contribution to defeating the Japanese and the mess-ups with communications really unnerved them. However, the world often works in a balance and Triebel's frustration contrasted decidedly with Dealey's elation aboard Harder,

> This had been a dream come true. The Harder was in the middle of an enemy convoy and I felt like a 'possum in a hen house.[261]

Dealey expended the last of his torpedoes during this action and left for Pearl Harbor while Pargo and Snook headed for a new patrol area. After several days of fruitless searches Snook finally got a chance at redemption on the night of November 28th. Pargo made contact with the enemy and Snook quickly homed in on Pargo's radar to get moving in the direction of the enemy convoy. Triebel was extremely motivated writing,

> Made radar contact 4 miles on Pargo. This was done intentionally coming in on their radar sweep. I believed they knew where the

convoy was and didn't want to get left chasing my own shadow 10 miles on a flank again.[262]

At about 8:00 pm Snook made visual contact with the convoy and joined Pargo on the port flank but then moved to the starboard, but Pargo had already moved there. Once Snook found out Pargo's new position, she went back to the port flank. The earlier confusion was back, hopefully it would not play a role in this new attack.

Snook moved in to attack the convoy and set up and easy shot, but as they moved in the lookouts on Snook thought they saw Pargo in the way.

Snook pulled back figuring that Pargo would take the shot. After about an hour of hearing nothing, Snook moved in again to take a shot at the enemy ship. But just as Snook was about to shoot a lookout once again shouted that he saw a submarine, which could only be Pargo. Again, Snook's attack was called off. This time Triebel pulled out of the area for about three hours. Again, they heard no action from Pargo so they reasoned that the small ship that kept getting in their way was not Pargo. Triebel decided if that little ship were in his way again, he would blow him out of the water.[263]

Finally, Snook moved in for another try at the tanker. Just as he got him in his sights the men on the bridge of the Snook saw a large explosion in the middle of the convoy. Pargo had struck. Triebel now reasoned that the little ship that had caused them so many problems was indeed a small escort and not the Pargo. Snook fired six torpedoes into the main group of the convoy. As luck might have it, they got only one hit and that was on the ship that Pargo had just hit. Triebel ordered Snook to turn, and he fired his four stern torpedoes into the convoy and got one hit. At that exact moment though, they lost radar contact with Pargo. After all that had Snook destroyed Pargo? Was Fred Warder, Ian Eddy, and the entire crew of Pargo killed by an errant shot from Snook? It seemed impossible that Fred Warder, after such a great career, would be dead by a shot from a submarine under his overall command.

Triebel was concerned to say the least, but this was war and he had to carry on with the attack despite what he might think about Pargo. He shook off any doubts and moved in to attack the remaining ships of the convoy. Just after midnight he let go four torpedoes against the remaining tankers. Many explosions and flame lit the sky in a pyrotechnic show that nearly blinded the men on the bridge. After the initial flash and fireball, debris rained down upon the ocean – no survivors could be seen.

Quickly Snook's front six torpedo tubes had already been reloaded as they got back in amongst the convoy. Snook turned and fired another full six-torpedo salvo and got four hits on one ship, which instantly disintegrated. A small escort vessel came out to do battle with Snook, but when Snook brought its stern torpedoes to bear and took two shots at the little Japanese ship, it ran off. Far from being intimidated by the Japanese anti-submarine ship, Snook turned and gave chase. That must have been quite a shock to the Japanese crew – the Americans had become very bold and relentless in their attacks since the first frustrating moments of the war.

Just then, Snook was rocked violently by a massive explosion. The crew on the bridge held on for dear life as they were nearly tossed into the sea. About 5,000 yards away a colossal fireball went into the sky exploding so violently that the men on Snook theorized that the ship must have been a tanker carrying high-octane aviation fuel. The men on Snook also figured that the Japanese tanker must have been sunk by Pargo indicating that their friends were still alive. Just at that moment, and much to the relief of Triebel, Snook's radar found Pargo confirming that Fred Warder was still alive. It had been a good night's work with a few of the enemy sunk, but more importantly both Snook and Pargo survived despite the once again poor communications. After this second effort of "coordinated" attacks it was obvious to everyone that communications had to be fixed for attack groups to achieve maximum effectiveness.

Despite those problems the attack group sank seven enemy ships, three were credited to Harder and two each to Snook and Pargo. Lockwood thought that the patrol was a complete success while Warder wrote that, "It is regretted that greater damage was not inflicted [on the enemy]." Warder also noted that the presence of three American submarines seemed to confuse to a certain degree anti-submarine operations of the Japanese. He praised each of the commanding officers and their crews for all of the hard work stating that it had been a great pleasure to work with them.

* * *

When Warder returned to Pearl Harbor aboard the Pargo he was confronted with another severe problem. The office of the State Tax Commissioner of West Virginia had gone through his files and discovered that Fred Warder had not filed a tax return in 1939 with the State of West Virginia. The commissioner truly wanted to be helpful and included a form with his form letter for Fred Warder to fill out and return with payment of taxes. It was a good thing that the tax commissioner was nearly six thousand miles away when Fred received the impertinent and incorrect letter. Warder answered the commissioner,

> This is to inform you that I have not resided in West Virginia since I was seventeen years old; that I own no property in West Virginia, that I have received none of my income from West Virginia sources, and that my total connection with the State is the fact that my mother resides in Grafton. In accordance with the foregoing, I am not returning the return, which you forwarded to me.[264]

Then Fred got another cold slap in the face when he found out that his insurance company had cancelled his life insurance policy *retroactively* because of his combat duty. Mary thought that was understandable to a certain extent, but it really burned Fred up. He reasoned that he had been dutifully sending in his premium payments while unbeknownst to him, he actually no longer had insurance. Even in wartime America looking out for number one never went out of fashion. Even a war hero and minor celebrity like Fred Warder got the shaft from time to time. The company, National Life Insurance Company located in Montpelier, Vermont, did write and say that they would return his premium payments to him. That did not mollify Fred and had him longing for the days when he was at sea and only had to contend with the Japanese.[265]

* * *

Like his leaky submarine during the first year of the war, Fred Warder, as with all of the Warder's, were busy putting patches on the leaks in their lives. The latest disaster came to Mary and the family back in Baltimore. Mary's landlord at the Deepdene house decided he wanted it back and gave her notice to leave the place. Mary of course was disappointed. She had high hopes for staying at that one house for the "duration" and now those hopes were completely dashed. Mary thought of moving to Hawaii, but the cost would have been prohibitive and taking the children to an active war zone did not seem like the best idea to her. Her next idea was San Francisco. That made a lot of sense as Fred would be only a short plane flight away in Oahu, plus the Navy had a huge base at Mare Island where all Pacific Ocean submarines went for overhaul. Uncertainty about Fred's movements caused Mary to scotch that idea. The only option remaining was to once again hunt down a house in the Baltimore area. Considering Mary's past bad luck with renting and the reluctance of east coast landlords to rent to people with children, she new that the experience was going to be bad.

After some initial looking around Mary decided that finding another place to rent was hopeless. She decided to buy a house. That would be difficult with no money though. Once again Fred's sister Sue Pattison came to the aid of Mary and Fred and offered to put up the down payment on a house for Mary, which Fred could pay back over the space of about eight months. Mary contacted a real estate agent and began looking for a house. After thinking longer about the problem though, Fred decided that he would rather borrow money against his life insurance for the down payment. Then indecision caught him again; he thought that if he were killed in action Mary would need the extra money from the life insurance since the company had taken away his indemnity clause, therefore it was back to the Sue Pattison plan.[266]

After searching for a few weeks Mary found a charming little two-story house on Greenleaf Road, about a mile from the Deepdene house. That was perfect because the children could continue attending classes in their same schools. The rooms were tiny, but everybody got their own room, that is until Fred's Aunt Margaret moved into the house due to health problems. That did not bother Mary or the rest of the family as Margaret was a gentle woman who spent most of her time sewing and mending clothes. Because the move was local Bessie could easily follow the family to their new home, which made Mary and the four children especially happy. The house had a big back yard where Mary planted a "Victory Garden." Unlike Fred she was not blessed with a green thumb but being smart she simply planted plants that defied poor treatment. Consequently, the Warders had lots of Eggplant. Mary and Bessie simply had to come up with a variety of ways to cook their one variety of vegetable from their Victory Garden.

Just as with their last house the Warders enjoyed great neighbors who gathered on the tree shaded sidewalks to exchange a little conversation and swap ration coupons. Mrs. Sweeny who lived across the street was and especial favorite. She always waved to the kids and liked to watch them play. She was a good conversationalist for Mary and Bessie when they took a break from the day and sat on the front porch. Mrs. Sweeny had a car, which she and Mary did errands in from time to time. Sometimes the kids were invited on the shopping excursions, which they enjoyed because it meant a ride in the car, a very special treat.

Mary met many new friends while keeping her old friends from the last house. The four children also made new friends and the move proved to be a huge success. Grace sent a very nice letter to her father,

> Dear Daddy, I love the new house that mother bought and I hope that you will to, Susan and I have lots of fun with the children. Mary and Fred and I all go to school, Love Grace.

Fred answered her,

> I thank you for your most sweet note. I am very glad you love the new house. I am sure I will too; just so you and all the family live in it.[267]

Things went well in the new house, but other things did not change, most notably Fred Jr.'s penchant for practical jokes and other assorted mischief. In the back of one of the closets there was a removable panel. On one particular day Mary needed to take Mary Jr. out for some errands. Bessie had fallen very ill so Fred Jr. was to watch over the two little girls for a short period of time. He had been warned to never go behind the panel in the closet, but curiosity, or mischief, got the best of him. When Mary came home and found Fred Jr., Grace, and Suzy behind the panel she decided this bad behavior needed special attention. She directed Fred Jr. to write to Fred Sr. about the panel that they were directed to never go behind. Fred Jr. wrote to his father,

> We got curious so we decided to explore it. Just as we were coming out mother got home and we all got in trouble for disobeying her, so she wanted me to write to you and explain the whole thing, and then she wants you to write back and tell what my punishment should be.[268]

Fred Sr. thought the letter from Fred Jr. to be, "Quite the treasure." Fred Sr. promised Mary to write Fred Jr., "along the lines you suggest." After a few weeks Bessie recovered so there would be less opportunity for Fred Jr. to cause mischief.

With the "hat" picture on the wall, the kids in school, the new neighbors all acquainted, and Bessie helping, Mary could sit back and enjoy the new house. She felt so good and secure in her new surroundings that she even bought letterhead with the new address printed on it. Fred sent her congratulations on the new home after Mary sent him a detailed description of it. Shortly after that though, the pressure of home ownership hit Fred very hard. Money worries abounded in his now fertile imagination as advice flowed from Pearl Harbor to Baltimore.

Mary had to buy a few things for the new house while Fred wanted to save money for an upcoming tax bill, for leave, for insurance, and also to save for a cash "reserve." Mary understood that very well and did her best to economize, but there were certain necessities one just had to have, such as a bicycle for Mary Jr. Fred Sr., no longer confined to his submarine decided he could be a big help to Mary in this situation. As far as the bike purchase, Fred wrote,

> I would give the second-hand column a good whirl on this as I imagine new bikes are practically unprocurable.[269]

Fred was right; bicycles were on the rationing list and could only be purchased with a permit. Purchases were basically reserved for people who needed a bicycle for work. The very unpopular Leon Henderson, head of the Office of Price Administration (OPA), was behind that regulation. To help promote the new regulation the intrepid Henderson had himself photographed on a "Victory" bicycle, but in his great patriotism he took it one step further; firmly planted on the handlebars of his Victory bicycle was the shapely figure of the young and beautiful Betty Barrett, a stenographer who worked for the OPA. After a few maneuvers such as, "Look Ma no hands," the fun-loving commuting duo disembarked extolling the virtues of bicycle rationing and "car" pooling, which in that case amounted to something more like "bike" pooling.[270] Whether the OPA had anything to do with it or not a bike was purchased for Mary Jr.

Home ownership indeed opened a whole new window of discussion for the formerly vagabond family. Shortly after the move to Greenleaf a correspondence concerning schools came up. Mary thought that Mary Jr. would do very well at Notre Dame, which is a preparatory school as well as a lady's college in Baltimore. Fred's reply to that suggestion is a classic in the genre of husband-and-wife relations,

> Naturally I want the children to have every advantage; but can we afford such schools just now? By the way, where are they all going to school just now?[271]

Fred severely undermined his own case when he admitted to falling behind on his payments to Sue, "Due to some big mess bills, the result of a good bit of entertaining which my boss insists on doing."[272] Sue did not mind about the money at all. She perfectly understood the pressure the war brought onto her now famous brother and his family. Maybe everybody in the rest of the country did not pull together all the time, but the Warders always looked after each other through thick and thin. After all that Mary and Fred had been through since the dark days of Pomona a few nickels and dimes were not going to cause any serious problems. Being depth charged for sixteen straight hours changes ones perspective to a certain degree.

Finally in August 1944 Fred started to hear rumors that he was to be reassigned to shore duty back in the United States proper. He requested that if indeed he was to be reassigned out of combat that he be sent to the Baltimore area, however there would not have been a lot for him to do there, other than take over as commandant of the Naval Academy, a prospect that he absolutely dreaded. When he did finally get his orders, they were almost too good to be true; he was going to New London, Connecticut to run the submarine school. For Mary it was not exactly York where she Fred and the family had spent such happy times, but it was a very close facsimile. The only problem was the house, which they had been forced to purchase.

Fred and Mary decided to try and find a place to rent in Groton, which was very close to New London on the Thames River. They would only begin to move after Fred actually took up his post; the two knew by now that Navy orders changed rapidly at times and they wanted to be as sure as one could be that his new assignment was actually going to stick for a longer period than the three-day Long Beach, California assignment of 1940. Once Fred was firmly established at the submarine school the house in Baltimore would be rented and Mary and the four kids would move north, and the family would finally be completely reunited.

Before the great day a few letters arrived from Fred that really touched everybody in the family.

> Please remember me in your prayers – not to keep me safe but for God to help me do my duty and be a strong man worthy of such splendid children and such a lovely mother.
>
> I wish I could rake leaves up for you and I think the house cleaning would be a welcome occupation; although if I had the chance I'd give Bessie the day off and send Suzy out to play and say "To hell with the housecleaning."

> I love you more than ever. I hope you don't find my presence around the house too much of a strain. I honestly haven't felt so well for years as I did when I was with you. And the memories of the songs the children sang, the things they did and said, the things you did and said make me feel awfully good.

Then he addressed the real apprehension that so many men and women felt after losing control of their lives due to the war. Except for two short leave periods Fred and Mary had not lived together for the last four years, he wrote apprehensively,

> You must not be frightened about this period of shore duty – five years (sic) has been a long time but I know we can learn to live together better than we ever have before. I have become more and more to appreciated how really wonderful you are (sic).

Fred was a bit worried about what he thought to be his deteriorating appearance.

> I must go and get a haircut. It grows like hell on the sides and neck but there's little of it left on the top. If I get home you will find me much older, I'm afraid; but much happier than I've ever been before to be with my dearest girl in the world.[273]

Then finally the great day came. Fred came home and raked some leaves just as he said he would, but he mainly wanted to relax and enjoy his family. Some of Mary's friends in the neighborhood came by to say hello, and one neighbor boy was so intrigued by the famous sea raider next door that he crept into the house and went upstairs and stared at Fred Warder as he slept. What a thrill! In addition to being on display to the neighborhood boys interested in military matters, Fred found time to read stories to Grace and Suzy, toss the football around with Fred Jr., and of course play plenty of Parcheesi games.

After the family spent a wonderful three weeks together Fred returned to Pearl Harbor for a short period then proceeded to New London, Connecticut where he took over command of the Submarine School. Along with that command came a promotion in rank to Captain. What a thrill it was for Mary to pin the eagles onto Fred's collar. He enjoyed the moment but considered the promotion to be the most temporary in nature directly tied to his duties at the submarine school, and if not that, then certainly tied to the war. Fred was certain that after the war he would be reduced in rank back to Commander, as is the custom. When Fred had calling cards printed up he specifically requested that the area before his name where his rank would appear, be left blank so that he could simply fill in the appropriate prefix with a pencil no matter what his rank might be.

While Fred got some temporary bachelor quarters in New London, Mary began to making arrangements to rent out the house in Baltimore and move north. Because Fred had arrived to his new duties during the school semester it was decided that the children would finish out the fall semester in Baltimore, then join Fred at the Submarine School in December.

A few letters went back and forth between the Submarine Base and Baltimore, but more importantly Mary went back and forth between the Submarine Base and Baltimore a few times. What a great elixir that was for both Fred and Mary to spend a little time together alone as Fred tried his level best to avoid the obligatory parties thrown almost constantly by his fellow officers at the Submarine Base.

The search for housing was easier for Fred in the New London area that it had been for Mary in the Baltimore area. After not too much hunting they found a house to move into on Ramsdell St. in Groton within walking distance of the Thames River and just a short drive for Fred to the Submarine School in New London. Mary and Fred loved the new place. It was a big frame house, and the property was farm-like, which appealed to Fred. He had a big area in the back of the house where he could keep a garden. Over the next year he grew every kind of vegetable with the favorites being lettuce, broccoli, and corn. The children also liked the garden especially since their dad was doing the gardening – no more eggplant, which had been Mary's staple crop back in Baltimore. A barn with a hayloft located at the back of the property completed the ideal image of the kind of place that a gentleman farmer would reside.

For Mary the house was big and came with some furniture to compliment her own that would be shipped up from Baltimore. The children had rooms of their own and there was lots of space for indoor living and games, an important advantage considering the winters in Groton and New London could be brutal. It got so cold at times that the Thames River completely froze over. There was a wood stove that kept the kitchen warm and cozy during the cold winters. The stove also doubled as a "good behavior" device; any of the children who needed to be disciplined would make the trek to the woodpile and collect enough wood to feed the stove. Especially bad offences required the malefactor to chop the wood into stove-sized pieces. Because of his high rate of mischief and tomfoolery Fred Jr. accounted for much of the chopped wood that made it into the stove. The house also came with a refrigerator, so the Warders said goodbye once and for all to their icebox.

Finally in December the entire family moved up to Groton, the reunion was happy and permanent, or at least as permanent as can be hoped for by the family of a Navy officer during wartime. December means Christmas and the Warders went and bought a large Christmas tree to make up for the Christmas' recently lost. Luckily the OPA did not think to ration those. That Christmas in Groton was the first that the entire family spent together since the days that Fred was in charge of building the famous ship Seawolf at Portsmouth, NH. It was a magical time for Mary and Fred. The four children were happy and settled, and yes excited about the gifts in the stockings and under the tree. Mary's piano was shipped north, and she filled the holiday season with carols as the family gathered around the piano to sing along with her playing. As much as Fred and Mary wanted to avoid too much socializing, inevitably they went to a few parties and gave a few parties, just enough to have fun and do their duty, not so much as to become drudgery.

The holidays are traditional times for family portraits and the one taken of the Warders about that time speaks volumes. Mary Sr. is seen even more beautiful and radiant than ever. Suzy is unusually pretty while Grace's sweet smile is cuter than a Norman Rockwell painting. Fred Jr.'s blond hair made him look like the cherub that his sisters swore at times he was not, and Mary Jr. had completely matured from an awkward preteen to a truly attractive and confident looking young woman. Her thick wavy hair looked much like her mothers.

Fred Sr. had changed the most. Even the more relaxed environment of the submarine school could not take away his care worn face with only the slightest hint of a smile. Three years of fighting on the front lines etched a grimness into his eyes noticeable to his family. It is not the fighting that takes it out of men like Fred, but rather the constant responsibility for other men's lives that run them down. Fred had worked everyday of every week since December 7, 1941, in the relentless pursuit of perfection in order to keep his men as safe as possible in battle. No matter how hard they all tried to survive, many did not, including Fred's good friend Sam Dealey who lost his life when Harder sank with all hands. It is hard to take that kind of pressure even occasionally but taking it constantly for three years can irreparably hurt a person without them ever knowing it.

After Christmas the family easily fell into a routine that suited them all very well. The kids attended school, which was just a short walk from their house. During the summer there was a beach close to the house where the kids could play as the Thames flowed by. Often Fred took the children to the Navy base where they enjoyed a movie or bought comic books. The Ships Service Store also sold milk shakes that the children really loved. Fred liked deep-sea fishing and had many opportunities to go out with his friends and "catch dinner," and was often accompanied by Fred Jr. who enjoyed the sport as well. When Fred and the children were gone Mary visited with other submarine wives, went for walks, and relished the days. She was very happy.

Fred Warder had spent the last seven years of his life training crews on his own ships and now he was the head instructor for all of the submarine crews in the United States Navy. He was a natural teacher so his new job at the submarine school suited him very well. Fred did not mind the paperwork too much and like his previous job as Division Commander he had ample opportunities to go to sea if only for a day cruise of "hands on training" and evaluation.

Once the word got around that Fred Warder was in command of the submarine school letters pored in from friends, friends of friends, vague acquaintances, and anybody else who thought they could make some kind of connection to him, requesting duty at the school. An Admiral wrote to Fred on behalf of a former aid; Harold Prebele asked Fred to consider a friend named Francis; William Brady thought that if he mentioned that he was from Fairmont, West Virginia that Fred would get him to the school. Another man wrote that he had been on ten war patrols and needed a break plus, "My wife has a baby girl for me to see." Parents wrote him requesting land duty at the school for their sons that were in combat. It was never ending, and Fred could not blame people ground down by combat to request shore duty for awhile. Many of Fred's former crewmembers asked to come to the school; Fred always tried his best for those men that he had previously led in battle. Not only did Fred help his old shipmates get to the school when requested, but due to his excellent efforts at the school he helped the Submarine Service in general as was noted by his friend Elton Grenfell, the commander of Submarine Squadron 44, who said the graduates from the Submarine School seem to be of much higher quality since Fred took over.

Amidst the tumult of requests and compliments Fred continued to show why his men loved him so much; he never forgot them. Bill Deragon on Pipefish was getting concerned about his wife Betty and she was getting worried sick about her husband – the pressure had been growing for over four years and she literally could not take it anymore. Deragon, who had been Warder's X/O on Seawolf, found out that Betty had been asking Fred about him (Bill). Deragon sent his apologies to Fred, who did not need any apologies; Fred remembered how Betty had been such a great friend and help to Mary when the pressure had gotten to her. Fred wrote Bill,

> Betty has not been making a pest of herself, as you put it, in the least, we are always glad to hear from her and you and I can't blame her for getting worried a little bit now and then.[274]

Fred went out of his way to help Bill Deragon get shore duty over at Portsmouth, New Hampshire, much to the relief of Betty. Deragon had been at sea for the entire run of the war and was run down. With her husband's new assignment Betty and Mary were able to visit from time to time, just like the old days when the two "girls" would occasionally meet in New York for a nice weekend of shows and late dinners.

Another person that was in serious need of help was Mrs. Watts. She had been in Long Beach when everybody got stranded there in 1940, had been a huge help to everyone, and made all of the correct decisions for Mary at that most critical time. Nearly five years later Mrs. Watts wrote Fred and literally begged him to get her husband to the West Coast where she lived in Hynes, California. Fred did not hesitate and wrote the Detail Officer at Terminal Island on Mrs. Watts behalf,

> An old shipmate of mine, Lt. (jg) Evan Watts, who commissioned my last ship with me as an electrician's mate and went to China with me in 1940 where he was subsequently transferred to Pike, has about 13 patrols under his belt in Pike, Stingray, and Chub. I happen to know that he has had a belly full. He is 36 years old. His wife is caring for a sick father in Hynes, California (as well as two kids) and cannot very well come east with him to new construction. If it can be arranged, I would very much like to see Watts made available to shore establishments for shore duty at Terminal Island.

The detail officer obliged Fred's request and Watts and his wife were reunited on the West Coast. After 13 war patrols Evan Watts survived the war!

Rudy Gervais, Warder's trusty helmsman during his time as CO on the Seawolf also needed help with shore duty. Gervais had been on 11 war patrols and earned a bronze star with combat distinction. He confided to Fred in a letter that he was so worn out and that he could not get on another boat. Warder got him to shore and after the war wrote a very nice general letter of recommendation to help Gervais get a start in civilian life.

While Fred did his part to help old crewmates, Mary worked away helping their families. When James Adkins, or "Catty" as he was known on the Seawolf, was on patrol as CO of Cod, Mary helped his wife "Fritzy" with the christening of his twin daughters. Afterward Mary kept in close contact with her and gave whatever help and support that Mrs. Adkins needed. Fred wrote to Catty assuring him that his wife was okay, and that Mary was lending a hand to her. That is the way of the Navy; when Mary needed help in Pomona, the wives and friends of crewmembers helped her out. Now she was in the position to help – and she gave everything she had to everyone who asked.

Fred Warder and Mary considered helping old crewmates to be their privilege and a very positive experience. This unfortunately was mixed in with the worst side of warfare, the killing and loss and grief that so many had to suffer before the Untied States finally won the war. Many family members with a son or husband overdue on patrol appealed to Fred for information on almost every subject possible to relieve their pain and anxiety. Fred always did his best to console a grieving family member or track down items the family might be looking for. Ruth Tucker was a typical example. Her son Ensign Samuel Tucker was on the Robalo when it sank after hitting a mine near Palawan in the Philippine Islands. Miraculously four men, including Tucker, were able to escape the submarine before it sank and swam ashore where the Japanese unfortunately captured them. The Japanese held the four men in the Puerto Princess POW camp where they were tortured for information. On August 15, 1944, they were taken aboard a Japanese destroyer and never heard from again. What Mrs. Tucker wanted was a picture of her son in uniform, as she did not have one. Fred searched the school files and did come up with a group photo that featured Ensign Tucker in uniform. He sent it to her as a small consolation for her son's heroic work in the war.

Seawolf crewmember families also appealed to Fred for information about relatives either at sea or lost. David Butler had served on the Seawolf during the first year of the war. When his current ship Tullibee was reported overdue from patrol David's wife contacted Fred to get some desperately wanted information. That ship sank when the torpedo it fired made a circular run and blew it up. Only one man survived to tell the story, a gunner's mate named Kuykendall. Fred sent her a very nice condolence letter in which he extolled her husband's virtues and informed her that he had recommended Butler for the Silver Star. Warder also enclosed three pictures of ships sinking due to action by the Seawolf at Davao Gulf. The pictures were taken using a special rig attached to the periscope. By sending the pictures Fred gave the families physical evidence of the contribution they had made during the war, a small consolation, but something at least.

Fred lent a hand in other ways to help people better endure their losses. On one occasion Kate Smith came to the submarine base to give a concert and caused quite a sensation. She had already been very famous before the war started with a nightly radio show on CBS, but her singing of Irving Berlin's song, "God Bless America" put her in a pantheon of her own. Fred was not her biggest fan, however he did play congenial host to her before her concert at the base. Fred also arranged for Alice Boucher to attend the concert. Her son had been on Tang when its torpedo made a circular run and blew it up in the same circumstances as the submarine Tullibee. Mrs. Boucher wanted Kate to sing the Navy song "Anchors Away" because it was her son's favorite song. Mrs. Boucher told Fred she would feel closer to her son, who she had not seen for 23 months, if Kate would sing that one song. Fred did not attend the concert but received a nice thank-you letter from Mrs. Boucher for looking after her at the submarine base and getting her tickets to the show.

While Fred took care of these serious matters other things of a more comical nature came his way. The Netherlands awarded him the Bronze Cross for his service in the defense of The Dutch East Indies. An embassy official mailed him the Cross, then later wrote wanting it back. After further examination of Warder's case the Dutch decided that he deserved the Bronze Lion, not the Bronze Cross. Dutifully Fred sent back the Cross then some months later received the Lion. Fred was non-pulsed over the Dutch Decorations; but he was concerned about American decorations and wrote the Navy Department for authorization to wear the Philippines Defense Medal with a gold star for his service in the defense of those islands, which was granted.

Fred was not the only Warder that collected medals for valor during the war. His brother John, who was in the army fighting in Europe, received a Bronze Star for gallantry and was wounded in action. A fragment from a shell or grenade cut him pretty badly. There was no leave for him, rather he was quickly patched up in a field hospital and sent back into the battle line, as was the custom in World War II. John sent a few souvenirs to Fred Jr. including a German helmet. He asked Fred Sr. if it would be okay to send his son a Nazi dagger – Fred Sr. did not like that idea at all, so the dagger stayed in Germany.

Frank, another of Fred's brothers, was fighting in the Pacific. When Fred received letters from his brother, he tried to figure out his exact location going only by the circumstantial evidence in his letters as they were all censored as far as geographic locations were concerned. At one point Fred thought Frank was at Tawi Tawi, but later figured out he was on Zamboanga, both were places Fred visited prior to the war and during his first seven war patrols. On August 3rd, 1945 Fred sent Frank a whole list of people to look up while he was in the Philippine Islands; "A Russian with a Filipino wife and two kids that own the Dessicated Coconut Co," an "Augustinian father named Connery," and the "McCrary's in Iloilo or Panay," were just a few of the people that Fred wanted Frank to drop in on and say "hello" to.

On August 6th an atomic bomb was dropped on Hiroshima. After reports came to the Japanese government that only one plane was involved in the air raid, they realized that the Americans had cracked the secrets of the atom and were able to release its ferocious energy at will. Despite the great devastation of that atomic attack on Hiroshima and the exponentially greater devastation of the conventional air raids against Japan that preceded it, the war went on. On August 8th Fred found out that his brother was near Davao Gulf and asked him if he would go to the dock and see if he could find one of the ships that Warder sank there. On August 9th a second atomic bomb exploded over Nagasaki, and six days later on August 15th a cease-fire was called. On September 2nd, 1945, representatives of the Empire of Japan climbed aboard the U.S.S. Missouri to sign a formal surrender. The calamity of World War II was over.

Epilogue

If one were to study only Fred Warder's correspondence, it would never have been known that the war ended. There is no mention of atomic bombs, Victory, duty changes, or of the amount of points accumulated for an early discharge. Fred's correspondence reveals no special happiness or joy; there is no elation in the mundane letters and orders that continued to flow from his desk. Everyday after that 15th of August Fred Warder continued to put on his uniform and report to his duty post. Mary continued to look after her family and lent assistance to any others who were under Fred's command and former crewmembers.

The men that Fred Warder generally dealt with were graduates of Annapolis, officers first, with a clear vision of their duty. The war was over, but they continued the job of protecting America's freedom. They prepared for the next war or attempted to stop the next war through preparedness. After Victory in Europe and Victory in Japan a new and virulent disease spread across parts of the world – totalitarianism as usual – but in the guise of communism. Soon a crisis came, the Berlin Blockade, then a strange new war – the Cold War.

Since the day he walked out of Bancroft Hall Fred Warder either prepared for war or fought in war. For his efforts to keep America and the world free, he was rewarded with more responsibility, first as a Squadron Commander, latter he joined the surface fleet as the Commanding Officer of the cruiser U.S.S. Columbus, then Chief of Staff for the Atlantic Submarine Command (COMSUBALT), ending up some years later as a Rear Admiral, then as the Commander of Submarines in the Atlantic. He trained his men as he trained himself, studying endlessly and working relentlessly.

Through all these assignments Mary gave her time and organized moves from this post to that. She gave moral support and befriended Navy wives as well as continued to raise and encourage her family, all of whom achieved success. She was Fred's foundation and made it possible for him to go out into the world and slay the dragons that came out of their caves. Mary worried about Fred and advised him on his career. She was the person that constantly warned him to be careful about what he said to his superiors and repeatedly told Fred just prior to World War II, "Your place is in a submarine fighting the Japanese."

Mary and Fred endured separations, strange posts, and extreme danger as they sacrificed together in service of the Americans. Both overcame human frailties common to human existence; they did those things by their own choice and will, and neither ever intimated that they ever regretted it.

About the Author

Sam Stavros graduated from The Claremont Graduate University. He was a speech writer and taught history at Cal State San Bernardino and Chaffey College. He has been an invited speaker to many gatherings of scholars speaking on topics ranging from submarine warfare to geopolitics and U.S. History.

NOTES

[1] Personal papers of FW.
[2] Ibid.
[3] Carlo D'Este, <u>A Soldier's Life</u>, New York, Henry Holt and Co., 2002, p. 133
[4] Personal papers of FW
[5] Ibid.
[6] Personal Navy file of FBW.
[7] Calvert, James, <u>Silent Running</u>, New York: John Wiley and Sons, p.10
[8] Personal papers of FW.
[9] Ibid.
[10] Elizabeth Norman, <u>We Band of Angles</u>, New York: Pocket Books, 2000, p.3.
[11] Ibid. p.5.
[12] Interview with Hank Thompson.
[13] Personal letters of F.W.
[14] ibid.
[15] ibid.
[16] Deck Logs of the U.S.S. Seawolf
[17] Personal letters of F.W.
[18] ibid.
[19] Personal correspondence of FBW.
[20] Interview with Hank Thompson
[21] Personal letters of F.W.
[22] Ibid.
[23] David Brinkley, <u>Washington Goes to War</u>, Ballentine Books: New York, 1988, p. 46
[24] Ibid. p. 48
[25] "What Do the Women of America Think About War?" Ladies' Home Journal, February 1940, p.12
[26] Ibid. p. 13
[27] Graham White, <u>FDR and the Press</u>, University of Chicago Press: Chicago, 1979, p.51.
[28] Ibid. p. 52
[29] Cissy could not have been too impressed with Roosevelt from the beginning though. While riding in Cissy's private train, Roosevelt's

Endnotes

Secretary of Agriculture, Henry Wallace (later Vice-President) went into the bathroom and found a gold plated flushing handle. He unscrewed the handle and went back to the party declaring, "No wonder people in the United States are so upset when the wealthy travel with gold-plated toilet handles."
[30] Brinkley, Washington, p. 183
[31] Ibid. p. 22
[32] White, FDR, p.52
[33] Ibid., p. 44
[34] At the time O'Donnell was suing pro-Roosevelt publisher J. David Stern of the *Philadelphia Record* for libel. Stern had referred to O'Donnell as an anti-Semite and a Naziphile. Most of the shocked reporters at the news conference thought Roosevelt did it in order to help his friend Stern out. This was not FDR's most shining moment. (From, White, FDR).
[35] Allen Winkler, Home Front U.S.A., Harlan-Davidson: Wheeling, 2000, p.51
[36] The Voge's were well to do so they could afford private transportation and housing in order to get around Adm. Hart's order that all dependents must leave the Philippines.
[37] Oakland Tribune, Wednesday, May 14, 1942, front page
[38] White, Graham, FDR and the Press, University of Chicago Press: Chicago, 1979, p. 116
[39] Oakland Tribune, Wednesday, January 13, 1942, front page
[40] Long Beach Independent, Friday, January 24, 1941, front page.
[41] Berg, Scott, Linderbergh, Berkley Books: New York, 1998, p. 359.
[42] Ibid. p. 362.
[43] Ibid. p. 414.
[44] Ibid. p. 423
[45] Ibid. p.427
[46] Personal Papers of F.W.
[47] ibid.
[48] ibid.
[49] ibid. January 14,1941
[50] ibid.
[51] Winston Churchill, Speech to the house of Commons, Nov. 10th, 1942.
[52] Personal papers of FW
[53] A few days later Fred Received from Bill a very nice letter saying that he, Bill, and his wife Margaret were patching things up. Also enclosed were some snapshots of the kids Bill had taken while everyone was together in Maryland.

[54] ibid.
[55] ibid.
[56] Deck Logs of the U.S.S. Seawolf, July 1, 1941
[57] Personal letters of F.W.
[58] Ibid.
[59] Winston Chruchill, speech in the House of Commons, June 18, 1940.
[60] Personal papers of Fred Warder.
[61] Ibid.
[62] Warder was successful in keeping Capece on the Seawolf, and a good thing too. During the 4th War Patrol, Capece's quick thinking saved the ship and for that he received a silver star.
[63] Ibid.
[64] This exceptionally exciting action took place off of the Japanese home island of Kyushu. A B-29 had ditched into the ocean on its way home from a bombing run. When Gato surfaced to rescue the airmen an enemy plane came in for an attack. Instead of diving Holden ordered the deck guns manned and they shot it out with the enemy plane and successfully rescued the U.S. airmen. (See Clay Blair, "Silent Victory," p. 840.
[65] For more on this subject see Longitude, by Dava Sobel.
[66] Ibid.
[67] Personal papers of F.W.
[68] ibid.
[69] Theodore Roscoe, United States Submarine Operations in World War II, United States Naval Institute, Annapolis, 1949.
[70] The message of the 27th read, "This dispatch is to be considered a war warning…The number and equipment of Japanese troops and the organization of the naval task forces indicates an amphibious expedition against either the Philippines, Thai, or Kra Peninsula or possibly Borneo."
[71] William Manchester, American Caesar, Little, Brown, and Co., Boston, 1978, p. 192
[72] Gordon W. Prange, At Dawn We Slept, Penguin Books, 1991, p. 185
[73] ibid, p. 187
[74] John Toland, But Not In Shame, New York:Random House, 1961, p.11
[75] Manchester, MacArthur, p. 197
[76] Roscoe, Submarine Operations, p.23
[77] Manchester, MacArthur, p. 180
[78] Ted Morgan, F.D.R., New York: Simon and Schuster, 1985, p.465.
[79] Manchester, MacArthur, p.201.
[80] Toland, Not In Shame, p. 12

Endnotes

[81] Manchester, MacArthur, p.208
[82] ibid., p.210
[83] Roscoe, Submarine Operations, p.23
[84] Clay Blair, Silent Victory, J. B. Lippincott Co., New York,1975, p.107
[85] The U.S.S. Seawolf, p.28
[86] Submarine War Patrol Report.
[87] ibid.
[88] Toland, But not in Shame, p.65
[89] ibid.
[90] Eckberg, Seawolf, p.31
[91] Claude Conner, Nothing Friendly in the Vicinity, Savas, Mason City, 1999
[92] About an hour after this contact Ekberg did figure out that the sounds he was hearing, far from being two Japanese Submarines talking to each other, were in fact some reef fish – probably croakers. Ekberg, Seawolf, p.32
[93] Submarine War Patrol Report.
[94] Ibid.
[95] American submarines carried three alarms on their intercom. The Klaxon (ah-oo-ga) for diving, a rising siren for collision, and ships bells (bong, bong, bong) for battle stations. This last alarm was ofte referred to as the "Bells of St. Mary's."
[96] Eckberg, Seawolf, p. 36
[97] War patrol report.
[98] ibid. Warder later reported, also in the war patrol report that upon further consideration he thought the ship was a fleet supply ship of the Kamtakawa type.
[99] Eckberg, Seawolf, p.67
[100] Later Warder reported that sound had reported two explosions but he did not remember having that information at the time.
[101] Submarine War Patrol Report.
[102] Ibid.
[103] Peter Padfield, War Beneath the Sea, John Wiley & Sons, Inc., New York, 1995, p.186.
[104] Blair, Silent Victory, p. 42
[105] ibid., p.50
[106] ibid., p.150
[107] ibid., p.254
[108] Roscoe, Submarine Operations, p.258. The South West Submarine Command actually stuck with the magnetic exploder all the way until ordered to stop in March of 1944 nearly 3 years after the war started and long after

everybody, even the Bureau of Ordinance new that the exploders did not work. Chapter 20 of T. Roscoe's book gives a great account of all things torpedo during WWII and should be the first place people look for information on that topic.

[109] Padfield, War Beneath the Sea, p.350
[110] Karl Doenitz, Memoirs, The World Publishing Co., Cleveland,1959, p. 89
[111] ibid., p. 93
[112] Toland, But not in Shame, p.84. Manchester, American Caesar, p.212.
[113] Blair, Silent Victory, p. 118
[114] ibid., p. 119
[115] Personal interview with hank Thompson.
[116] Ibid.
[117] A few patrols later when Seawolf was in Fremantle for repairs one of the men who stowed away was working on the outside of the Seawolf under water. He popped up out of the water in front of an astonished Henry Thompson who recognized him from Corregidor. They exchanging the minimal greetings and went their separate ways.
[118] War Patrol Report
[119] ibid.
[120] Ekberg, Seawolf, p. 62
[121] War Patrol Report
[122] ibid.
[123] A case in point is Richard O'Kanes' experiences described in his book "Wahoo" in which his first CO, Marvin G. Kennedy, seemed (according to O'Kane) to take delight in knocking him for even supposed errors in navigation. Warder's opinions are from his personal correspondence, other sources are from interviews of crew members.
[124] The crewmembers of Seawolf tended to be quite successful in their navy careers. Holden, Warder, and Kisella all retired as admirals.
[125] War Patrol Report.
[126] ibid.
[127] Eckberg, Seawolf, p. 66
[128] West Point Atlas of American Wars, Vincent Esposito ed.
[129] Toland, But Not In Shame, p. 164
[130] Eckberg, Seawolf, p.72-73
[131] Personal papers of FW.
[132] Ibid.
[133] Ibid.
[134] Ibid.

Endnotes

[135] Personal papers of F.W.
[136] Ibid.
[137] Ibid. This quote out of order, July 4, 1941
[138] Ibid.
[139] Ibid. July 4, 1941
[140] Personal papers of F.W.
[141] Brinkley, Washington goes to War, p.71
[142] Ibid. p. 108
[143] Ibid. p. 109
[144] Ibid.
[145] Personal papers of F.W.
[146] She actually addressed all of the V-Mail to the Postmaster of San Francisco, California
[147] Personal papers of F.W.
[148] Ibid.
[149] War Patrol Report. The charts were made around 1890 by Germans and the Dutch who had colonial interests and aspirations in the Pacific. The Americans simply copied their charts.
[150] Toland, Without Shame, p.220
[151] Morison, The Rising Sun in the Pacific, p.312
[152] Clay Blair contends in Silent Victory that in fact Hart initiated his own relief and that Adm. King in Washington opposed the move but Roosevelt concurred with the British and the Dutch that Helfrich should command. Also according to Blair, "Hart was appointed to the general board and helped with the Pearl Harbor investigations. He was later appointed United States Senator from Connecticut filling out the term of Francis Maloney who died in office."
[153] From personal interview.
[154] After awhile Deragon who was the executive officer simply had Casler do the navigation as he was much better at it. Despite this laps by Deragon Warder continued to heap praise on his executive officer. Warder was able to get the most out of his crew understanding their strengths and emphasizing those while minimizing their weaknesses.
[155] Warder lists the place as Benoa which judging from his charts was on the Cape of Tafel. The Japanese landings were closer to Sanur. While Warder made the observations they were closer to Cape Tafel (listed as Tafel Haek on his chart) but the whole of the coast would be visible to him.
[156] Morrison, The rising sun in the Pacific, p.323. The soundman Ekberg wrote in his book Seawolf that there were probably about 15 Japanese ships

in the area. In fact there were three and Warders charts and report mention only two and possibly three.

[157] War Patrol Report
[158] War Patrol Report.
[159] ibid.
[160] Personal interview.
[161] personal interview.
[162] Morrison, Rising Sun, p. 322.
[163] War Patrol Report.
[164] ibid.
[165] ibid.
[166] ibid.
[167] Toland, Shame, p.258.
[168] Morison, The Rising Sun , p.361.
[169] Toland, But Not In Shame, p.255
[170] War patrol report. The negative tank was broken and it is very likely the speed and angle of the planes would actually have been used to save the ship during this problem but the war patrol report is clear that the negative tank was flooded.
[171] Submarine War Patrol Report.
[172] ibid.
[173] ibid.
[174] ibid.
[175] ibid.
[176] ibid.
[177] From the personal papers of Fred Warder.
[178] Ibid.
[179] Ibid.
[180] Winkler, Allan, Home Front U.S.A., Harlan Davidson: Wheeling Illinois, 2000.
[181] The Grafton Gazette, May 1, 1942
[182] From the personal papers of Fred Warder.
[183] Personal papers of FW
[184] ibid.
[185] Blum, V Was for Victory, p.54.
[186] ibid.
[187] Personal papers of FW.
[188] Ibid.
[189] Winkler, Allen, Home front U.S.A, p.50.

Endnotes

[190] Interview with FW daughter, Grace
[191] Personal papers of FW
[192] Ibid.
[193] Personal papers of FW.
[194] The Evening Capital, August 23, 1942.
[195] Ibid.
[196] Brinkley, David, Washington Goes to War, p. 118
[197] ibid.
[198] Personal Papers of FW
[199] Interview with Hank Thompson.
[200] War Patrol Report.
[201] The exactness of time can be used as a sort of barometer to Warder's temper. When he puts the month and day of his last warning in a report he is pretty mad. When he includes the hour after the month and day, as with the problem in front of Surabaya, then he is really mad. If he includes the minute after the hour then everybody can just forget it!
[202] Ibid.
[203] Ibid.
[204] Maley, Seawolf, p. 130
[205] Interview with Hank Thompson
[206] War Patrol Report, first endorsement.
[207] Blair, Silent Victory, p. 290
[208] O'Kane, Wahoo.
[209] Personal interview with Hank Thompson
[210] War Patrol Report
[211] ibid.
[212] ibid.
[213] ibid.
[214] ibid.
[215] ibid.
[216] First endorsement to the Submarine War Patrol Report.
[217] Clay Blair, Silent Victory, p.266
[218] The Evening Capitol, Feb. 18, 1943
[219] Padfield, Peter, War Beneath the Sea, John Wiley & Sons: New York, p.205
[220] Brinkley, Washington Goes to War, p.127
[221] Kennett, Lee, For the Duration, Scribner's: New York, 1985, p. 138.
[222] Brinkley, Washington Goes to War, p. 130
[223] The Evening Capital, June 17th, 1943

224 The Evening Capital, June 26th, 1942
225 Ibid, June 29th, 1942
226 www.gtexts.com
227 Brinkley, Washington Goes to War, p.132
228 Blum, John Morton, V Was for Victory, Harcourt Brace Jovanovich, New York, 1976, p. 186
229 Morgan, Ted, FDR, Simon & Schuster: New York, 1985, p. 595
230 Speech by President Roosevelt, October 13, 1942
231 Yellin, Emily, Our Mothers War, Free Press: New York, p. 205
232 F.W. papers, letter dated July 5th, 1942.
233 Ibid. July 22, 1942.
234 Allen, Stookie, Heroes of Democracy, 1942
235 Wnkler, Allen, The Politics of Propaganda, Yale University Press: New haven, 1978, p., 22
236 ibid.
237 Winkler, Propaganda, p.23
238 New York Herald Tribune, October, 9, 1941, [Lilley], Winkler, Propaganda, p.23
239 Personal papers of FW
240 ibid.
241 These ships were basically outrigger dugout canoes that were rigged. The natives that used them were excellent sailors. On one occasion a crewmember of Seawolf clocked one of these boats at 13 knots.
242 The Voge speed spread was a chart that helped correct minor errors due to an enemy ships speed. Sometimes it worked and sometimes it didn't. Named after Warder's good friend Richard Voge.
243 War patrol report.
244 In fact every member of a submarine crew had to qualify for all of the other jobs aboard the ship. With such small crews, about 66 men, there was always a chance that disease, or an injury in battle required any member of the crew to step into someone else's job. Just another reason why submariners were paid significantly better than crew on the surface fleet.
245 ibid.
246 ibid.
247 Herbert Bix, Hirohito and the Making of Modern Japan, p.447
248 ibid.
249 ibid.
250 War Patrol Report
251 Personal papers of FW

Endnotes

[252] Ibid.
[253] Ibid.
[254] Blair, Silent Victory, p. 514
[255] Submarine War Patrol Report of Pargo.
[256] Sturma, Michael, Death at a Distance, Naval Institute Press: Annapolis, 2006, p. 158
[257] Submarine War Patrol Report of Snook
[258] Ibid.
[259] War Diary of Coordinated attack Group
[260] Ibid.
[261] Submarine War Patrol Report of Harder
[262] Submarine War Patrol Report of Snook
[263] Ibid.
[264] Ibid.
[265] Ibid.
[266] Ibid.
[267] Ibid.
[268] ibid.
[269] Ibid.
[270] Van Wert Times Bulletin, Front page, January 14, 1942
[271] Personal papers of FW.
[272] Ibid.
[273] Ibid.
[274] Ibid.

CPSIA information can be obtained
at www.ICGtesting.com
Printed in the USA
BVHW061044111022
649148BV00016B/1133/J